Knitting
America

A Glorious Heritage
from Warm Socks to High Art

Susan M. Strawn

Voyageur Press

For Bill and Vicky Oltmanns

First published in 2007 by Voyageur Press, an imprint of MBI Publishing Company LLC, Galtier Plaza, Suite 200, 380 Jackson Street, St. Paul, MN 55101 USA

ISBN-13: 978-0-7603-2621-3

Editor: Michael Dregni
Designer: Sara Holle

Printed in China

Credits:
On the front cover: Grandma teaches her granddaughter to knit, circa 1920s. (Photograph © Underwood & Underwood/Corbis)

Inset on the front cover: A bouquet of yarn skeins. (Photograph © Solveig Hisdal) Warm socks. (Photograph © Chris Hartlove) *Spirit Throne* by Karen Searle. (Photograph © Karen Searle)

On the frontispiece: Knitting friends, circa 1930s.

On the title page: Currier & Ives's engraving, *The Knitting Lesson*.

Inset on the title page: Knitting during the Great Depression. (Library of Congress)

Library of Congress Cataloging-in-Publication Data

Strawn, Susan.
Knitting America : a glorious heritage from warm socks to high art /
By Susan M. Strawn.
p. cm.
Includes bibliographical references and index.
ISBN-13: 978-0-7603-2621-3 (hardbound w/ jacket)
1. Knitting--United States--History. I. Title.
TT819.U6S77 2007
746.43'20973--dc22
2007019906

Contents

Foreword   7

Introduction   Knitting America   9

Chapter 1   The First American Knitters   11

Chapter 2   Victorians Knit in a Culture of Domesticity   23

Chapter 3   Knitting for the Civil War   39

Chapter 4   Traveling Stitches   51

Chapter 5   Knitting for an Age of Optimism   73

Chapter 6   The Knitting War   91

Chapter 7   The Knitting Doldrums of the 1920s   109

Chapter 8   Back to the Knitting Needles in the 1930s   121

Chapter 9   An Army of Knitters   137

Chapter 10   The Family that Knits Together . . .   155

Chapter 11   Worldly Knitting   171

Chapter 12   Knitting Redefined   183

Endnotes   198

References   205

Index   206

Acknowledgments   208

About the Author   208

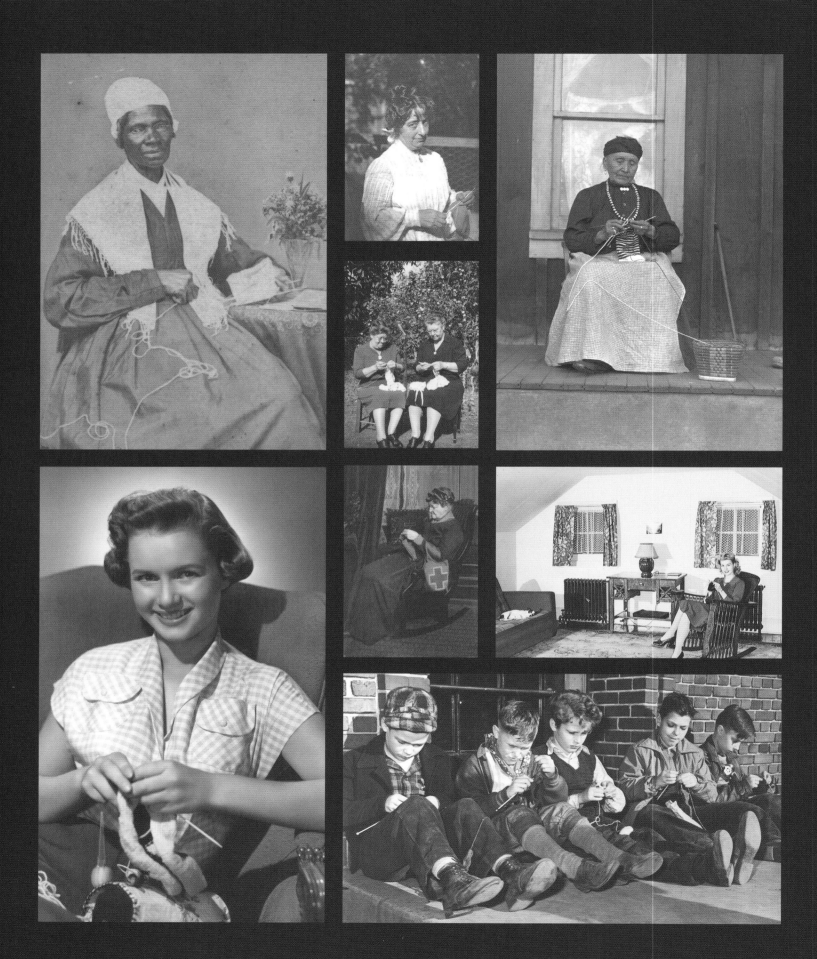

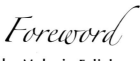

Foreword

by Melanie Falick

When I began to knit as an adult — after several false starts during childhood — I was immediately curious about the lives of knitters and how I could study history, in particular women's history, by way of knitting. At the time — this was in the late 1980s — there were fewer knitters (certainly fewer knitters who were "outed") and definitely fewer books about knitting being published than there are today. While I was curious about the history of knitting in the United States, I found it easier to explore its history in countries outside of it, in places like the Shetland Islands in Scotland and the Orenburg region of Russia. In part, this was because I had a fairly serious case of wanderlust at that time and was always eager to travel abroad, and in part because information about these foreign knitting traditions was more readily available. I loved to knit but I had the feeling that most of our society regarded it as inconsequential, as not having any significant impact on American lives.

I distinctly remember lying on my bed in my small New York City apartment searching for stories about knitters in the United States in Richard Rutt's 1987 book, *A History of Hand Knitting* — only to be faced with this statement: "Information about the history of hand knitting in the United States is hard to find." A few years later I happened upon a paperback copy of *No Idle Hands: The Social History of American Knitting* by Anne Macdonald (first published in 1988); this book gave me my initial glimpse into domestic knitting history, was certainly more helpful than Rutt's book, and whetted my appetite for more. But more was slow in coming.

Having been asked to write a foreword for *Knitting America*, I have had the opportunity to review this comprehensive text before publication. While it doesn't surprise me that Susan Strawn has created such a fascinating book — when I first met her, when we both worked for Interweave Press (she as an illustrator and stylist and I as an editor), she immediately impressed me with her commitment to excellence and her eagerness to take on new challenges — I am still in awe of the scope of her accomplishment here. After leaving Interweave, she earned her Ph.D. and clearly honed her research skills.

What I find most fascinating about this book is how Susan has placed the history of knitting within the context of American history, so we can clearly see how knitting is intertwined with such subjects as geography, migration, politics, economics, female emancipation, and evolving social mores. She has traced how a melting pot of knitting traditions found their way into American culture via vast waves of immigration, expanded opportunity for travel, and technology. She has shown how knitting has provided solace during difficult times, from the Great Depression to the days following September 11. She has documented the significant contributions knitters have made during periods of war, especially the Revolutionary War, the Civil War, and World Wars I and II. She has demonstrated how the first American knitters created clothing that was crucial for survival, how knitting evolved into a symbol of feminine propriety and then later into a symbol of rebellion, how some American women used knitting as a means of earning income at times when other types of employment were not open to them, and how today, while it can still be a method of earning a living, it has become primarily a mode of creative expression. Along the way she illustrates this history with a plentiful supply of visual imagery (much of it rarely seen before), including reproductions of paintings, photographs, and/or advertisements on nearly every page.

I know that in the years to come I will refer back to this book many times, rereading certain passages and marveling over images — maybe the Pacific Northwest Tulalip Indian on page 50 or Grace Coolidge, the only first lady known to have entered her knitting in county fairs, on page 111, or the song lyrics for the musical sensation of the 1910s "Listen to the Knocking at the Knitting Club" on page 74, or the advertisement from 1918 on page 87 for the newest invention (and one of my favored tools), the circular knitting needle. I know that Susan, now a committed and generous scholar, hopes that her book will inspire other writers to delve even deeper into the rich topic of American knitting history. I believe that will happen. But first we must take a bit of time to appreciate her validating work and to thank her for sharing it with us.

Melanie Falick
Editorial director of STC Craft; author of *Knitting in America, Kids Knitting, Weekend Knitting,* and *Handknit Holidays,* and co-author of *Knitting for Baby;* former editor-in chief of *Interweave Knits* magazine

Opposite page:
American knitters — snapshots through time.

Knitting America

This is a book that tells many stories about knitting in America. There are stories about ways that knitting was brought to America and helped provide for the early settlers who spread across the land. There is a story about the role knitting played in one of America's first best-selling books, the captivity narrative of Mary Rowlandson. Yarn and knitting needles in portraits of American women tell the story of personal industry and of dedication to home and family. And there are stories too numerous to mention about knitting during America's many wars — all except one war. The story of American knitting also holds many success stories about immigrants who founded yarn companies and about knitting instructors and designers who carved out careers in the knitting industry.

Bishop Rutt, the eminent historian of hand knitting, wrote, "Information about the history of hand knitting in the United States is hard to find." I understand how he felt. The history of knitting can be elusive. In the past, knitters have seldom thought to mention such an ordinary, everyday part of life as knitting. And most things that are knit are practical. They are intended to be used up and worn out, not preserved under glass. While writing this book, I learned that knitting was there in the historical record, but I had to look closely and develop a certain savvy about finding it. Once I did, my dilemma changed from desperate searching to coping with an encroaching avalanche of information about knitting that appeared in the historical record.

Without technological advances in the way our civilization stores and retrieves knowledge, this book would have taken a lifetime to research and write. So many scholarly articles and books have been digitized and can be searched for references to knitting (or "stocking" or "mitten"). In the past, this simple task carried out now in a few keyboard strokes would have required extensive travel, research permission, and weeks of reading. The presidential papers at the Library of Congress, for example, have been transcribed, so online keyword searches uncovered the history of women who sent hand-knit stockings to President Abraham Lincoln. And I discovered more stories about knitters who are otherwise lost to history.

Collections of photographs, many digitized and searchable in online databases, often raise more questions than answers about knitters and knitting. Why was a Japanese-American woman photographed knitting in a World War II internment camp? Similarly, collections of hand knits, seldom digitized or searchable online, hold stories of the families who preserved and donated them to museums. If knitting is intended to be used and worn out, why are so many everyday pieces of practical hand knits donated to museums? Without the librarians and collection curators, the fragile stories in the photos and textiles would also be lost to history.

One purpose of this book is to entertain. Another is to consider knitting as a topic worthy of serious research. If you close your eyes and place your finger on any page of this book, you will find a topic for a thesis, dissertation, or biography. More than anything else the stories in this book are intended to honor the craft of knitting and take knitting beyond its often trivialized stereotype.

Opposite page: Grandma passes down to her granddaughter knowledge on how to spin and knit. (Photograph © Underwood & Underwood/Corbis)

Chapter 1

The First American Knitters

The unremarkable and intimate stuff of everyday life, knitting and its story in early America must be teased from the historical record a bit at a time. Letters and diaries, paintings and memoirs, account books, wills and inventories that survived through the centuries reveal the story of knitting, though in fleeting details. Knitting receives an occasional mention in only the most meticulously kept diaries of a compulsive knitter who recorded inches knit on

Needlework tools include a silver knitting needle case, 1700–1800 (upper left corner) and a silver, heart-shaped knitting sheath, 1790–1840 (lower left corner). (Winterthur Museum)

a stocking or mitten each day. Resisting the seductive myths, knowledge about knitting grows thanks to documents, clothing, and patterns that reveal knitting heritage.

Before the arrival of European explorers and settlers, there's no evidence that the people already living on the North American continent — the most isolated of the world's continents at the time — had developed their own knitting traditions. Icelandic sailors and explorers may have been the earliest European arrivals. The Spanish — seekers of gold, silver, and native labor — founded Saint Augustine in 1565, colonized South America, and had settled Santa Fe by 1610. Spanish settlers introduced hardy desert *churra* sheep, and the Pueblo people used their wool for weaving and, likely, for knitting learned from the Spanish.

Europeans from other knitting nations arrived along the Atlantic Coast, enticed by the letter on American exploration printed and distributed by Americo Vespucci throughout Europe. In 1607, the Virginia Company attempted — and failed — to establish the first English village at Jamestown, Virginia. Dissident English Puritans settled successfully in Plymouth, Massachusetts, in 1620. Others

Opposite page: Knitting signified the early American feminine ideal of an industrious housewife dedicated to home and family. In this portrait entitled *Mrs. Ammi Ruhamah Robbins, 1812* by painter Reuben Moulthrop, Mrs. Robbins appears to have been knitting a stocking in the round using cotton or linen yarn. (Detroit Art Institute)

Historical Pattern
1600s Monmouth Cap

In 1979, Kirstie Buckland published her observations of the Monmouth cap from the Monmouth Local History collection in Costume: The Journal of the Costume Society. *According to Buckland, this cap was "believed to be a genuine specimen and the only survivor." Her description follows:*

"It is seamless stocking stitch throughout, with a flat double brim knitted together at the edge, which continued into a loop, the crown is finished off with a small button, and it is knitted in coarse, thick, 2-ply wool, felted, thickened and shorn. It may have been dyed after or during felting. The most noticeable feature is the shape which is achieved with mathematical care and simplicity; all in plain knitting, and in multiples of ten and twenty, it could not be simpler for an illiterate novice to learn. It follows a carefully head-hugging, helmet-shaped pattern suggesting that this was important. It is in excellent condition but very small, eight inches deep, twenty-two inches (55 centimetre) and only fifty-nine stitches in circumference at the junction of crown and brim, making roughly 2½ stitches to the inch (one stitch per centimeter) after shrinking. It is arrogant to presume that the knitter made a mistake, but it is obviously more successful with sixty stitches. It follows the shape of the wearer's head, curving where he pulled it down to his ears. It was not designed to flatter — was it intended to be worn inside a helmet?"

Buckland also refers to the "small top-knot" on the cap, so perhaps the yarns at the top of the cap were finished into the "button" to which she refers earlier.

This knit cap is believed the only true example of a surviving Monmouth cap. Knit in the round using fine brown 2-ply wool yarn, the cap was fulled and measures 8 inches deep and 22 inches (59 stitches) in circumference at the brim. (Monmouth Local History Collection, Monmouth Museum, Wales)

soon followed: the Dutch in New York, more Puritans in the Massachusetts Bay Colony, Swedes Delaware, French in Maryland and Louisiana, Quakers in Pennsylvania, and waves of settlers from France, Ireland, and Barbados in the Carolinas. By 1700, North America was home to some two hundred thousand Europeans, many of whom were indentured artisans who provided labor in the colonies. By 1700 as well, colonists had brought thirty-one thousand African slaves as servants and laborers in fields of rice, tobacco, and indigo.

Knitting in the Colonies

The first colonists brought simply the same clothing they wore in their mother countries and dressed according to occupation and social status. In 1607, the Virginia Company advised that each man en route to Jamestown take a knit Monmouth cap and three pairs of silk stockings (plus three shirts, three falling bands, one waistcoat, three suits of lightweight cloth, four pairs of shoes, and one pair of garters). Stockings had come into fashion during the early sixteenth century and the middle classes adopted them from the wealthy. These fashionable silk stockings, worn with knee-length breeches, suggest the Jamestown men expected a much warmer climate.

Fifteenth-century artisans in Monmouth, Wales, first knit the caps, typically in natural shades of fine brown wool from local Ryeland sheep. The

caps warranted mention as an "honorable badge of service" for a Welshman in Shakespeare's *Henry V* (1599). English knitters copied the style, and British soldiers and sailors soon wore the practical, warm Monmouth caps. The extant Monmouth cap in the Monmouth Local History Collection at the Monmouth Museum, Wales, was knit in the round using heavy, two-ply wool with a flat double brim, well-fulled, and finished at the crown with a small loop knit from the last few stitches and caught down into the knitting.[1]

The Jamestown expedition failed due, in part, to the lack of proper clothing and perhaps not enough warm knit stockings. A 1622 London broadsheet — titled *The Inconvenients that have happened to Some Persons which Have transported Themselves from England to Virginia, without Provisions Necessary to Sustain Themselves* — advised future colonists take warmer clothes.[2] The Massachusetts Bay Company heeded the advice and sent more suitable garb with subsequent Puritan convoys during the 1630s. Each immigrant was given (among much else) four pairs of stockings, a woolen cap, and two red knit caps.[3] The stockings brought to America were not necessarily hand knit, or even knit at all. Some seventeenth-century stockings were cut and sewn from woven fabric. Sturdy sewn-fabric stockings were cut on the bias, a tailor's technique that lends stretch for a snug fit. The knitting machine was invented in 1589, but its use was controversial. Machine, or frame, knitters turned out fine silk stockings for fashionable men and women, but they threatened the livelihood of England's

American colonists owned and wore fine hand knits that were European in origin. These Women's mitts were knit in cotton and probably brought to America from the Netherlands or England circa 1700. (Colonial Williamsburg Foundation)

hand knitters, many of whom were impoverished rural women in desperate need of money earned with home knitting. There was an extensive hand knitting industry in seventeenth-century England: Sarah Fell's account books record many hand-knit stockings purchased by the Fell family, and traveler Celia Fiennes saw widespread hand knitting, including stockings, throughout rural seventeenth-century England.[4]

The woolen caps were most likely hand knit, however, and Americans imported thousands from England. Early Plymouth records do not mention knitting in the colony, but knitting was a common skill in England, so Plymouth settlers likely took up needles and yarn. When the Weavers' Guild of Boston compiled knitting patterns for costumes worn at Plimoth Plantation — a contemporary reproduction of the settlement — it based designs on vintage depictions or extant English hand knits from the same era. The Weavers' Guild patterns include three styles of English caps: a thrum cap, a flat cap, and a cap similar to the Monmouth. Shown in seventeenth-century woodcuts and paintings, a thrum (or thrummed) cap was knit with ends of single lengths of yarn drawn at random through the knit stitches and knotted — a thrifty use for leftover yarns. A flat cap was knit in wool in the round, fulled, and blocked. The Weavers' Guild knitters located two flat caps at the Metropolitan Museum of Art and two at the Museum of London. The Victoria & Albert Museum has one of many flat caps found at late medieval and renaissance sites. This cap was knit, fulled, cut, and re-sewn to create a double brim. Such caps were the subject of the Cappers Act of 1571: Every English resident older than six years and of a lower status than "gentleman" had to wear a wool cap made in England on Sundays and holidays or face a fine. This was one of many acts passed during the Tudor reign to protect the cap-making industry.

For Plimoth Plantation costumes, the Weavers' Guild of Boston knitters based five additional patterns on knit pieces excavated from the Gunnister archaeological site of a young man buried in a Shetland Islands peat bog. Although the Gunnister grave dates to the late seventeenth century, rural styles changed slowly, and people presumably wore similar knits earlier in the century. Based on detailed analyses of the hand knit pieces from the Society of Antiquaries of Scotland, the Weavers' Guild knitters designed a small, finely knit drawstring purse, gray with a red-and-white pattern; gloves with gauntlets; knee-length stockings; a heavily fulled cap with turn-up brim; and a cap without a brim, structurally similar to the Monmouth cap but with a pile created by tight loops of unspun fiber knit into the cap that obscures the knitting. They also designed an undershirt knit in the round after a child's earth-brown knit shirt, mittens based on fragments of a child's mitten, and garters (in garter stitch) — all patterned after pieces in the textile collection at the Museum of London.[5]

Knitting soon became part of a colonial girl's education, as one of many domestic skills that prepared her

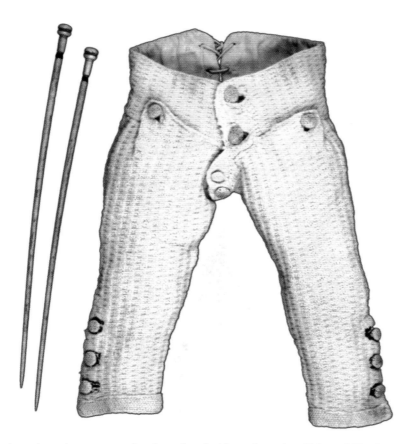

Boy's knee breeches, circa 1790, knit either in America or Europe in cotton and lined with linen. (Colonial Williamsburg Foundation)

A 1771 woodcut depicts the capture of Mary White Rowlandson during the attack on her home in 1676. Rowlandson had her knitting and needles in a pocket tied beneath her skirts. (American Antiquarian Society)

for the role of wife and mother. Edward Kimber visited America during the early 1700s and observed, "After dinner they retir'd, the Boys to School, and the Girls to their Spinning and Knitting."[6] Children as young as five or six learned to knit, often stockings. A girl from a wealthy family might attend school during adolescence, where she would stitch samplers and further hone her needlework skills. As adults, women from less wealthy or rural families bartered their hand knit items for clothing or food. From the 1740s through the 1760s, colonial merchant Jabez Carpenter kept records showing some customers settled accounts with hand knit clothing, such as Susannah Reed, who paid her account balance with five pairs of hand knit mittens and a pair of stockings.[7]

English colonists used cloth and clothing, including knit stockings, as ceremonial gifts or payment for allies among the New England Indian tribes. Colonists who moved into the frontier regions, in turn, adopted practical Indian deerskin leggings and breech cloths. Frequent disputes among English settlers and Indian tribes escalated into the bloody Metacom's Rebellion, better known as King Philip's War. Both sides committed atrocities and took captives. On February 10, 1676, thirty-eight-year-old Mary White Rowlandson and her three children were taken captive during an attack on Lancaster, Massachusetts. Rowlandson was shot in the side by the same bullet that fatally wounded Sarah, the six-year-old daughter she carried in her arms. For eleven weeks and five days, she moved frequently with her captors. Rowlandson wrote that "because of my wound, I was somewhat favoured in my load; I carried only my knitting work and two quarts of parched meal." When captured, she had carried her knitting in her pocket, a separate piece of clothing tied around her waist beneath skirt and petticoat. In 1682, Rowlandson told of the importance of her knitting in her captivity narrative titled, "The Soveraignty and Goodness of God, Together with the Faithfulness of His Promises Displayed."[8]

A pastor's wife, Rowlandson considered captivity a test of faith and refused to knit on the Sabbath: "I was at this time knitting a pair of white cotton stockins for my mistress; and had not yet wrought upon a Sabbath day; when the Sabbath came they bade me go to work; I told them it was the Sabbath day, and desired them to let me rest, and told them I would do as much more to morrow; to which they answered me, they would break my face." One of Rowlandson's captors removed stockings from a victim following a battle and brought them to Rowlandson. "Then came an Indian to me with a pair of stockings that were too big for him," she wrote, "and he would have me ravel them out, and knit them fit for him." When Rowlandson knitted for her captors, she received more food and clothing. One captor asked her to "knit a pair of Stockins, for which she gave me a quart of Pease," while another "asked me to knit him three pair of Stockins, for which I had a Hat, and a silk Handkerchief." She suffered from hunger and counted herself fortunate to be able to knit in exchange for better fare. Rowlandson left a record of knitwear adopted into her captors' dress: One man wore "white Stockins" with girdles of wampum on his head and shoulders, and a woman wore "fine red Stokins and white Shoos."[9] She also recorded kindnesses shown to her by Philip, the Pokanoket sachem, and knit a shirt and cap for his son. Rowlandson was ransomed and released in early May 1676, the place marked by a boulder still known as Redemption Rock.[10] Though her youngest daughter died, Rowlandson's other two children were released.

The colonial population included large numbers of African slaves. Between 1619 and 1807 — England abolished slave trading in 1807 — some four hundred thousand slaves were imported into North America. Slave owners bought coarse, low-quality, European-style clothing for their slaves, and account records include knit Monmouth caps. None of the Monmouth caps appear to have survived, although a reference appears in a 1768 advertisement for a runaway servant who might have been wearing "a Monmouth cap, a brown linen shirt and trowsers."[11] Advertisements for runaway slaves also describe clothing, as evidenced in a 1775 newspaper advertisement listing "thread stockings" worn by a runaway.[12] Thread stockings, knit from linen, were better quality than plaid stockings, which were bias-cut from woven cloth[13] and were worn by most slaves. Presumably, thread stockings meant this particular runaway slave worked in the household.

African slaves were also knitters. Documents — newspapers, diaries, account books, wills — from Maryland and Virginia show slaves made textiles, including knitting for their own families. Although some slaves learned to spin and weave in Africa, the plantation mistress or white employees usually taught slaves to knit. John Mason of Virginia recalled that during the 1770s his father's slaves made their own coarse clothing and stockings, and they knit finer textiles for the white family, especially the children.[14] Martha Forman of Rose Hill, Maryland, taught her youngest house girls to knit, and they made stockings for all fifty slaves on her plantation. Harriet Batten, one of the Forman house slaves, learned to knit at age five and, when she was eight, she knit more than half the stockings worn at Rose Hill.[15] Martha Washington's personal knitter, a dower (inherited) slave named Lame Peter, taught slave women to knit. George Washington wrote his overseer to keep an eye on Peter, who tended to knit stockings that were too small for their intended wearers.[16] Thomas Jefferson, who suffered from the cold and arthritis much of his life, wore hand-knit slipper socks, presumably made by slaves at Monticello. During the eighteenth century, knitting was part of the curriculum for black children in schools that the Bray Associates, an English missionary organization set up in Virginia and North Carolina. In 1760, the Bray school hired Ann Wager to teach both boys and girls in their Williamsburg, Virginia, school; she was to teach the "Girls to Sew knit, &c. as well as *all* to read & say their Catechism."[17]

Throughout the seventeenth and eighteenth centuries, well-to-do colonists could afford to wear expensive British imports, including frame-knit stockings. Women who lived in rural areas were more likely to make their own hand-knit stockings. Colonists had flax for linen and even experimented with silk. Sheep were scarce during the colonial period, so the northern colonists often mixed wool with linen (called linsey-woolsey[18]), while southerners mixed it with cotton, which was available on a small scale during the eighteenth century. Disputes with Britain were ongoing after the Parliament of England passed the Woolen Act of 1699, which intended to protect the British textile industry from fledgling ones in the American colonies. The act prohibiting the colonies from selling or exporting certain textiles was an effort to keep the colonies in their place as only a source of raw materials for Britain's powerful textile industry giants. When more disputes arose with

Britain, colonists agitated to ban luxury goods and boycott British textiles. Slaveholders turned over the job of making cloth and clothing to the slaves themselves after the colonies boycotted British imports.[19]

Revolutionary Knitting

More and more colonists made and wore their own clothing, first as a symbol of resistance and then as an open revolt against Britain. In 1769, the Virginia Merchants Association advocated a ban of British goods, including luxuries like silks and woolen worsted, but also stockings.[20] Although women were not heroes in battle, they fought for independence by establishing spinning groups and spinning their own yarn to make sure Americans were "cloathed with the work of our own hands." Instead of embroidery lessons during school, Virginian Betsy Ambler Brent knit stockings. New York City teenager Charity Clarke knit "stockens" from homespun yarn her friend gave her and said that she "felt Nationly."[21]

Rebellion over taxation without representation peaked in 1773 at the Boston Tea Party, marking the beginning of the War of Independence. The first shots were fired at Lexington and Concord, Massachusetts, and on July 4, 1776, the colonies adopted The Unanimous Declaration of the Thirteen United States of America. The War of Independence would last eight and a half years. George Washington was elected commander in chief, and his first duty was to maintain the American Continental Army — never more than sixty thousand men — in the field.

This fragment, presumed to be the bottom of a waistcoat front, was knit of silk and gilt metal in the early seventeenth century, probably in Europe. (Colonial Williamsburg Foundation). Gift of Kathleen A. Epstein

Top: A waistcoat sleeve fragment, knit of silk and gilt metal in the early seventeenth century, probably in Europe. (Colonial Williamsburg Foundation) Gift of Kathleen A. Epstein

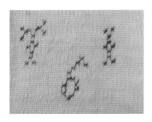

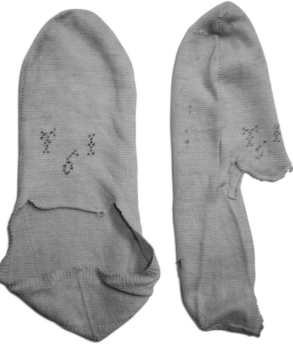

Hand-knit slipper socks worn by President Thomas Jefferson. His initials, "T J," and the numeral "6" are embroidered in cross stitch. Jefferson suffered from the cold, and the number indicates he had at least six pairs of slipper socks, likely slave knitted. Throughout the seventeenth and eighteenth centuries, both men and women wore hand-knit stockings. Family members knit some stockings; knitters with cottage businesses also sold hand-knit stockings. Although machine-knit stockings were available, hand-knit stockings were worn by preference, for economic necessity, or as a political statement. (National Society Daughters of the American Revolution)

Clothing shortages for soldiers in the Continental Army were a chronic, often desperate problem. Throughout the war, Washington wrote heartbreaking letters to Congress pleading for more troops and clothing — notably stockings for the soldiers' bare and bleeding feet. In September 1777, Washington wrote to the Pennsylvania deputy quartermaster, "You are hereby authorized to impress all the Blankets, Shoes, Stockings [and other Articles of Cloathing] for the use of the Army, that can be spared by the Inhabitants in the Counties of Bucks, Philadelphia and Northampton, paying for the same at reasonable Rates, [or give Certificates]."[22] Again in October 1777, he begged Congress for "Supplies [that] may be obtained to relieve our distresses, which in the Articles of Shoes, Stockings and Blankets are extremely great."[23] He wrote to Patrick Henry in December 1777, "We had in Camp not less than 2898 Men unfit for duty by reason of their being barefoot and otherwise naked."[24] Washington's pleas for stockings, shoes, and blankets continued throughout the war, particularly when brutal winters bore down on his ragged army. If they were fortunate to have more than rags in which to wrap their feet after their shoes wore out, Washington's soldiers wore fabric stockings or leggings. Washington's sister-in-law sent stockings she had knit to the general in April 1777, and he wrote back to his brother John, "I thank her for the trouble she has taken in knitting the Stockings."[25] Stories abound about Martha Washington knitting for the soldiers when she joined her husband at Valley Forge. A lovely story — and even a painting — traces no further back than

Colonial Revival periods of the nineteenth century. The collection and archives at Mount Vernon hold no evidence that she was a knitter. Knitting was utilitarian; Martha Washington was a wealthy woman known for other needlework more appropriate to her genteel station in life, particularly embroidery and needlepoint chair seats.

Most women in colonial America were subservient to husbands. The American Revolution, however, brought many women into public life. Rhoda Farrand of Parsnippany, New Jersey, was among these women. According to the story handed down to Eleanor A. Hunter, Rhoda's great granddaughter, Rhoda organized women to knit hundreds of warm woolen stockings after her husband wrote to her about the soldiers' bleeding feet in Morristown, New Jersey:

> "We are here for the winter, in Morristown,
> And a sorry sight are our men today
> In tatters and rags with no signs of pay.
> As we marched to camp, if a man looked back,
> By the dropping blood he could trace our track;
> For scarcely a man has a decent shoe,
> And there's not a stocking the army through;
> So send us stockings as quick as you can,
> My company needs them, every man,
> And every man is a neighbor's lad;
> Tell this to their mothers, *they need them bad*."

Rhoda began knitting stockings at once, while her son drove her to neighbors to recruit more knitters:

> She turned to her daughters, Hannah and Bet:
> "Girls, each on your needles a stocking set:
> Get my cloak and hood; as for you, son Dan,
> Yoke up the steers as quick as you can;
> Put a chair in the wagon, as you're alive;
> I will sit and knit, while you go and drive."

"Knit," said Rhoda to all, "as fast as you can." The rush was on to knit stockings for the soldiers:

> On Thursday, they knit from morn till night,
> She and the girls, with all their might.
> When the yarn gave out, they carded and spun,
> And every day more stockings were done.
> When the wool was gone, then they killed a sheep —
> A cosset — but nobody stopped to weep,
> They pulled the fleece and they carded away,
> And spun and knitted from night until day.

When the stockings were knit, Rhoda and her son Dan delivered them to the soldiers in Morristown, New Jersey:

Martha Washington, the wife of General George Washington, knitting during the Revolutionary War. This reproduction of the painting *Washington, Our First War Time Knitter* was printed between 1900 and 1920, one of several American Colonial Revival movements. Stories about Martha Washington knitting for the soldiers trace to nineteenth-century writing, not to extant knitting or papers that indicate she actually was a knitter. (Library of Congress)

On Monday morn, at an early hour
The stockings came in — a perfect shower —
A shower that lasted until the night;
Black, brown and grey ones, and mixed blue and
    white.
There were pairs one hundred and thirty-three,
Long ones, remember, up to the knee;
And the next day Rhoda carried them down
In the old ox-wagon to Morristown.
I hear, like an echo, the soldiers' cheers
For Rhoda and Dan, the wagon and steers,
Growing wilder yet for the chief in command;
While up at "salute" to the brow flies each hand,
As Washington passes, desiring them
To thank Mistress Farrand in the name of his
    men.
But the words that her husband's lips let fall,
"I knew you would do it!" were best of all.[26]

The details here are embroidered perhaps, yet grounded in historical accuracy. Letters, diaries, and journals describe Washington's armies marching miles through heavy rains and muddy roads, their feet wrapped in rags and many without shoes. Washington spent two winters at Morristown, where soldiers who were cold, starving, and unpaid took up arms and began marching on the Continental Congress in Philadelphia until he convinced them to turn back.

The 1776 Revolution created a dynamic and rapidly growing republic, although not all Americans had won. Loyalists who fought for the British felt betrayed, and many immigrated to Canada. Native American Indians were forced to cede large tracts of land to the new government and were pushed west of the Mississippi River. Thomas Jefferson's draft for the Declaration of Independence addressed slavery, accusing Britain of being responsible for the African slave trade — although Jefferson himself held slaves at Monticello. Southern congressional delegates struck the anti-slavery phrase, fearful their slaves would be freed. The British slave trade ended in 1807 and New England states passed laws to ban slavery — 13 percent of American blacks were free in 1820. Southern states, however, considered slavery an economic necessity, laying the seeds for the Civil War.

Knitting in a New Republic

The war over, the new nation became a republic. The first presidents — George Washington, John Adams, Thomas Jefferson — led the nation through the War of 1812 and dramatic westward expansion. Americans who ventured into new territory worked at keeping up appearances, and eastern merchants supplied the frontier with all manner of goods — cotton and worsted-wool stockings, cotton and linen fabric, ribbons, cloaks, buttons, and frying pans — all floated on keelboats along rivers or pulled in carts across the mountains. Silk stockings appeared in orders from frontier Ohio as early as 1790. Still largely a barter economy, J. B. Robinson advertised in 1821 he would sell carding wool in exchange for frontier products

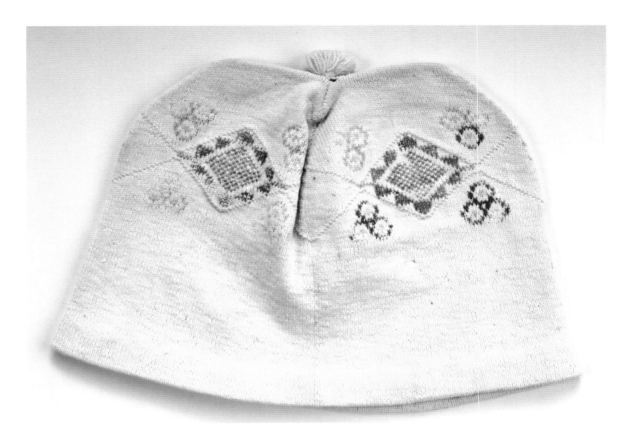

In addition to stockings, knitters made nightcaps. Amos Plimpton (1795–1852) of Massachusetts wore this hand-knit, hand-embroidered cotton nightcap, circa 1830. (Historic Deerfield Collection, Deerfield, Massachusetts)

like wheat, corn, and beeswax. Although the finery of life sounds incongruous with frontier life, settlers wanted to build the kind of society that needed silk stockings, stylish coats, fine tea, and silver table-spoons.[27]

Frame knitting machines were in America by 1773, although hand knitters continued to make stockings and mittens at home for their families and to sell or trade. The Historic Deerfield collection holds knit gloves and stockings made in the Nathaniel Robinson spinning factory in Pawlet, Vermont, in 1820. David Barrows of Germantown, in present-day Philadelphia, recorded details of his life as a frame knitter from 1841 to 1851, including yarn purchased and numbers of mittens and stockings knit.[28] Hand-knit stockings were kept in demand by Americans like Abigail Robinson who purchased them. A single Quaker woman from Newport, Rhode Island, Abigail kept meticulous accounts of her life from 1794 to 1834, including the amounts she paid for hand-knit stockings. In 1803, she bought yarn for three pairs of stockings for her nephew and paid four shillings to Rebecca Goddard for knitting two pairs. She paid in cash rather than barter, particularly to poor neighbors who needed money they earned from knitting.[29]

Martha Ballard was an industrious midwife and knitter who lived on the Maine frontier. From 1785 to 1812, she kept a detailed diary — weather, illness, death, weaving, spinning, mending, knitting, and pre-

siding as midwife at more than eight hundred births. Knitting was part of her daily routine, as her diary entries list:

I have done my housework and knit a mitten for Cyrus Except the thumb.
Mended Mr. Ballard's mitts & knit some.
Clear & warm. I have workt in the gardin, knit some, boiling soap. . . Mr. Wiman made us a present of 12 fish.

False labor during delivery number fifty-one took her to the expecting household four times before the baby finally arrived. While she waited, Ballard "settled into her knitting, producing two pairs of gloves and five and a half pairs of mittens."[30]

In well-to-do urban families, daughters enjoyed knitting as part of the genteel life in refined house-holds. Knitting was one of many diversions in the daily life of Frances Baylor Hill, who in 1797 wrote in her diary, "Got up early knit a little, read, wrote a let-ter to Cousin Betsy Hill by Papa, cut out a piece of linning and sew'd on Mama's apron." In 1787, Lucinda Lee recalled young ladies who dressed up and gathered at afternoon tea parties, each toting their knitting and sewing work.[31] Perhaps these young women added knitting to hope chests that would one day furnish their own households. Prosperous matrons were also at leisure to create knit finery, their

This colorful hand-knit cotton nightcap, circa 1830, belonged to Amos Plimpton (1795–1852) of Massachusetts. (Historic Deerfield Collection, Deerfield, Massachusetts)

Knitted silk sewing case made by Mary W. Alsop of Middletown, Connecticut, in 1814. Worked in blue letters at the top, under a flap, is the name "L:ALSOP," and on the other side the initials "M:A. 1814" are knit at the fold of the flap. Lined with striped silk, the sewing case has flannel half circles for sewing needles and a pocket to hold thimble and thread. Inside one pocket is a handwritten card that reads: "Needlebook Knit and made by Great Grandmother Mary Wright Alsop for her Son Joseph W. Alsops wife Lucy Whittilsy Alsop." Women with leisure time for needlework could knit such finery as gifts. (Winterthur Museum. Gift of Francis du Pont)

slender knitting needles kept stylish silver knitting needle cases.

"Poetry" mittens also demonstrated knitting expertise. Blue-and-white homespun-wool poetry mittens at the Smithsonian National Museum of American History date to the early nineteenth century. There is shag knit at the wrists, and a poem is knit throughout the mittens, starting at the wrist of one, spiraling to the top, and continuing from the wrist to the top of the second mitten. The name William Watson is found on each thumb, possibly the name of the poet. The knitter designed the mittens using Xs to separate poetic lines:

One thing you must not borrow nor never give away X For he who borrows trouble will have it every day X But if you have a plenty and more then [*sic*] you can bear X It will not lighten yours XX if others have a share X You must learn to be contented then will your trouble cease X And then you may be certain that you will live in peace X For a contented mind is a continual feast.[32]

Practical business or fancy work for home and family, American knitting fell into the traditional woman's sphere. Republican motherhood was the new model followed by women who nurtured the home and raised the next generation of citizens, while men competed in the marketplace and public life. Then in 1837 came the coronation of England's Queen Victoria, an event that would usher in knitting as part of a new cult of domesticity.

These wool baby mittens were knit circa 1827–1834. Eighteenth- and early nineteenth-century knitters made mittens by the dozens for the family or to sell. These mittens were probably worn by one or all three sons of Caroline Elizabeth and Judge Andrew Galbraith, appointed United States District Judge of Wisconsin in 1838. (Wisconsin Historical Society)

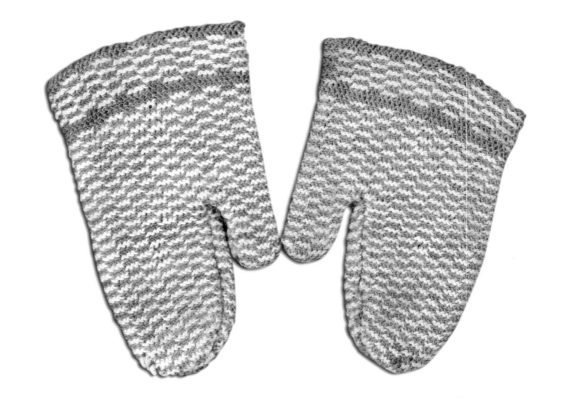

A proficient though anonymous knitter made these "poetry" mittens in the early nineteenth century. The mittens are knit of blue and white homespun wool yarn, with shag knit at the wrists. The poem begins at the wrist of one mitten, spirals to the top, and winds from the wrist to the top of the second mitten. The name "William Watson" on each thumb is presumed to be the name of the poet. (Smithsonian Institution, National Museum of American History)

Chapter 2

Victorians Knit in a Culture of Domesticity

How to Knit and What to Knit.

☞ GIVEN FOR ONLY 4 SUBSCRIBERS AT 25 CENTS EACH PER YEAR.

This is the best book yet published on Fancy Knitting. It teaches how to knit, giving description clear, concise, and easily understood. Everything illustrated. Shows cuts and gives Five Different Ways of casting on stitches. Tells how to knit plain' knitting, and to purl or seam, how to pick up a stitch, and how to repair a half-knitted stitch; gives two ways to increase, tells how to slip a stitch, how to narrow, how to cast off and how to join ends; gives careful directions for knitting stockings, gives different ways of forming the heels and toes. Tells how to insert a new heel and sole in an old worn stocking; gives directions for common and artistic darning that will imitate the knitted stitch. Gives directions for numerous styles for fancy borders for stockings, mittens, etc., etc.; squares for quilts, afghans, and many other things.

We send this book for 4 subscribers, or 25 cents.

When Queen Victoria came to the throne of England in 1837, she brought a refreshing return to the importance of family. During her long reign, she set a tone of domesticity and gentility in England and America. Women admired her love for her husband, her large family, and her devotion to home and duty. The mistress of the middle-class Victorian home and family sought to create a haven of culture and serenity. American women followed styles of dress set by Queen Victoria, too. The queen's bridal gown was white satin trimmed with orange flower blossoms and a veil of white Honiton lace. She dressed her little sons in sailor suits, a style that American mothers adopted for their sons. More families lived in cities during the Victorian era, and men worked in professions that paid well enough to buy exotic or domestic bric-a-brac for the home and hire servants from the waves of new immigrants to tend elaborate Victorian décor and social ritual.

The cult of Victorian domesticity drove a wedge between home and work: men earned a living and women kept the home. In a March 1850 article entitled "The Sphere of Woman," the popular *Godey's Lady's Book* advised readers that "the prudent woman reigns in her family circle, making happiness and every virtue possible, and spreading harmony and peace throughout her domain. What is the highest happiness of man, but to carry out what he knows to be right and good, and to have full control over the means to this end? And where are our dearest and inmost ends in life, but in the household?" *Godey's* advised the Victorian woman not to stray from her home sphere: "As the sexes were designed to fill different positions in the economy of life, it would not be in harmony with the manifestations of Divine wisdom in all things else, to suppose that the powers of each were not peculiarly fitted for their own appropriate sphere. Woman gains nothing — she always loses when she leaves her own sphere for that of man."[33]

"The best book yet on fancy knitting," promised *The Ladies' Home Journal* in August 1885. The magazine sent *How to Knit and What to Knit* to any reader who recruited four subscribers, or mailed in 25¢.

Opposite page:
Mrs. Brown, a wealthy Victorian-era woman, posed for her formal portrait while knitting. The 1869 painting titled *The Brown Family* by Eastman Johnson depicts Mrs. Brown as the epitome of Victorian domestic propriety. (Fine Arts Museum of San Francisco, gift of Mr. and Mrs. John D. Rockefeller III)

During the second half of the nineteenth century, sentimental Gothic or Romantic Victorian literature like this engraving entitled "Happiness", found in *Godey's Lady's Book and Magazine* in 1862, depicted women as angelic sentinels of the home. The idealized Victorian woman was expected to find joy in her role as mother. Knitting signified this young mother's commitment to home and family under humble circumstances. Like many women who lived in rural areas and needed to knit stockings and mittens for the family, she was never without knitting needles in her hands.

Victorian-Era Knitters

The knitter exemplified the idealized image of dedicated, industrious Victorian wife and mother. Beginning in the White House, several First Ladies were devoted knitters. Eliza McCardle Johnson, wife of President Andrew Johnson and first lady from 1865 to 1869, adhered to the conventional idyll of the mid-nineteenth-century Victorian woman. She spent much of her time knitting, reading, or visiting with family, when she was not occupied soothing her husband during his post–Civil War administration. Similarly, Ida Saxton McKinley, first lady from 1897 to 1901, suffered from ill health and often confined herself to private quarters in the White House. She knit hundreds of bedroom slippers (the National First Ladies' Library has a pair) that charities auctioned for considerable sums.[34]

Oral histories show that many Victorian-era knitters who lived in rugged, rural areas were made of stern stuff. Elizabeth E. "Grammy" Miller was a Scotch-Yankee woman born in 1848. She married, gave birth to four sons, lived on a Vermont farm, and was never without her knitting, as she remembered:

> Mother and I knit all the long stockings for the women and girls and the footins and mittens from yarn I had spun. Land sakes, the footins, double mittens and single mittens I have knit. After I was married and the children were growing up, I was never without a pair of needles in my hands. In the fall I had somebody came in to help while I did up the fall spinning.
>
> . . . always colored my own yarns and I would make the boys' stockings striped grey and some other pretty color like blue to go with it. The legs were knit with a row of color and the feet plain. When I went out to a sociable or a farmers' meeting in the evening, I always took my knitting. We had a spanking pair then and when we were out in the carryall I knit up hill and down. My knitting went everywhere but to church. The only vacations I had in those days was when the children were born.[35]

Still, knitting was a pleasure for many women. The lyrics of an 1880 ballad, "Knitting the Scarf," romanticized the tender image of a young Victorian woman knitting for her absent lover.[36] Victorian-era poet Caroline Gilman idealized her time with needle and yarn in her poem "My Knitting Work:"

> My knitting-work! my knitting-work! a confidant art thou,
> As smooth and shining on my lap thou liest beside me now;
> Thou know'st some stories of my thoughts the

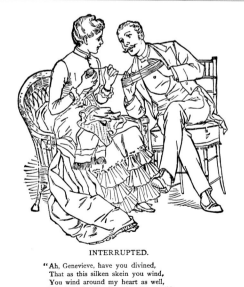

INTERRUPTED.

"Ah, Genevieve, have you divined,
That as this silken skein you wind,
You wind around my heart as well,
The thread of love's entangling spell?
Those smooth, soft hands, so dainty white—"
"I wash them morning, noon and night,
As you do yours, young man, I hope,
In lather made of IVORY SOAP.''

"Come Baby, Come," was the title of this 1880 engraving from *Godey's Lady's Book and Magazine*. Idyllic Victorian domestic bliss required little more than a humble cottage if a caring family dwelled within. The Victorian moral that money does not buy happiness dismissed the hardships of rural life.

Left: Knitting was a domestic skill that could attract a suitor to court a young Victorian woman as prospective wife, as shown in this Ivory Snow advertisement from 1887.

Portraits of wealthy Victorian families often showed a mother with her knitting, a symbol of her dedication to her domestic role. *The Hatch Family* by Eastman Johnson from 1871 is an imposing group portrait with three generations of the Hatch family in the library of their Park Avenue residence in New York City. (The Metropolitan Museum of Art, gift of Frederic H. Hatch)

many may not know,
As round and round the accustomed path my careful fingers go.

Sweet, silent, quiet knitting-work! Thou interruptest not
My reveries and pleasant thoughts, forgetting and forgot!
I take thee up and lay thee down, and use thee as I may,
And not a contradicting word thy burnished lips will say.

My moralizing knitting-work! thy threads most aptly show
How evenly around life's span our busy threads should go;
And if a stitch perchance should drop, as life's frail stitches will,
How, if we patient take it up, the work may prosper still.

Poet Opal Blaisdell Lenox hints at the very real person — all knitters can relate — beneath the idealized veneer of another Victorian knitter:

Milady, at the open window, sits
With countenance serene and look demure,
Her downcast eyes contributing allure.
The blush upon her cheek that glows and flits,
Adds glamour that demoralizes wits;
And waning sun with touch so light and sure,

Photography became another art medium during Victorian times. In "Portrait of the Artist's Mother," photographer Frances Stebbins Allen created an artistic study of light and form when he posed his mother with her knitting. (Frances Benjamin Johnston Collection, Library of Congress)

Makes of her hair a golden halo pure.
But modestly, Milady simply knits,
Intent upon the swiftly rhythmic flash
Of gleaming needles that is never stopped —
While world and I adore her beauty fair.
But now I rise and quickly close the sash,
For I have noted that a stitch is dropped,
And World — you must not hear Milady swear!

Victorian knitters often assembled albums with needlework samples and instructions for making favorite patterns. The Joseph Downs Collection at the Winterthur Archives in Winterthur, Delaware, has several of these tributes to Victorian industry that knitters no doubt shared with one another and handed down within their families. An album of knitting, crocheting, and tatting instructions from 1832–1888 includes 118 pages of instructions for making stockings, socks, shawls, baby clothes and shoes, bags, sofa cushions, and a bed rest, as well as twenty-two worked samples and a page depicting various stitches. Mrs. Charles Spencer prepared a fifty-six-page book, circa 1880, containing instructions for more than twenty knitting and crocheting patterns, along with six samples of fancywork designs pinned onto the pages. Another twenty-page album of knitting, crocheting, and lace-making instructions from around 1891 is attributed to Mrs. C. D. Mowry of

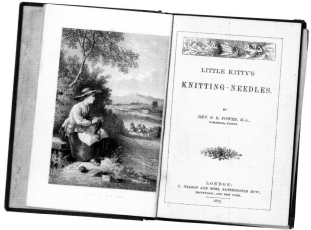

The good Reverend P. B. Power wrote *Little Kitty's Knitting-Needles* as a parable of a young girl helping the poor with the power of her knitting. Published in London and New York in 1875, it was a religious tract in disguise.

Mount Vernon, New York — or possibly she obtained the book from someone else. The album includes instructions for making lace, decorative edging, a diamond insertion, infants' shirts and socks, baby shoes, and a knit cape. The surviving album contains four finished samples and occasional comments on the patterns, such as, "I don't like this one."[37]

Godey's Lady's Book
American women relied on the many new self-help publications to guide them in Victorian propriety for home, wardrobe, childcare, and needlework. In *Mrs.*

This Bachelik Pelerine was short and open at the back with "prolonged . . . shawl-like ends in front" and a hood that "when thrown back, forms a kind of cape." *Godey's Lady's Book and Magazine,* December 1870.

Right: Miss Frances S. Lambert's books were among the most popular of the scores of Victorian-era needlework books. Advances in printing technology and growing leisure time for middle-class women drove the success of Victorian self-help books, including the needlework manuals that typically reinforced moral and religious values. Miss Lambert was English, but the lack of copyright protection allowed American publishers to print and distribute her books without her permission — "numerous petty piracies" she called them. Her other publications included *The Ladies' Complete Guide to Needlework and Embroidery* and *My Knitting Book.*

A reader received *Knitting and Crochet,* a needlework manual edited by Jenny June, in return for recruiting new subscribers to *The Ladies' Home Journal* in 1886.

Fig. 1.

Beeton's Book of Household Management, published in 1861, Mrs. Beeton instructed the growing number of middle-class families (the middle class tripled between 1851 and 1871) in social rules required in their new stations. Among her instructions for such details of behavior as retiring for the night and letters of introduction, she assured the Victorian wife and mother that "light or fancy needlework often forms a portion of the evening's recreation for the ladies of the household."[38] In *Letters to Young Ladies* (1854), Mrs. Lydia Huntley Sigourney advised the practice of needlework for refinement and accomplishment. In 1852, J. and J. L. Gihon published *The Ladies' Guide in Needlework:*

a Gift for the Industrious Containing Instructions on Canvas Work, Knitting, Netting and Crochet Work, Millinery and Mantua-Making, Embroidery and Applique. In 1886, N. D. Whitney & Co, Publishers (Boston) provided instruction in *The Lady's Book of Knitting: New and Easy Patterns of Useful and Ornamental Work.* The book claimed it was "compiled and edited by a lady expert, who has conscientiously tested all of them." She recommended the best pattern for turning a heel to inexperienced stocking knitters, reassuring them that "the heel seems to present mountains of difficulty" that "in reality the mountain is but a mole-hill after all." Miss Lambert, an Englishwoman, wrote several needlework books. In *Decorative Needlework* (1846), she provided an array of knitting stitches and patterns for insertions, shawls, caps, muffs, muffatees (wrist warmers), stockings, bags, bed covers, and cushions.[39]

Foremost among the advice magazines was *Godey's Lady's Book.* Published from 1830 to 1898, it offered a bible of guidance for all aspects of home and family, including needlework and fashion. In 1830, *Godey's* printed poetry; beauty tips; stories that were, in truth, thinly disguised morality plays; music; household hints and recipes ("receipts"); the latest London fashions; and a handful of embroidery and lacework patterns. Women's fashions in 1830 called for especially large, puffy sleeves over which a shawl was worn for warmth. The properly outfitted Victorian woman required a walking dress, carriage or promenade dress, evening

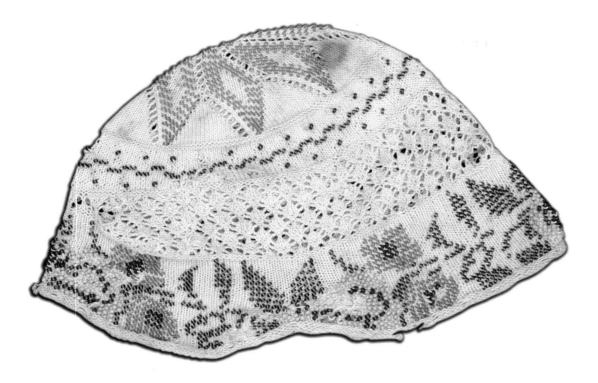

The Victorian knitter who wished to apply knitting to creative new uses needed to look no further than the knit egg holder in *The Art of Knitting*, 1892.

This rabbit penwiper could be knit using strategically placed increases and decreases to craft the shape of a rabbit. "A very good imitation of the fur of this little animal is made by knitting in loops with the single Berlin wool wound double, which loops are afterwards cut and carefully combed out," noted *Godey's Lady's Book and Magazine*, November 1870.

dress, morning dress, and more. Shawls were the height of Victorian fashion until 1870.

As the century progressed, *Godey's* incorporated much more knitting into its "Work Department" in every issue. By 1850, "The Work Table" was initiated, a feature that emphasized crochet, embroidery, and hair work. The column included only one knitting pattern in 1850, a "Necktie" scarf knit in blue and white Shetland wool with the ends joined together, drawn up, and embellished with tassels.[40] In 1853, *Godey's* article "History of Stockings" traced the invention of hand-knit stockings to Spain. According to *Godey's*, William Lee invented the framework knitting machine after he was expelled from university and was reduced to living on the income his wife could make by hand knitting stockings.[41] By the 1860s, *Godey's* expanded to include knitting patterns in each issue printed during the Civil War years, yet oddly, there were no patterns to knit for the soldiers. Instead, practical hand knits for home and family included stockings, winter cuffs (wristlets), baby socks, knee warmers, fingerless hunting gloves, driving gloves with fabric-lined palms, and knit "braces," or suspenders. *Godey's* also devised patterns for clever little luxuries, such as a lace "Railway Stocking," a Norwegian morning bonnet, gentleman's necktie, a woman's waist-length "Winter Spenser" top, a woman's Sontag jacket,[42] opera hood, silky bag purse, and more. Fashionable styles of gloves, mittens, and caps changed during the century, and women needed knitting patterns that kept them up to date.

Godey's Work Department generated an impressive range of patterns for miniatures, exotics, and other Victorian frou-frou during the 1870s. Most intriguing were patterns for knit artificial flowers — a white garden lily, fuchsia, heart's-ease, and others.[43] *Godey's* recommended the flowers as ornaments for trimming caps and bonnets and provided instructions in excruciatingly fidgety detail. A single fuchsia flower required four calyx sections each knit with split China silk and supported with bits of fine wire. In addition, the knitter fashioned pistol, stamen, corolla, and leaves (each a forty-eight-row repeat) on fine wire supports attached to a stem. To achieve the full handsome effect, instructions advised using several shades of colors and different sizes for leaves, buds, and flowers.

In addition to knitting, tatting, embroidery, and crochet, there were instructions for paper flowers, pincushions, fans, glove boxes, watch pockets, and ornamental boxes. A pattern for a "Gentleman's Knitted Shirt" appeared early in 1870; knit in white wool, this style would be called a slipover sweater today. Victorians were still warming chilly knees with knit knee caps in the 1870s. A dedicated wife could whip up a pair of suspenders in gray cotton. And for the Victorian woman, there were knit dainty slippers — with cork soles — to pull over her boots for evening parties. Or she could immerse herself in lace knitting a pelerine in fine white Shetland wool.[44]

Patterns for Victorian oddities defy imagination. *Godey's* offered a pattern for a crocheted boa with knit

Muffatee from Miss Lambert's *The Hand-book of Needlework*, 1846. As she noted, "Two colours are generally used — say red and white. They are prettiest in German wool."

[THE STANDARD FILIERE.]

Knitters used different types of filieres, or gauges, with graduated openings to determine needle sizes. There was no universal standard during the Victorian era, so Miss Lambert developed her Standard Filiere to assist knitters who used patterns in her needlework manuals.

This knit knee cap used 1½ ounces of fine white wool. *Godey's* included such practical, everyday knitting projects along with fancy work in the ongoing section called "Work Department."

Historical Pattern
1880s Ladies Fancy Silk Mittens

Ladies' Fancy Silk Mittens, using Florence Knitting Silk to make elegant lace-patterned mittens.

This pattern comes from How to Use Florence Knitting Silk No. 4, *1882.*

Legend: *tto = thread thrown over as if you were about to purl.*

s and b = slip and bid: slip one stitch, knit the next, and pass the slipped stitch over.

n = narrow: knit two stitches together.

Materials: 1 ounce Florence Knitting Silk No. 300, and five No. 19 knitting needles.

Cast on 82 stitches, and knit one round plain.

2d round, k 1, tto, k 1, tto, k 1, tto, k 1, tto, k 1, tto, k 1, tto, k 1, p 2, repeat until 10 stitches remain, then k 8, p 2.

3d round, s and b, k 9, n, p 2, repeat until 10 stitches remain, then k 8, p 2.

4th round, s and b, k 7, n, p 2, repeat until 10 stitches remain, then k 8, p 2.

5th round, s and b, k 5, n, p 2, repeat until 10 stitches remain, then k 8, p 2.

As 4 rounds are required to complete each shell pattern, the 6th, 7th, 8th, and 9th rounds are a repetition of the 2d, 3d, 4th, and 5th rounds in the order named. This shell is repeated in the mitten shown 17 times, but if a longer wrist is desired, more shells can be added at pleasure. The twist pattern shown in the centre of the back is continued as follows, viz.:

10th and 11th rounds, same as 2d and 3d.

In the 12th round, the last 10 stitches are disposed of in the following manner, namely: Slip off the first 4 stitches on the fifth or extra needle, knit the next 4, then the 4 from the extra needle, and purl the *2* stitches remaining to complete the round. This operation must be repeated in every 12th round. One shell stripe each side of the twist pattern is to be continued up to the same point.

In commencing the thumb the stitches for this purpose must be so chosen as to bring the fancy work on back of mitten as near as possible to the centre of the same. In the right-hand mitten, the thumb is on the left-hand side of the fancy work, and in the left-hand mitten the reverse.

When you have 27 stitches in thumb, knit 3 rounds plain (except fancy back), and at the end of the 3d plain round cast on 4 extra stitches. Now slip the 27 thumb stitches on a piece of twine, tie securely, and with remaining stitches continue the hand, narrowing in each round once at the point where extra stitches were made, until 74 stitches remain.

To finish hand when sufficient length has been obtained, decrease as follows, viz.: Having 79 stitches, begin at corner of needle, k 7, n, k 7, n, k 7, n, k 7, n, k 7, n, k 7, n, k 7, n. Knit the rest of this round plain.

2d round plain.

3d round, * k 7, n, repeat to * and knit 7 rounds plain.

11th round, * k 6, n, repeat to * and knit 6 rounds plain.

18th round, * k , n, repeat to * and knit 5 rounds plain.

24th round, * k 4, n, repeat to * and knit 4 rounds plain.

Now narrow once on each needle in every round until only 4 stitches are left on a needle, then narrow twice on each needle and cast off. When decreasing once on each needle only, do not narrow at the same point in every round, but at a different place in each successive round.

To finish the thumb, place the 27 stitches on the three needles, and pick up 4 stitches from the base of gore formed between the hand and thumb by casting on the 4 extra stitches, knit once around and narrow once in each of the next 4 rounds at the point where the gore is; then knit 50 rounds plain, and finish by narrowing once on each needle in every round, until all the stitches are disposed of.

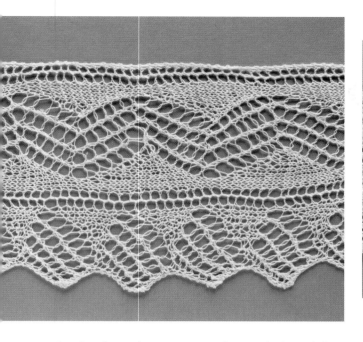

head and ears, button eyes, and tiny whiskers. A knit rabbit pen wiper imitated fur with knit loops of white Berlin wool singles, cut and combed after knitting.[45] What was left for the knitter who had met her family's needs for suspenders, shirts, slippers, boas, and rabbit pen wipers? A knitting basket! She could knit a basket using a simple slip-stitch pattern in maize, bright scarlet, dark scarlet, claret, and black yarns, then quilt a satin lining with custom pockets, add a quilted satin lid edged in quilled ribbon, and finish with whalebone handles covered with calico and wound with ribbon. "This very useful basket has been much admired," *Godey's* advised readers, "and is very easy to make."[46]

The number of needlework patterns in *Godey's* Work Department dwindled during the last two decades of the nineteenth century. Patterns leaned toward the practical. Knitters could make drawers for children using fine white Scotch wool yarn and steel needles or a knit shade to attach to a gentleman's straw hat.[47] In the final year of publication, *Godey's* dropped needlework altogether.

Lace Knitting

Victorians bore a special love for lace knitting. Some knitters assembled lace sampler workbooks, occasionally surviving today in vintage textile and museum collections. Miss Eugenia Pruden, born in Michigan in 1845, knit tiny lace samples in fine white cotton thread and assembled her lace pattern book with meticulous care to name each pattern with the date and donor.[48] And, given the number of patterns found in Victorian-era publications, every Victorian bed must have had a knit-lace counterpane spread — despite the time required. A replica 1890 knit bed-spread at the Warner House in Portsmouth, New Hampshire, has 1,024 knit squares made by 47 volunteer knitters.[49]

During the 1880s, needlework editors at the *Ladies' Home Journal* were smitten with lace knitting. Knitters found patterns for point lace, knit socks with shell tops, a coral tidy or antimacassar, fingerless lace-knit mitts, and lace edgings. Apparently, the *Ladies' Home Journal* considered the lace mitts quite a challenge. Pattern instructions concluded, "If any one gets into trouble over these directions, send 2 two-cent stamps to Mrs. H. E. Tucker, 610 Larimer St., Denver, Col., and she will try to help them."[50]

Any 1885 reader who recruited new subscribers to the *Ladies' Home Journal* qualified for a free knitting instruction and pattern book (also sold for 25¢, the price of a one-year subscription). Modestly promoted as "the best book yet published on Fancy Knitting," the magazine's booklet *How to Knit and What to Knit* gave directions for fancy borders, afghan squares, darning that imitated knit stitches, and variations for casting on, increasing, and forming heels and toes. In 1886, the *Ladies' Home Journal* sent a knitting and crochet book edited by Jenny June to any reader recruiting six new subscribers or four subscribers plus 10¢ cash. This book promised a great variety of designs and stitches, with two hundred illustrations and technical details that anyone could follow.[51]

The American silk industry marketed silk yarn to Victorian lace knitters. The industry had struggled to survive since its introduction before the American Revolution. Harsh winters, a mulberry blight, and labor-intensive production jinxed the profitability of sericulture. In 1855, Samuel Hill established the Nonotuck Silk Company, a silk productive enterprise

Lace knitting, such as this diamond pattern, captivated Victorian knitters, who used lace patterns for edgings, mittens and gloves, shawls, baby bonnets, and more. *The Art of Knitting*, 1892.

Butterick introduced its 1892 book *The Art of Knitting* with a sentimental illustration of a grandmother looking pleased about passing down her knowledge of knitting to her little scholar, her granddaughter.

Historical Pattern 1850s "Necktie" Scarf

Identified as a Necktie, the pattern for this scarf called for half an ounce each of blue and white Shetland wool and two blue-and-white silk tassels.

This pattern comes from Godey's Lady's Book and Magazine, *August 1850.*

Cast on 40 loops with blue; knit the first three rows alternately, pearl and plain.

4th row — Fasten on the white, slip 1, *a*, thread forward, slip 1, knit 1; repeat from *a*.

5th row (blue) — Slip 1, *a*, thread forward, slip 1, knit 2 together; repeat from *a*.

Every row is knit like the 5th, but alternately with blue and white, changing the wool at the beginning of each row. Knit until you have one yard and an eighth completed; then knit one row 2 loops together, and 4 rows of plain knitting with blue; cast off.

Join the two edges together on the wrong side; draw p the ends, and sew on the tassels.

that finally thrived. Renamed the Corticelli Silk Company in 1922, the firm manufactured silk thread, yarn, and ribbon until 1930. Victorian lace knitters who bought Florence Knitting Silk contributed to its success.[52]

A series of pattern books entitled *How to Use Florence Knitting Silk* showed knitters that this particular silk created elegant lace-knit edgings, stockings, and mittens. The Nonotuck Silk Company of Florence, Massachusetts, assured knitters that the "rules" for silk knitting were all "prepared by a person of large experience." Knitting with silk also became fashionable. Women were advised to follow the style "to carry Florence Knitting Silk to the summer resorts, there to be knit into stockings, while the knitter chats with friends on the hotel veranda." Florence Knitting Silk was sold in half-ounce balls, either fine or coarse, in a range of more than fifty colors, including "invisible" green, five shades of olive, bright yellow, drab, steel, slate, royal purple, and cherry.[53] Corticelli adver-

tised its silk yarn and silk mittens in the *Ladies' Home Journal* and offered the 1885 edition of its knitting book mailed to any address for "six cents in stamps."[54]

A Proliferation of Knitting Patterns

Victorian knitters had ample sources of patterns. On February 25, 1883, *The New York Times* headline "Gossip about Knitting" (page 4) lured knitters to instructions for ladies' gloves "daintily knitted in fine silk with No. 18 needles" for "wearing over their kid ones in cold weather." Patterns followed for a shoulder shawl and an open-work shell pattern for a baby's "boot," with further directions the clever knitter could follow to work the boot into a sock using Shetland wool. Yet instructions did not include pictures of the finished pieces, and knitters must have kept faith that diligently following row-by-row directions led to the desired gloves, shawls, or socks. Perhaps to inspire that faith, the article espoused the charm of knitting:

"Knitting is the one kind of fancy needlework which is never out of date. If few people to-day care to knit stockings and socks, there is still an indescribable charm in the knitting-needle which survives in our midst. Fancy knitting, delicate fabrics for the little ones, soft shawls, or head coverings grow beneath the hand, and new patterns are always desirable."

For 50¢ the Butterick Publishing Company sold *The Art of Knitting*, an 1892 compendium of Victorian knitting with more than two hundred and fifty illustrated patterns for mittens, gloves, shawls, hug-me-tights (Zouave jackets), counterpanes, lace edgings, rugs, doilies, purses, evening hoods, baby bootees and sacques, gentleman's neckties, hunting helmets, leggings, stockings, ladies' fancy mittens, petticoats, and so much more. Those who *really* loved to knit could find patterns for a knit egg holder, coffee strainer, pence (penny) jug, a beaded twine-ball case, toy balls, reins for a child, napkin (diaper) cover, baby bottle cover, infant drawers and chest protector, soldier and harlequin dolls, full-sized hammock, and a pot holder in the shape of an ear of corn.

Peterson's Magazine also published knitting patterns, each authored by the magazine's needlework doyenne, Jane Weaver. During 1860, Weaver's patterns included a knit lacy cuff, scarf braided from three seven-stitch-wide knit strips adorned with tassels, and a knit capuchin in "fine double zephyr." She offered several of the ubiquitous Victorian counterpanes — in

The Nonotuck Silk Co. published a series of knitting manuals encouraging knitters to select yarn from its line of Florence Knitting Silk for their mittens, stockings, and lace edgings.

Foot-Ball Sweater for a man is a slipover, knit in the round to the armholes. Ribbed borders are knit in double seed stitch. Although the popularity of sweaters is associated with World War I, this sweater appeared at least as early as 1892 in *The Art of Knitting*.

These baby's mittens dating from 1847 were knit from wool and worn by Marie Josephine (Gallup) Hunter of Courtland, Wisconsin. (Wisconsin Historical Society)

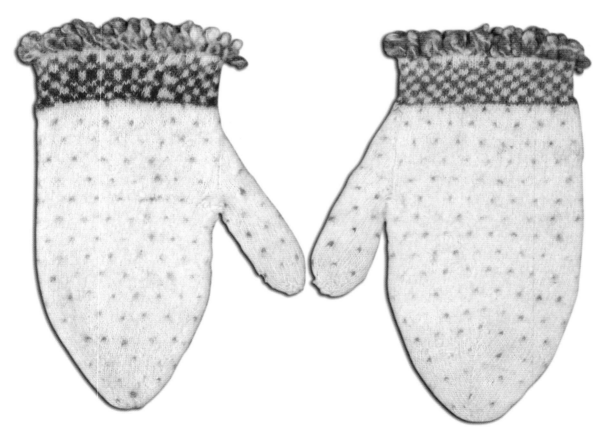

Fine seed-like beads were knit with silk thread for a lady's "reticule" or purse. Victorian women wore purses of various kinds, and their use increased or decreased according to the shape and size of skirts that were in style. (Washington State Historical Society)

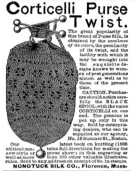

Publishers routinely copied patterns from one another's needlework manuals. Here's an 1885 advertisement for a Corticelli purse pattern in *The Ladies' Home Journal* and the identical pattern as it appeared in *The Art of Knitting,* 1892.

This knitted Pence Jug for "holding odd pennies" required small amounts of black and scarlet Germantown wool. *The Art of Knitting,* 1892.

knit shells, squares, and patchwork styles. In 1861, Weaver produced patterns for a knit leggin and a baby shoe and sock.[55] She shared the knitting pattern honors with Mrs. Warren, who designed a Norwegian bonnet and scarf, and Mademoiselle Roche, who promoted Thibet knitting on large needles for afghans.[56] During 1869, patterns attributed to Weaver included a girl's knit jacket, cravat, boy's gaiter, and an overshoe, presumably to wear around the home. In addition, patterns for a fabric knitting needle case and a knitting basket of cardboard stitched and embellished in cashmere yarn bore her signature.[57]

Weaver's productivity varied over the years. She slipped to one child's gaiter pattern during 1877, but the number of her patterns bounced back in 1879 to include a knit ball, dressing slipper, child's shirt, herringbone-stitch knitting, nightingale knitting, braces, shawl, and scarf. Her child's knit shirt is actually a pat-

tern-knit, short-sleeve, pullover sweater with scalloped edges. In her shawl pattern, she instructs the knitter to cast on seven hundred stitches, and she calls for eleven pounds total of mauve, white, and black wool (depending on the length, usually two and a half yards) to make her "Nightingale," a warm hooded wrap. By 1885, though, the only knitting pattern attributed to Weaver was a child's knit petticoat and in 1886, a child's Scotch cap knit in brioche stitch.[58] Was there really a Jane Weaver whose creativity generated all these patterns, or was she *Peterson's* equivalent of Betty Crocker, spurring four decades of Victorian knitting?

Beaded Purses and Knitting Styles
Bead-knit purses and reticules (drawstring purses) were popular with Victorian women. Home and fashion magazines provided instructions for making these purses, intended to hold a few coins, smelling salts,

handkerchief, and comb, and to be carried along for special occasions. A characteristic Victorian purse, often called a Miser's Purse, consisted of a narrow long tube — of knitting, crocheting, or netting — closed by two metal rings that slid over a short slit at the center. Early in the nineteenth century, a popular style of bead-knit purse was covered with intricate designs. The purses were worked with fine steel knitting needles using beads strung on fine yarn in sequence according to a chart, with each bead incorporated into a knit stitch following the pattern. Glass beads, sometimes transparent, and metal beads were used. "Beaded knitting" was distinguished from "bead knitting." In beaded knitting, the beads were knit at intervals to create patterns of rows. Bead knitting, a more complex process, inserted a bead into every knit stitch to create an often elaborate and realistic picture. Beaded knitting was used for baby socks and bonnets, as well as cuffs and collars.[59]

Historical Pattern
1890s Victorian Miser's Purse

This pattern comes from The Art of Knitting, *1892.*

Cast onto 1 needle 59 stitches and knit across plain. Second row: P2 together, th O [throw the yarn over the needle] and repeat until one stitch remains. Knit this. Repeat this row up to the 65th row inclusive. Now make 83 rows of plain knitting; then 65 rows of fancy knitting. Knit 1 row plain and cast off.

You will now have a long, flat piece, a little narrower at the center than at the ends. Sew up the edges, leaving an opening 2½ inches long at the middle. Join one end flatly and draw the other together as seen in the picture, and finish with steel trimmings.

Knit cape worn by Lucy (Luly) Elvira Bailey, circa 1860. This cape was likely knit by her mother, Lovilla Gordon Jones Bailey of Chicago. (Chicago History Museum)

Infant's Jersey to in zephyr wool for a newborn. Soft, wooly knits addressed Victorian concerns for healthy and comfortable children's clothing. *The Ladies' Home Journal*, August 1887.

Mrs. Jane Weaver's Nightingale Cape called for 11 pounds of knitting wool. *Peterson's Magazine*, March 1879.

Right: Child's knit slippers with satin ribbon ties, machine stitched to lambskin soles, circa 1900. (Wisconsin Historical Society)

And for the Victorian Child . . .

Victorians believed in dressing their children for health and comfort. In characteristic Victorian fashion, mothers received abundant childcare advice from physicians, educated women writers, scientists, and dress reformers. Most of these "experts" bemoaned the conflict between health and fashion. *Godey's* fashion editors advised readers, "We cannot enforce more earnestly than is necessary, perfect simplicity in the dress of children. They are not puppets made for the display of fine clothes; or Paris dolls, to be tricked out in the extravagance of the latest fashion."[60] And what could be healthier than soft, comfortable clothing knit with wool? Medical experts recommended wool worn next to the skin for children's health.[61]

Knitting patterns for children's clothing increased in number during the nineteenth century. In *The American Frugal Housewife* ("Dedicated to Those Who Are Not Ashamed of Economy"), Mrs. Child recommended that children "can knit garters, suspenders, and stockings."[62] In the 1870s, *Godey's* included a sampling of patterns for children: infant's socks, shell-pattern children's socks, baby gloves, teenaged girl's jacket, boys' gaiters, and a knit sponge that was presumably a baby's toy. A child's stocking pattern featured an entrelac pattern in red, white, and blue. Knit reins were attached to a cloth tied around the waist of a child, with little bells sewn onto the cloth appliqué in the shape of a horse. The earliest issues of the *Ladies' Home Journal* included knitting patterns for a baby's "bootee" and a newborn's "jersey" cardigan knit in garter stitch.[63]

Another Side of Victorian Life

Victorian women dedicated their time and talents to their homes and families, but they also brought their domesticity into public benevolence. Good wives and good mothers knit for their own families but also for the less fortunate. Women organized into thousands of voluntary benevolent societies in towns and cities across the nation. They knit and sewed gifts for the poor or sold their handiwork to make cash donations; they also solicited funds for schools, orphanages, homes for the elderly, soup kitchens, and more. Free black women in Massachusetts organized the Colored Female Religious and Moral Society of Salem to support and aid members who became ill or destitute. During the Civil War, both Northern and Confederate women answered the need for war support by knitting for the soldiers.

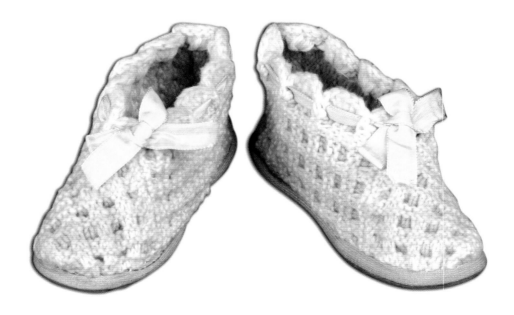

A girl's wool petticoat, 1885–1890, knit by Emma Augusta Waters and worn by her granddaughter Florence Catherine Hays of Beloit, Wisconsin. (Wisconsin Historical Society)

Baby's Sock with Imitation Slipper was a pattern from *How to Use Florence Knitting Silk No. 4*, 1882. It was knit in white silk with pink silk foot and edging.

A Victorian-era knitter wrote "Anna Loves James" in purl stitches on a pair of white cotton stockings, now well worn and carefully mended. (Washington State Historical Society)

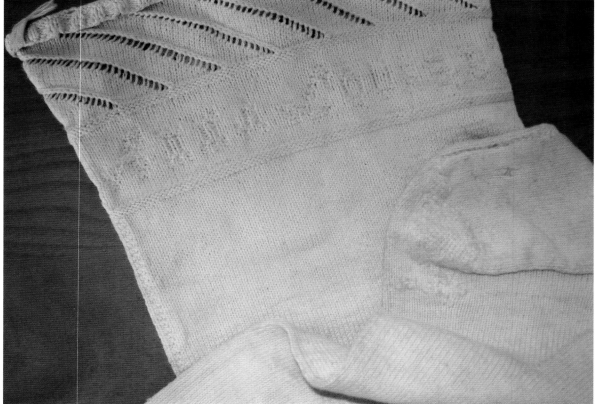

Babies' Knitted Sack, knit in "4-thread Saxony yarn in white and pale-blue," is knit in one piece and joined under the sleeves and along the side. *The Art of Knitting*, 1892.

Chapter Three
Knitting for the Civil War

Before the War Between the States, America was not a united nation. While the North had grown into an economic and industrial giant, the South relied on a one-crop economy — king cotton — based on slavery. The Victorian sense of moral righteousness over slavery permeated ideological and economic division between North and South. Abraham Lincoln wrote, "If slavery is not wrong, nothing is wrong." A self-taught circuit lawyer with humble origins, Lincoln opposed slavery on moral grounds, although his overriding goal was to hold the Union together. Confederate President Jefferson Davis argued for state rights and the economic necessity of slavery in the South. Slavery, Davis believed, served as a smokescreen for the North's hypocrisy: The North accused the South of exploiting blacks as slaves, but Northern bankers and industry exploited the South financially.

The Civil War began on April 12, 1861, when the Confederacy fired on Fort Sumter in Charleston, South Carolina. The war became one of the pivotal events in American history — and among the bloodiest. Nearly half of the nation's young men volunteered or were conscripted into military service, an estimated 2.6 million. By war's end, one in five were dead or wounded, the highest losses in any American war.

Whether Northerner or Southerner, abolitionist or slaveholder, white or black, rich or poor, Americans united in picking up their needles to knit for their Civil War soldiers.

The North: "Sanitary" Knitting

Poor Northern women on farms and in factories struggled without the husbands, fathers, and brothers who left to serve the Union Army. Some took in boarders or sewed shirts, while others knit hats, gloves, and mittens. In upstate New York, Semira Merrill tried to raise a little cash by selling hand-knit women's gloves and mittens, but her customers "found the price of 25¢ per pair beyond their means."[64]

A Civil War–era knitter from Louisville, Kentucky. A tax stamp on the back mark indicates the photo was taken between August 1864 and August 1866. (Colleen Formby Collection)

Opposite Page:
Eastman Johnson's 1861 painting *Knitting for Soldiers* captured the mood of the Civil War era on both sides of the fight. Young and old took up their needles and yarn to make everything from warm socks to bandages for their soldiers. (Collection of the New York Historical Society)

Sojourner Truth set aside her knitting for a moment while posing for a photograph on a print card, dated 1864. Born into slavery in 1797 in New York, she was originally named Isabella Baumfree by her Dutch slaveholder family. She gained freedom in 1826 when New York emancipated all slaves. Sojourner Truth was a tall, strong, imposing orator who touched a public nerve with her impassioned narratives on antislavery, women's rights, and temperance movements. Sojourner was illiterate, but her extraordinary life was recorded by an empathetic white woman, Olive Gilbert. (Library of Congress)

I Sell the Shadow to Support the Substance.

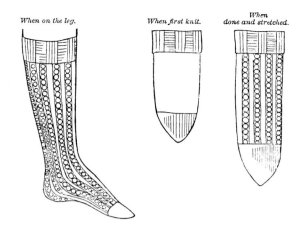

When on the leg.   When first knit.   When done and stretched.

Although newspapers published patterns and instructions to knit stockings and mittens for the soldiers, women's magazines like *Godey's Lady's Book and Magazine* ignored war knitting. Instead, magazines gave readers patterns for civilian use like the Railway Stocking, knit in cotton, an openwork lady's stocking made by dropping every other stitch off the needle and stretching out the stocking so the stitches run down to the ribbing. *Godey's Lady's Book and Magazine,* January 1861.

Left: The Knitted Winter Spenser required "seven skeins of dark fleecy four-thread, one skein each of gray fleecy, four shades." Perhaps the snug fit of this lady's jacket and the double row of what appear to be metal buttons reflect the inevitable military influence on civilian clothing during wartime. *Godey's Lady's Book and Magazine,* February 1861.

Northern women of the Victorian leisure classes, however, had the resources to volunteer for nursing and relief services. Two weeks after Fort Sumter, America's first woman doctor, Elizabeth Blackwell, led a gathering of three thousand women who organized the Woman's Central Relief Association, dedicated to defining the soldier's true needs and organizing the benevolent efforts of Northern women. Similarly, the U.S. Sanitary Commission tracked the health condition of soldiers and centralized donations from thousands of individual aid societies that sprang up in Northern towns and cities. Vermont's Walpole Soldiers' Aid Society stitched quilts, knit stockings, and made other comfort items. Mrs. Bardwell, who organized the society, led a typical antebellum life that revolved around household duties — knitting for her family and the poor. She wasted no time knitting soldiers' socks after Lincoln called up 1 million soldiers in fall 1861.[65]

Membership in these societies was nearly always white, although Northern black women organized their own relief groups. In Philadelphia, black women formed the Colored Women's Sanitary Commission and the Ladies' Sanitary Association of St. Thomas's African Episcopal Church. White women tended to focus on soldiers exclusively, while black women's aid societies also sent support to former slaves in the South.[66] Northern women usually sympathized with abolitionism and had organized anti-slavery fairs for decades before the Civil War. Sojourner Truth, a black abolitionist freed from slavery in 1827, delivered her famous "Ain't I a Woman?" speech to a feminist gathering in Akron, Ohio, in 1851. No exact transcript of her speech survives, but her words were later recounted. In part, she addressed the religious argument against equal rights for women: "If the first

woman God ever made was strong enough to turn the world upside down, all alone these women together ought to be able to turn it back, and get it right side up again! And now they is asking to do it, the men better let them."[67] The woman whose words electrified nineteenth-century audiences sat for a formal photograph in a knit shawl and cap with her current knitting project.

At times, women found themselves torn between the needs of anonymous suffering soldiers and soldiers from their own families or towns who wrote home asking for warm socks. Women often felt loyal to family or home regions and, at times, balked at sending knit donations to the Sanitary Commission for anonymous distribution. Fanny Pierce of Weymouth, Massachusetts, wrote to her soldier brother that "Aunt Susan has been knitting a pair of soldier's stockings which she wishes were for you." Hannah Lamb and many of her New England neighbors sent their donation of "countless soldiers' socks" to the army in the west; Lamb's were marked for Missouri, where her brother served as a military doctor.[68]

Northerners and Southerners alike believed the war would not last long. The Northern government was not prepared for prolonged conflict, and shortages plagued the states sending soldiers into battle. Machine-made stockings were plentiful but of poor quality, especially those with a seam running down the middle. The new Potter's knitting machine made acceptable seamless stockings, but the machines themselves could not be manufactured fast enough for the growing numbers of soldiers. The Union Army needed woolen knit socks, and the Sanitary Commission decided women could solve this shortage with hand-knit stockings delivered to the Commission for distribution.[69]

Stunned by early Southern victories, Northerners organized to support soldiers destined to face winter in the field. In October 1862, *The New York Times* conveyed the Sanitary Commission's request that "the energies of the patriotic ladies of the land be now

Historical Pattern
1865 Union Army Socks

This pattern comes from "Directions for Knitting Socks" in the United States Sanitary Commission Bulletin, Volume I, Number 31 of February 1, 1865. This modern interpretation for experienced knitters is by Karin Timour, who has conducted extensive research on materials and methods for knitting Civil War socks. Copyright © 2007 by Karin Timour.

Yarn: 5 ounces 3/8 Jagger Spun yarn (1490 yards per pound). Contrasting heels and toes: 3 ounces of contrast color.

Needles: Use a set of five American size 1 needles (2.25 mm) or size to make gauge.

If you prefer to knit with four double point needles, one circular or two circulars, adjust these instructions accordingly

Gauge: 9 stitches to the inch, 11 rows per inch.

19th Century Sizes: Some people believe "people were smaller then" — but the average height of soldiers in the Civil War was 5' 8" — most wearers will fit into the size feet included in this pattern. What *has* changed is how much modern people weigh versus Civil War soldiers. While you may not need to change the size of the foot, you might well have to change the size of the leg.

The original pattern provides instructions for making three sizes: small (10 inch foot); medium (11 inch foot); and large (12 inch foot).

Leg Size: We tried on socks made to each size to see how large a leg they could comfortably fit. The "small size" can stretch to snugly fit a leg that is up to 13 inches around. The "medium" will fit a leg up to 14 inches around and the "large" a leg up to 15 inches around. If the person wearing the socks doesn't want a really tight fit around his leg, you may want to adjust accordingly (see below).

How many stitches to cast on for a good fit in the leg:

1. Measure from the floor up the wearer's leg 13 inches. Using a tape measure, measure how big around the leg is at this point (circumference).

2. Multiply this number by your stitches per inch (from your gauge swatch).

3. Subtract 30%. Your new total is the number of stitches to cast on.

Foot Size: If the wearer has a foot that is smaller than 10 inches long or larger than 12 inches long, you'll need to alter the length of your sock. Either have them stand on a ruler to give you the exact length, or make a tracing of their foot and use that to measure.

Ribbing: Use either a) knit one, purl one or b) knit two, purl two until your ribbing is 3½ inches long.

Leg: Knit leg in stockinette, keeping one stitch at the beginning of each row in purl, forming your "seam stitch" down the back of the sock leg until leg is 6½ inches long.

Heel Flap: Locate your purl (or seam) stitch. This will be the center of your heel flap. Divide instep stitches from heel flap.

Cast on 65 stitches: Heel flap will be 33 stitches
Cast on 70 stitches: Heel flap will be 35 stitches.
Cast on 75 stitches: Heel flap will be 37 stitches.

Cast on any other number: Divide the total number cast on in half (you need to have an odd number, because your seam stitch will be in the middle) to determine heel flap total.

Contrasting Color Heels: You can choose to start your contrast color at start of heel flap, after an inch or inch and a half of heel flap.

Heel Flap Construction Choices: This pattern includes a choice of two ways to make a heel flap:

Version A:

Row 1: Slip first stitch, knit straight across, remembering to purl the seam stitch when you come to it.

Row 2: Slip first stitch, purl straight across; remembering to knit the seam stitch when you come to it.

Repeat these two rows until your heel flap is three inches in length, and end ready to start a right side row.

Version B: This version of the heel flap will add durability to your heel flap.

Row 1: Slip first stitch, knit straight across, remembering to purl the seam stitch when you come to it.

Row 2: Slip first stitch, then purl one stitch and slip one stitch – alternate purling and slipping stitches across the heel flap. Knit the seam stitch when you come to it.

Repeat these two rows until your heel flap is three inches in length, and end ready to start a right side row.

Turning the Heel: Discontinue seam stitch.

Mentally divide the number of stitches by four:

If your heel flap is 33 stitches, one quarter is 8 stitches.

If your heel flap is 35 stitches, one quarter is 9 stitches.

If your heel flap is 37 stitches, one quarter is 10 stitches.

Start with the right side of the heel flap facing you:

Row 1. Slip one, then knit until (8; 9; or 10) stitches remain unknit on the needle. Knit the next two stitches together. There should now be (7; 8; or 9) stitches remaining unknit. Flip work so wrong side is facing you.

Row 2: Purl back until (8; 9; or 10) stitches remain unpurled. Purl next two stitches together. There should now be (7; 8; or 9) stitches left unpurled. Flip work so right side is facing you.

Row 3: Look for the "gap" that was made by knitting two stitches together in two places on this heel flap. Continue alternately knitting and purling across, each time knitting or purling together the two stitches on either side of the "gap."

Knit until (7; 8; or 9) stitches un-knit. Knit the next two stitches together (one from either side of the "gap"). You should now have (6; 7; or 8 stitches left unknit) Flip the work so that the wrong side is facing.

Row 4: Purl until(7; 8; or 9) stitches remain unpurled. Purl the two stitches together from either side of the "gap." You should now have (6; 7; or 8 stitches left unpurled). Flip so right side is facing you.

Continue until all stitches have been knit off. 17 stitches should remain on the needle at the bottom of the heel.

Pick Up Stitches along the Left Side of the Heel Flap: If contrasting color used for heel, at this point switch back to main color.

Hold the sock so that you are looking into the sock, with the needles holding the instep stitches (the ones that will form the top of the foot), the farthest away from you. The bottom of the sock should be closest to you. Move half the stitches at the bottom of the heel to another needle. If you have 17 stitches left, put 8 stitches on the left-hand needle (Needle 1) and 9 on the other (Needle 4).

Pick up stitches along left side of heel flap and put them on Needle 1, knit straight across instep stitches (Needles 2 and 3) and pick up the same number of stitches along the right-hand side of heel flap (Needle 4).

Joining the Heel to the Foot: Needle number 1 holds half the stitches left at the bottom of the heel and all the stitches picked up along the left side of the heel. Needle number 2 holds half the instep stitches. Needle number 3 holds the second half of the instep stitches. Needle number 4 has all the stitches picked up on the right-hand side of the heel and the remaining half of the heel stitches.

Knit as follows:

Row 1: Needle 1: Knit until 3 stitches are left. Slip one, knit one, and pass the slipped stitch over the knit stitch. Knit the last stitch.

Needle 2: Knit straight across.

Needle 3: Knit straight across.

Needle 4: Knit the first stitch, slip one, knit one, pass the slipped stitch over the knit stitch and knit remaining stitches on that needle.

Row 2. Knit all stitches on needles 1, 2, 3, and 4.

Repeat Rows 1 and 2 until remaining stitches equal the number of stitches cast on. If using the original Sanitary Commission's cast on, this will be 65; 70; or 75.

Knitting the Foot: Knit foot until it is $2^{1}/_{2}$ inches shorter than finished length of foot.

Toe: If making of contrasting color, switch colors now.

Row 1: Knit 6 stitches, slip one, knit one, pass slipped stitch over the knitted stitch. Repeat across row. If odd stitches remain at end of row, knit plain.

Row 2–7: Knit six rows plain.

Row 8: Knit 5 stitches, slip one, knit one, pass slipped stitch over the knitted stitch. Repeat this the entire row. If there are odd stitches left at the end, knit them plain.

Row 9-13: Knit five rows plain.

Row 14: Knit 4, slip one, knit one, pass slipped stitch over the knitted stitch. Repeat this the entire row. If there are stitches left at the end, knit them plain.

Row 15–18: Knit four rows plain.

Row 19: Knit 3, slip one, knit one, pass slipped stitch over the knitted stitch. Repeat this the entire row. If there are stitches left at the end, knit them plain.

Row 20–22: Knit three rows plain

Row 23: Knit 2, slip one, knit one, pass slipped stitch over the knitted stitch. Repeat this the entire row. If there are stitches left at the end, knit them plain.

Row 24–25: Knit two rows plain.

Row 26: Knit 1, slip one, knit one, pass slipped stitch over the knitted stitch. Repeat this the entire row. If there is one stitch left at the end, knit it plain.

Row 27: Knit this row plain.

Row 28: Knit two together. Repeat this the entire row.

Break off yarn, thread through darning needle and weave in ends. Weave in all ends when colors changed.

"To Run the Heels and Toes:" In the original pattern the last step is to "run heels and toes." "Running a heel" is a 19th century term for a way of reinforcing the heels and toes. The knitter would take a darning needle, thread it with sock yarn, and then use a "running" stitch all over the inside surface of the bottom of the toe and the bottom and sides of the heel. Don't make a knot at the end of your "running yarn." Don't go all the way through the sock — just shallowly dip the needle down so that it slides under the surface of the inside of the sock. You can take fairly large "running stitches" and just go back and forth inside first the heel and then the toe. To make sure that you don't accidentally sew the sock closed, it's a good idea to insert a darning egg, a light bulb, or a potato inside the sock to help hold it open.

Gentleman's Neck-Tie in Brioche Knitting. Perhaps women knit such patterns while they waited hoping for the end of the war and for men to return home. *Godey's Lady's Book and Magazine*, January 1865.

turned to the knitting of socks and the making of underclothes for the soldier." Patriotic ladies volunteered nobly to previous calls for nursing, hospital work, and every other service. Now, soldiers who relied on government supplies risked going to battle without warm undershirts, drawers, and socks. "Chill November and freezing December are almost upon us," *The New York Times* noted in 1862, calling on women to provide warm underclothes, including knit socks, for the soldiers: "Our army is now somewhere between a half a million and a million strong; and every soldier in it should have at least two pairs of warm woolen socks. This, as will be seen, will require close to two million pairs — which is sufficient to keep active all the knitting needles in the country for a long time. . . . Women will knit and sew — and great will be your reward."[70] Knitters responded with impressive numbers of socks and mittens. Women in Bernardston and Deerfield, Massachusetts, organized groups to knit socks for the soldiers, as did boys at the Westboro Reform School.[71] In one year, the Northampton, Massachusetts, Ladies Army Aid Society alone sent 432 pairs of socks and 91 pairs of mittens, and the Aid Society in the small community of nearby Florence sent 54 pairs of wool socks.[72]

Popular fiction spurred the moral connection between patriotism and knitting stockings for the soldiers. In the moral tale "Blue Yarn Stockings" in *Harper's New Monthly Magazine*, a Northern woman rejected the suitor who laughed at her knitting. When he trifled with her knitting, he trifled with her patriotism and godliness. A soldier in "A Pair of Stockings from the Army" wore his hand-knit stockings as a reverent symbol of female generosity and affection. In "Joe Hale's Red Stockings," a recuperating soldier married the young woman who slipped a note with her name into the toe of the red stockings she knit for the Sanitary Commission.[73] In reality, donations to the Sanitary Commission sometimes carried such messages as "Socks sent home in the knapsack of a dear brother who fell at Antietam" or "Stockings knit by a little girl 5 years old, and she is going to knit some more." One knitter waxed poetic in the message she attached to her soldier's stockings:

> Brave sentry, on your lonely beat
> May these blue stockings warm your feet
> And when from wars and camps you part
> May some fair knitter warm your heart.[74]

Women obtained yarn and patterns from central distribution points and worked alone or during meetings. Young single women appeared to enjoy the social cohesion of knitting with a group, while others with children worked at home and knit stockings when time allowed. In Pennsylvania, the ladies of the Richmond

Knitting for the Soldiers

By Mary J. Upshur, 1862

Knitting for the soldiers!
How the needles fly!
Now with sound of merriment,
Now with many a sigh.

Knitting for the soldiers!
Panoply for feet —
Onward bound to victory
Rushing on retreat.

Knitting for the soldiers!
Wrinkled, aged crone
Plying flying needles
By the ember stone.

Crooning ancient ballads,
Rocking to and fro;
In your sage divining
Say where these shall go.

Jaunty set of stockings,
Neat from tip to toe,
March they with the victor,
Lie with vanquished low.

Knitting for the soldiers!
Matron — merry maid,
Many and many a blessing,
Many a prayer is said,

While the glittering needles
Fly "around — around,"
Like to Macbeth's witches,
On enchanted ground.

Knitting for the soldiers
Still another pair!
And the feet that wear them
Speed they onward — where?

To the silent city
On their trackless way?
Homeward — bearing garlands?
Who of us shall say?

Knitting for the soldiers!
Heaven bless them all!
Those who win the battle —
Those who fighting fall.

Might our benedictions
Speedily win reply,
Early would they crown ye
All with victory![95]

A Knitter's Letter to President Abraham Lincoln

Dear Sir
Please allow an oald Ladey of ninty One years of age to presnt you a very humble testimoney of esteeme & confidence in the shape of a pair of socks knit with my own hands & allow me to say that I remember the tryals passed thrugh in revolution days. I lost two Brothers out of three that was in the servis of the cuntery. besides Uncles & a number of cousins. & my prayer to Him that doethe all things well, that holdethe this nation in the hollow of His hand & hath continued my life to this time, & had Enabled me to worke almost dailey from the commcmnt of this rebelion to the present hour for the soldiers (God bless them) that you might be rich- ley indoued with that wisdom which you have so much kneaded to enable you to bare so grate responsibilities & to do that that is for the good of our bleding Country & I do pray that you may live to see this rebelion ended & with it slavery (which I do abomonate) wiped from our land, & long thereafter to witness & Enjoy the fruits of your labour — you will pardon this intrusion upon your time & beleive me ~~your~~ to be your frind & freind of my bleding countery;
Sarah Phelps.
Groton. N. H. Jany. 1865.[96]

Letter written by 90-year-old Sarah Phelps of Groton, New Hampshire, to Abraham Lincoln. A pair of her hand-knit stockings accompanied the letter.
(Abraham Lincoln Papers, Library of Congress)

Soldier's Aid Society recruited women to knit stockings for which the state government paid 25¢ a pair.[75]

Support for the war took other forms beyond sewing and knitting. In Melrose, Wisconsin, local farmers donated wheat to a women's organization that sold it at a market and used the proceeds to buy supplies for soldiers.[76] Coordinated efforts raised millions of dollars at fundraising fairs, and people donated all manner of goods sold for cash to help soldiers. After 1863, the best known were the sanitary fairs benefiting the Sanitary Commission, with some reaching manic levels. The largest was held at the Chicago Sanitary branch, a massive combination of fair and exposition. Donated produce and livestock alone were said to fill one hundred wagons. Despite the massive scale, donations retained their personal tone, including hand-knit socks.[77]

Although many women were knitters before the war, not all women had appropriate patterns for socks and mittens. In December 1861 *The New York Times* broadcast the call for patriotic ladies to knit mittens and provided instructions calling for "large needles;

gray or blue yarn, such as used for socks." The mittens had separate fingers for thumb and forefinger, designed for firing a rifle.[78] In 1862, a Massachusetts newspaper acknowledged, "Some of the ladies in Springfield say they would make mittens for the soldiers if they only knew how. We give the following 'receipt' for their especial benefit."[79] Patterns were mailed to knitters who could not travel to town. The U.S. Sanitary Commission's "Directions for Knitting Socks" called for knitting in the round on four needles with a purl stitch seam down the back and no decreases to shape the calf and ankle. The sock has a square heel and round toe, and three pairs required one pound of wool yarn.[80] The pattern used size thirteen needles; nineteenth-century needle numbers increased as needle diameters decreased, so this was equivalent to today's size one ($2\,1/4$ mm). In general, finer knitting needles (or "pins," as they were sometimes called) were made of steel, and coarser needles of ivory, whalebone, or wood. Knitters measured needle size with commercial knitting gauges; the Bell Gauge marketed by Walker & Company was a favorite.[81]

Among the thousands of sock knitters was eighty-three-year-old Mrs. Abner Bartlett of Medford, Massachusetts, who began to knit in September 1861 and produced more than three hundred pairs of stockings for the soldiers by February 1865. She sent President Lincoln the three hundredth pair, which he kindly acknowledged in writing. Other women sent hand knits along with letters of admiration to Lincoln. In February 1865, ninety-one-year-old Sarah Phelps of Groton, New Hampshire, sent her "very humble testimony of esteeme & confidence in the shape of a pair of socks knit with my own hands." At the age of eighty, Lucy A. Thomas sent the president hand-knit gloves accompanying a note that read, "Sir this pair of Gloves was knit Expressly as a present to your excellency by Mrs Lucy A. Thomas, widow & relict of the late Hon. Ira Thomas of Adams Jeff Co. N.Y." In 1864, Mrs. H. S. Crocker sent Lincoln her expression of esteem in the shape of a patriotic hand-knit scarf, writing that "the scarf is some of my own knitting and inventing. I tried to knit a Spread Eagle over your name but did not succeed." A non-knitter, Philena M. Upham of Leicester, Massachusetts, wrote the president, "I am unwomanly enough not to love to knit." Instead she sent him his own copy of the book she had written for the hospitals.[82]

The First Lady Mary Todd Lincoln is not remembered as a knitter, either, although not for want of knowledge. Typical of a Victorian woman's education, she learned to knit when she was young:

> Mary . . . was a studious little girl who had "a retentive memory and a mind that enabled her to grasp and thoroughly understand the lessons she was required to learn." She usually finished her homework before Elizabeth [Mary's stepmother's niece], and was soon clicking her knitting needles with the ten rounds of "cotton stocking" that both girls were required to knit each evening.[83]

Mrs. Lincoln focused her attention not on knitting, but on pressing her husband into political life.

The South: "Socks for the Soldiers"
The Civil War swept further into the South and disrupted lives of Southerners far more than those in the North. Every Southerner felt the blows of wartime sacrifice and hardship. Poor white women of the Southern hill country suffered the loss of husbands and sons and had to work the small farms that produced little in the best of times. Women who were mistresses of plantations were left to manage the agriculture and slaves, often on land that became a battleground. Southern women kept the home front in many ways — as nurses, farmers, and even spies or soldiers by disguising themselves as men — and they knit for the soldiers, as their Northern sisters were knitting for their army. Before Confederates attacked Fort Sumter, Southern women organized aid societies that rolled bandages and made cartridges. The citizens of Fairfield, Texas, were making canteen covers and knitting socks to get their men ready for the first call to arms.[84] Nearly every Confederate town organized a soldier's relief association or soldier's friend association. Relief organizations sprang up in churches, Sunday schools, and missionary and benevolent organizations. In Montgomery, Alabama, a synagogue formed the Hebrew Ladies Soldiers' Aid Society. Another Alabama society issued a call for wool donations, promising to knit it into soldiers' socks. In August 1861, a Virginia woman was the voice of many Confederate women during the early months of the war: "We are now very busy making clothes, knitting socks for the soldiers. Each lady proposes making one hundred garments — some are making mattresses, preparing bandages and knit nightshirts and comforts for the wounded — all are doing the most they can to add to the comforts of the soldiers."[85] The Southern states never had an organizational powerhouse like the Sanitary Commission, though, perhaps due to their more scattered, rural population.

Many Southern women were knitters before the war: Mrs. C. G. Richardson (nee Hattie Brunson) of South Carolina learned to knit stockings when she was five years old; Mrs. William Long Craig's mother had earned money knitting socks; in Georgia, Josephine Wood's mother carded and spun all the yarn used to knit the family's stockings; and Ella Lassiter, a black woman born into slavery in Georgia, recalled that her plantation mistress knit stockings for her as Christmas gifts.[86] Several former slaves interviewed during the 1930s for the Works Progress Administration Ex-Slave Narratives refer to knitting. A former slave woman from Kentucky recalled, "I been knitting socks and sewing and piecing quilts ever since I was eight years old." Another Kentuckian said she always wore stockings, hand-knit in fine yarn and usually striped for summer wear, and in winter she wore plaid linsey-woolsey. Slaveholders valued their slaves' spinning, sewing, and knitting skills, as evidenced by a Washington, D.C., slaveholder's praise in 1884 of the sewing of a slave woman and her two daughters, adding "both can knit stockings."[87]

Southern women proved especially prolific diarists during the war, and many wrote about their knitting. In *A Blockaded Family: Life in Southern Alabama during the Civil War*, Parthenia Antoinette Hague wrote that the women in her family became adept at knitting "ornamental woolen notion" like capes and sacques. She carded and dyed lamb's wool clippings in handsome colors, and she knit them into flower designs and fancy borders for gloves, hoods, and shawls.[88] Perhaps the most informative and respected

A Civil War soldier's hood knit from short pieces of different yarns for Major John T. Gilmore, a Confederate Army surgeon under General James Longstreet's troops in Knoxville, Tennessee. During the Civil War, the South was cut off from Northern textile industries and Southern ports were blockaded. As the war progressed, Southerners suffered from drastic shortages of fabrics and yarn. Many resorted to using scraps of yarn and torn fabric to knit pieces such as this hood. (McClung Museum, University of Tennessee)

of all the Civil War diaries is that of Mrs. James Chesnut (Mary Boykin). Chesnut was a Southern woman of intelligence, wealth, and privilege who enjoyed the social circle of Confederate president and Mrs. Jefferson Davis. She kept a fiery and personal account of her life immersed in distinguished Confederate society from the day she learned Lincoln was elected president and through the turmoil leading to the war's end until her final entry on August 2, 1865. During that time, Chesnut accompanied her husband on many of his military operations and spent time in various Southern towns. Chesnut balanced her personal traumas with adept descriptions of the larger struggles the South faced during the war. In August 1861, knitting socks for the soldiers had already become part of her established routine when a Captain Shannon — who had not yet seen action — called on her: "He seemed to find my knitting a pair of socks every day for the soldiers droll. He has been so short a time from home he does not know how the poor sol-

dier needs them." Knitting flowed through her life as naturally as reading and light conversation:

> I do not know when I have seen a woman without knitting in her hand. "Socks for the soldiers" is the cry. One poor man said he had dozens of socks and but one shirt. He preferred more shirts and fewer stockings. It gives a quaint look, the twinkling of needles, and the ever-lasting sock dangling.

Chesnut was fortunate to be able to afford knitting yarn. Later in September, she sent a little boy to buy wool for her knitting: "He was so pleased; he called himself my 'Confederate Agent.'"[89]

Shortages plagued the Southern home front. The few textile mills in the South diverted production for tents, bandages, and clothing for the soldiers, yet there was a shortage of labor to work the mills. The naval blockade largely prevented import of textiles and export of what cotton could be produced. Confederate cur-

Knitting gave her something to do while her family tried to keep safe. In her diary she wrote:

> Aug. 4. Thurs. The shells have ben flying all day and we have stayed in the cellar. Mama put me on some stockings this morning and I will try to finish them before school commences.
>
> Aug. 5. Friday. I knit all the morning. In the evening we had to run to Auntie's and get in the cellar. We did not feel safe in our cellar, they fell so thick and fast.
>
> Aug. 19. Fri. Auntie went down to Grandpa's this morning and I missed her so much. That is the only place I had to run to. I have ben knitting on my stocking some to day.
>
> Tues. Sept. 6. This has been a dark gloomy day and we feel gloomy too.... I commenced knitting me a pair of gloves but I don't know when I will get them done.[93]

rency was based on paper money and not gold or silver, and inflation ran rampant. Women who could not afford exorbitant prices or chose not to buy factory goods scrounged their households for textiles and made do by reusing materials. Women wove their own homespun and made their shoes; stories abound of shoes made from odd materials like sail canvas or squirrel skins. As the war progressed, desperation set in. Women tore apart mattresses, re-carded the wool stuffing, and wove it into clothes. Leftover new wool scraps were carded, mixed with cotton, spun, and knit into socks. Even rabbit fur was blended with cotton and silk, and knit into gloves.[91]

During the final days of the war, Southern women and children in particular suffered serious deprivations. Cornelia Phillips Spencer in North Carolina and her neighbors used every possible resource to support the soldiers: "children went barefoot through the winter, and ladies made their own shoes, and wove their own homespuns; where the carpets were cut up into blankets, and window-curtains and sheets were torn up for hospital uses, where soldiers' socks were knit day and night, while for home service clothes were twice turned, and patches were patched again." Spencer believed women tried their best to keep up some semblance of normalcy under desperate times: "Mothers were still preparing boxes for their boys in the army; the farmer got his old battered tools in readiness for his spring's work; the merchant went daily to preside over the scanty store of thread, needles, and buttons, remnants of calico, and piles of homespun, which now constituted his stock in trade; and our little girls still held their regular meetings for knitting soldiers' socks, all unconscious of the final crash so near."[92]

From the first rumblings of war to Sherman's final sweep through a defeated South, knitting comforted soldier and civilian alike. Ten-year-old Carrie Berry knit stockings during the siege of Atlanta in 1864.

Knit socks, mittens, gloves, and scarves could also forge intimate links between knitters and soldiers, a link that, at times, helped a soldier survive. The father of Mrs. I. E. Doane walked for six months after he was released from a Yankee prison at the end of the war. After reaching his South Carolina home, he told her his own story about knitting: "a profitable little trading business he had developed while in prison. His initial stock consisted of some knit gloves, socks and other articles which his wife had sent him. It had been very cold that winter and these warm articles of clothing were in great demand."[94]

On April 1, 1865, General Robert E. Lee surrendered to General Ulysses S. Grant at Appomattox. The Confederate generals and soldiers had fought well in the face of a chronic lack of troops, and Southern civilians made enormous sacrifices for their cause. But as the losses mounted, the South simply ran out of resources. It had overestimated the economic importance of cotton. Belief that wartime cotton prices would rise proved ill-founded; cotton prices fell as more countries produced cotton, while other countries stockpiled cotton in anticipation of the war, and hyperinflation of Confederate money took its toll.

Although the Civil War failed to distribute human and economic rights equitably, the new Union made America a nation and — Northerners in particular — headed into the largest and longest geographic and economic expansion in human history.

Civil War
Reenactment Knitters

Across America, Civil War reenacting organizations portray the lives and remember the sacrifices of those who lived — and knit — during the era. Many seek deep, complex authenticity in dress, including hand knitting. In *Confederates in the Attics: Dispatches from the Unfinished Civil War*, Tony Horwitz met knitters at a Civil War encampment: "At a Confederate tent, I found a 'Soldiers Aid Society' where women clad as southern belles sat knitting socks. They sipped Confederate coffee (parched corn sweetened with dark molasses) and gossiped about their Northern counterparts." Details count in the search for authenticity: "Out here I'm obsessed with my clothes. It's like I'm searching for the Holy Grail, except it's not a cup, it's a bit of gray cloth with just the right amount of dye and the exact number of threads."[97] The Atlantic Guard Soldiers' Aid Society, a research-based civilian reenacting organization, is one of such that advocates for authenticity in knitting and provides knitting patterns, links to patterns, and vendor recommendations.[98]

Civil War reenactors knitting at a Sky Meadows State Park, Virginia, encampment. Barb Todd knits a sontag, and Colleen Formby knits a hood. (Colleen Formby)

Chapter Four

Traveling Stitches

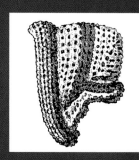

Americans were thinking big during the nineteenth century. Restless and expansive — both the joy and bane of the American character — they streamed across the continent, particularly after the Civil War. Although the New England states were also growing, the population of Ohio alone increased from 230,000 in 1810 to 2.3 million in 1860, while Illinois went from 55,000 in 1820 to 1.7 million in 1860. In their wake, they displaced indigenous populations even as 28 million more immigrants arrived on American shores between 1850 and 1915. The urban population jumped from 20 to 40 percent of the total between 1860 and 1900. Still, the United States remained a largely agricultural nation; the number of farms bloomed from 2 million in 1860 to more than 6 million by 1910, mostly in the Great Plains region. Ever more immigrants poured into the Midwestern states, leaving the South remarkably unchanged after the Civil War. The predicted migration of freed slaves to the North simply never happened. The Americans on the move, native-born and immigrant alike, carried with them their knitting knowledge and traditions.

A Lady's Travelling Cap. A woman of wealth and privilege like Susan Magoffin would have carried *Godey's Lady's Book* or Miss Lambert's needlework manuals on her travels. Although she did not record what she knit along the Santa Fe Trail, a traveling cap would have been most appropriate. *Hand-Book of Needlework* by Miss Lambert, 1846.

Knitting on Westward Journeys

Nineteenth-century movement across the nation was well underway long before the Civil War. The Homestead Act of 1862, the construction of railroads, and a booming export market for American goods opened land ownership and commerce for millions. In the mid nineteenth century, trade caravans in the American Southwest followed the Santa Fe Trail, a rough route from Independence, Missouri, across Kansas and Colorado to Santa Fe, New Mexico. Susan Shelby Magoffin, the first American white woman to travel the Santa Fe Trail, took along her knitting. From June 1846 through September 1847, Magoffin kept an extraordinary diary of the journey she undertook with her husband, Santa Fe trader Samuel Magoffin. Accustomed to wealth and privilege, Magoffin traveled in relative luxury in a private carriage attended by servants. "The life of a wandering princess, mine," she wrote.

Opposite Page: A Pacific Northwest Tulalip Indian woman, Magdeline Whea-kadim, knits with bulky yarn in the round using four needles, 1906. The knitter was the mother of Tulalip Chief William Shelton. (Photograph by Norman Edson, University of Washington Libraries)

Pioneer settlers in Cherry County, Nebraska, posed in 1901 with their prized possessions in front of their new sod house. The family portrait includes an ubiquitous frontier knitter, no doubt churning out stockings and mittens to prepare for severe winters ahead in the Nebraska Sand Hills. (Photograph by Solomon D. Butcher, Nebraska State Historical Society)

A BABY'S SOCK.

A Baby's Hood and Sock. During her pregnancies while traveling the Santa Fe Trail, Susan Magoffin undoubtedly knit tiny things — bootees, leggings, caps, blankets — in hopes of welcoming a healthy baby into her family. *Hand-Book of Needlework* by Miss Lambert, 1846.

Personal comforts surrounded her even during rough times: "We have rainy days any place and they are not more disagreeable on the plains than in N. Y. I have books, writing implements, sewing, kniting [*sic*], somebody to talk with, a house that does not leak and I am satisfied, although this is a juicey day *en al campo*!" Evidently, knitting was an everyday activity for Magoffin. On the third Sunday of her journey, she lost track of time on the trail and was alarmed to realize she was knitting on the Sabbath:

> Did I not in the very beginning of it forget — yes, and how can I be pardoned for the great sin — that it was the Holy Sabbath, appointed by my heavenly father for a day of rest — and classed it so much with the days of the week, that I regularly took out my week's work, knitting. Oh, how could I ever have been so thoughtless, so unmindful of my duty and my eternal salvation!

Magoffin made the best of travel through prairie storms, rain downpours, Indian scares, insect swarms, and miscarriages. After arriving in Santa Fe, she wrote about sharing her knitting with a Mexican woman who had shown her how to make tortillas:

> The old lady also brought over her knitting, which like the tortillas is done in a way tedious enough, notwithstanding, for curiosity to those at home, I learned how she did it. On showing her the much easier mode of the U. S. she seemed much surprised and delighted.[99]

Though Magoffin does not describe the particulars of the Mexican woman's knitting style, probably she worked in some variation handed down from sixteenth-century Spanish settlers who also introduced sheep and wool into the Southwest. What was Magoffin knitting? Her diary never tells. Perhaps she made the shawl that she wrapped about her head to protect herself from mosquitoes. Likely enough, she knit tiny sacques and bootees for the babies she miscarried during her journey.

Even before Magoffin's journey, missionaries traveled the American continent. Among the earliest adventurers into the Pacific Northwest were missionaries determined to bring religion to Native Americans — and some also brought knitting and sheep for woolen yarn. Six of the women who made the overland journey in 1836 and 1838 to establish the Oregon Mission kept diaries and letters. Eliza Spalding's letters describe the Nez Perce women whom she taught to knit, using wool from sheep the missionaries introduced:

> They have knit themselves yellow stockings, which colour I should not fancy for my own use, yet admire to see them in theirs . . . Jacob's wife, Abigail Ann and Matilda [Nez Perce women] have knit themselves leggins. Some appearance of civilization and improvement I think, we now really see.[100]

Although Spalding questioned the women's choice of color, she believed learning to knit was a step in the right direction toward betterment of the Nez Perce people. But why *yellow* socks? Perhaps the Nez Perce

Studio photo portrait of Mrs. Frederick A. Chapman, center, with her sisters, Fannie Merrill and Tryphine Goodson, circa 1880. Sitting for a photo portrait with knitting in hand was a popular convention, a sign of feminine productivity and membership in the growing numbers of families who had established middle-class homes on the plains and prairies. (Minnesota Historical Society)

women dyed wool yellow because the majority of regional wild plants yielded yellow dye. "I sometimes allow myself to feel," Mrs. Spalding added, "that perhaps God may be pleased to make use of the *weak things* to assist in building up His cause amongst this people." Knitting was one of the "weak things" in her arsenal for missionary work.

Waves of Immigrant Knitters

Massive immigration drove much of the increase in the American population throughout the nineteenth century. From 1815 until the Civil War, more than 5 million Europeans immigrated to the United States. Ten million more arrived by 1890, followed by another 15 million before 1915. The earlier immigrants came from Ireland, Germany, England, and Scandinavia, but after 1890 huge numbers arrived from Southern and Eastern Europe, including Russian Jews fleeing Tsarist pogroms. Many an immigrant brought knitting traditions from the old country. Photographs in the Vesterheim Norwegian-American Museum archive show Norwegian women knitting while still in Norway. Guro Olson, who emigrated in 1855 from Ullensvang, Hardanger, Norway, to Thor, Iowa, posed with her knitting twenty years after she arrived in America.

Immigrants brought not only traditional knitting skills and knowledge, but also hand knits from the old countries. Between 1892 and 1954, immigrants who arrived on the eastern shore came through Ellis Island.

Guro (Johaneson) Olson was one of many immigrants who brought knitting traditions with them from the old country to new homes in America. The Johaneson family changed their name from Johaneson to Olson when they emigrated from Ullensvang, Hardanger, Norway, in 1855. They settled in Thor, Iowa, where this photo was probably taken, circa 1875. (Vesterheim Norwegian-American Museum, Decorah, Iowa)

Norwegian immigrant women in Portland, North Dakota. In 1891 or 1892, photographer G. T. Hagen posed his mother spinning, a neighbor carding fleece, and a hired girl knitting what appears to be a stocking. Set in his studio with a painted backdrop, Hagen's photo shows that knitting was part of the bucolic image in this hand-tinted postcard. (Vesterheim Norwegian-American Museum, Decorah, Iowa)

"Sao sulla ho Mor Paa Rokken sin"   Photo by A. T. Hagen

Knitting was a long-standing tradition among Europeans who immigrated to America. In Mandal, Norway, Marie Koren with daughters Christiane, Lina, and Margrethe posed for a formal portrait dressed in their finest, Mrs. Koren with her knitting. (Vesterheim Norwegian-American Museum, Decorah, Iowa)

Archives at the Statue of Liberty National Monument at Liberty Island, New York, include such personal artifacts as two pairs of knit stockings from Italy, wool hand-warmers from Yugoslavia, a bed cover from Russia, and a shawl from Czechoslovakia. One pair of stockings from Abruzzi, Italy, was knit with orange and yellow linen yarn, a top band in a simple rib stitch; the second pair, also from Abruzzi, was knit in a cream color with an interlocking "L" pattern and scalloped border. The Russian bed cover has knit wool fringe in variegated shades of blue, green, pink, purple, rust, and beige. Marie Kovar knit the Czechoslovakian cotton shawl with green, red, and brown flower motifs along three edges.

Arriving in America, many immigrants found grueling work in expanding urban industries, while others surged westward to homestead land. Some traveled by steamboat, others along the overland trails. In 1859, an overland expedition handbook, *The Prairie Traveler*, advised "suitable dress" for those who undertook the journey. Each man needed four pairs of wool socks long enough to reach the knees; the author wore two pairs when he crossed the Rocky Mountains. Nowhere does he mention clothing recommended for women.[101] Homesteaders faced hostilities of nature — grasshopper swarms, prairie fires, blizzards, dust storms — and many built their first homes from sod turf cut out of virgin prairie. Women settlers found their lives absorbed in keeping homes, growing and preserving food, and clothing families against the harsh climate.[102]

Mormon pioneers blazed a trail from Nauvoo, Illinois, across the plains to Utah. Some Mormons began this trek as immigrants who first crossed the ocean. In 1867, Georgina Norr left Denmark for Utah

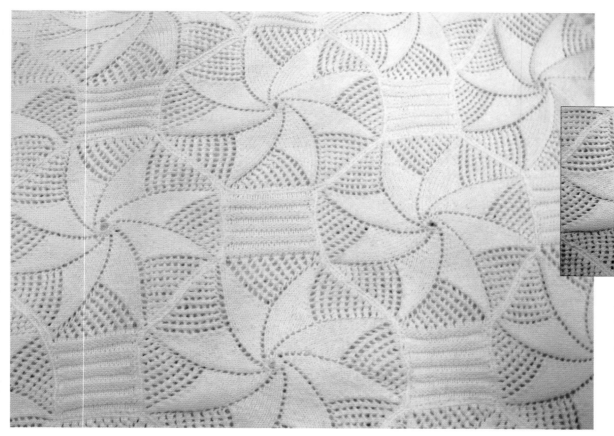

A pinwheel pattern counterpane hand knit by a Mormon pioneer woman. (Daughters of Utah Pioneers, Pioneer Memorial Museum)

A small red mitten, knit by a Mormon pioneer woman, circa 1834. Prolific knitting suited the Mormon pioneer spirit of industry and self-sufficiency. The abundant handwork of Mormon pioneer women is on display at the Pioneer Memorial Museum in Salt Lake City, Utah. (Daughters of Utah Pioneers, Pioneer Memorial Museum)

Left: Colorful stockings hand-knit by Mormon pioneer women. (Daughters of Utah Pioneers, Pioneer Memorial Museum)

as a small child, traveling the plains hungry and cold after her wool stockings burned to ashes when she dried her only pair beside a fire. Georgina's mother, when asked to donate to the early church in Utah, gathered wool from sage brush where sheep had passed, then washed, carded, spun, and knit stockings that she sold for 50¢ a pair. Presumably, Georgina did not lack for warm stockings in Utah.[103] For more than two months on her trek west in the early 1850s, Mormon pioneer Rachel R. Walker either walked or rode on a wagon and "spent much of her time knitting." Renowned for hard work, such Mormon settlers as Christina Oleson Warnick built homes, dug ditches,

plowed and planted the land, took in washing, and spun and wove cloth, and "always walked from one village to the next with her knitting in her hands." Children in the Larson pioneer family gathered around the fireplace while their mother read to them in the evenings. She propped the book, and a child turned the pages so she could knit while she read. Occasionally, she told them, "I'll have to stop while I turn the heel of the sock."[104]

Knit stockings brought on the westward journey wore out quickly with heavy use, and early settlers made do with bare feet or moccasins fashioned from skins. Women settlers knit replacement mittens and

"The Dropped Stitch" by photographer John H. Tarbell, 1897. The portrait of a knitter dressed in humble clothing and seated at the entrance to a log cabin suggests the hard life of many frontier women who took comfort in knitting — or at least made warm stockings and mittens for their families. (Library of Congress)

stockings, although manufactured stockings were readily available in nineteenth-century America for those who could afford them. Settlers with money to spend could buy merchandise — including machine-made stockings and other clothing — transported to frontier settlements by steamboat. The variety of cargo carried to settlers along the Missouri River was well documented in the steamboat *Bertrand* excavation. On its first voyage in 1864 from St. Louis destined for Fort Benton, Montana Territory, the *Bertrand* hit a snag at DeSoto Bend near Omaha, Nebraska, and sank in the Missouri River. No lives were lost, but all cargo went down with the ship. More than one hundred years later, excavation of the *Bertrand's* intact cargo recovered approximately eight thousand complete items or fragments of clothing, including unspecified numbers of woolen ankle-length manufactured stockings.[105]

Settlers and farmers also relied on peddlers for frontier commerce. Among them was Hyman Bernstein, who came to New York in 1870 and, unable to find a job, became a peddler who walked the country through Illinois, Indiana, Iowa, and some southern states. "Yes, I carried a department store on my back," he said, and in his pack he carried knitting needles and yarn.[106] Many such Jewish peddlers went on from selling out of packs or carts to owning general stores or even major department stores, where knitters bought yarn and needles. Bernhard Ulmann, a European immigrant, sold handkerchiefs and doilies from a pushcart in New York until 1870, when he opened his retail store in New York. Later, he founded Bucilla (an acronym for Bernhard Ulmann Company, Lace, Linen & Accessories), a company that grew to dominate knitting-yarn manufacture and sales during the early twentieth century.[107]

Many westward settlers described knitting as an important part of pioneer life. In Lincoln, Nebraska, Hattie Zellars and Tom Kelly remembered mothers who raised sheep and carded and spun wool for knitting. Harry Dixon, whose family arrived in North Platte, Nebraska, in 1878, said his mother knit all his stockings. At the age of five years, Mary E. Burleson traveled to New Mexico with her family in a wagon train of a hundred prairie schooners. They left a snug farm home in Missouri for a crude house where her mother spun the yarn to weave rugs that covered the dirt floor and to knit all the family stockings. When Mrs. W. M. Anderson and her husband arrived in Durango, Texas, in 1873, they struggled through crop failures, hailstorms, and drought. Mrs. Anderson spun wool, dyed with pecan bark, and knit their stockings. Similarly, James Thomas Wood, a child of Texas pioneers, remembered his mother also had to card and spin wool to knit socks for their family. The mother of Mrs. J. A. Hall, who came to Jackson, Nebraska, in 1855, sat and knit in the dark making stockings and mittens.

Women also sold their knitting. "Mother and sisters knitted woolen socks and mittens from yarn grown and spun by them, and sold hundreds of pairs," said J. L. Tarter, who was born in 1862 in Pulaski County, Kentucky. "A pair of hand knitted woolen socks sold for 25¢." In 1884, Mollie Grove Smith's family traveled by covered wagon to White Oaks, New Mexico, where her mother sold hand-knit mittens to their mail carrier for 50¢ a pair. In 1862, the grandmother of Ben E. Jenkins paid the pastor of their little Baptist Church by knitting all his suspenders and socks. Occasionally, a man referred to his knitting. In 1894, Uriah W. Oblinger wrote to his wife Laura, "If you have not knit me any mittens yet, I would rather you would knit me about two pair of woolen socks, as I can manage the mittens myself, for I don't want 'the mitten' from you at all."[108] Giving the mitten was a rejection, usually of a man's invitation or proposal.

Memoirs, diaries, letters, and newspaper articles indicate women wanted to keep up with finer fashion on the frontier, even in the face of clothing hardships, perhaps for novelty in a monotonous environment or as a topic of discussion that bonded otherwise isolated women. The demands of frontier life, however, required practical dress for their active lives, and even women who could afford to dress well often dressed down to fit in with less wealthy neighbors. Women settlers obtained knitting patterns from copies of *Godey's Lady's Book*, *Peterson's*, or *Harper's Bazaar* that they shared with other women or found at the ubiquitous milliner's shop that sprang up in nearly every town.[109] Some women on the prairies and plains worked in occupations or took up careers and business ventures considered appropriate for nineteenth-century women, particularly teaching and shopkeeping. Other women earned butter-and-egg money with home-based businesses, which included knitting socks. Westward immigrants included a relatively small number of African-Americans who escaped slavery before the Civil War or were freed afterwards. Typically, letters and memoirs of black women settlers reveal nearly identical concerns as white women settlers — setting up homes and caring for families. An untold number of black women worked as textile artisans during slavery, and presumably relied on such skills as knitting while homesteading or working in western towns.

Utopian Knitters

The image of American settlers crossing the prairies, carving out farms, and building towns has long invited the stereotype of the strong, rugged individual. In contrast, thousands of Americans, many from immigrant populations, established religious or secular utopian societies based on communal living. English lawyer and

An Amana girl and boy learning to knit, circa 1890. (Photograph by Bertha M. H. Shambaugh, Amana Heritage Society)

statesman Sir Thomas More first coined the term "utopia" in 1516 to describe a perfect human society. The majority of American utopian societies established communal groups whose members lived together with shared beliefs and simple worldly goods owned jointly rather than individually. Many American utopias trace their origins to persecuted Protestant sects that immigrated to America seeking land and freedom of religion. Secular utopian societies often rejected religion and modeled their idyllic worlds on ideas derived from the Age of Enlightenment. They had in common the belief that they could create a model community on which the rest of the country could be built, embracing different strategies to achieve this goal — whether religious or secular, authoritarian or egalitarian, industrial or agricultural and self-sufficient, based on marriage and family or celibacy.

Small numbers of communitarian societies settled in America before 1800 — New England colonial Puritan villages were founded on covenants, for example — but the grand utopian movement and communitarian idealism in America was widespread between 1820 and 1850. Utopian settlements clustered in the Northeast and Midwest, with a few in the Southeast and Pacific Northwest. Life in utopian communities revolved around village or church activities interwoven with careful attention to farms, gardens, and handcrafts — including knitting. Knitters are found among nearly all American utopians. At Old Economy Village, home to the Harmony Society, women knit bonnets, mittens, collars, and socks.[110] Similarly, women of the Bishop Hill Colony, Illinois, knit wool mittens and stockings — called "foot clothing" — like those brought from their native Sweden. By 1850, the colony sold the women's hand-knit stockings and mittens, and bought more sheep for wool, as well as large quantities of knitting needles. Colony women dyed their own wool using leaves, bark, moss, lichens, or purchased madder, logwood, indigo, and gambier. The demands of communal living left little leisure time for making luxury textiles, but women knitting practical socks and mittens fit the utopian ideal very well indeed.[111].

American utopians generally believed in simple living to avoid distractions from spiritual matters. Utilitarian knitting for home and family was intertwined with this utopian ideal. Busy hands and hard work were among the theological ideals of most religious utopias, and knitters appeared to have contributed more than their share of productive work. Journalist Charles Nordhoff observed during his nineteenth-century travels among utopians, "What puzzled me was to find a considerable number of people in the United States satisfied with so little."[112]

Separatists of Zoar

In 1817, the first Separatists of Zoar left Germany and followed their charismatic leader Joseph Baumeler to America, hoping to find religious freedom. Assisted by Philadelphian Quakers, they settled on land in Ohio. To survive the hard years, they pooled resources and lived communally. By 1852, the Zoarites held more than $1 million in assets. Zoar women continued the prolific knitting of their German heritage, raising sheep and dyeing and spinning their own wool. The collection at Zoar Village State Memorial includes wire needles and knit stockings, mittens, gloves, wristlets, and shawls, plus abundant knit lace. Most stockings are red or blue, one pair with "Zoar 1888" knit into the top. A pair of men's mittens has a looped pile surface; another was knit in plaid.[113] Though no example exists, a drawing in the *Index of American Design* — a Depression-era Works Progress Administration project — shows a leather pocket worn by a Zoar knitter on her apron belt to hold the ends of knitting needles, perhaps to help her knit faster.

The Believers of the Shaker Villages

Commonly known as the Shakers, their formal name is the United Society of Believers in Christ's Second Coming. Their founder was Ann Lee, a young factory worker from Manchester, England, who married a blacksmith and bore four children. When all four children died, Lee grew to believe that sexual relations between men and women were the source of the world's evil. She envisioned a utopia composed of sinless individuals living as brothers and sisters. In 1774, she and eight followers immigrated to America and established a hardy, creative settlement based on simple principles of celibacy, sexual equality, separation from the world, communal property, and direct experience of God. The number of Shakers peaked in the 1840s with nearly six thousand members in eighteen communities clustered in New England and the Southeast.

Knitting was important in Shaker life, and the followers were prolific. Consistent with other Shaker handcrafts, the superior craftsmanship and the uncluttered design quality of Shaker knitting were much admired. Shaker sisters knit large numbers of mittens, gloves, stockings, and socks of cotton, linen, or wool — some for community use, others for sale. Their knitting "pins" (fine wire needles) measured less than size 00 and produced extremely fine knitting. In 1838, for example, one order of sisters in Watervliet, New York, knit forty pairs of stockings and sixty-five pairs of "footings" (the foot part of a stocking). Occasionally, a knitter gained a reputation for especially fine work; Ada Cummings of Sabbathday Lake designed an especially well-fitted stocking gusset.[114]

Shaker sisters also knit fingerless mitts, wristlets, shawls, washcloths, cushions, and rugs. Knitters did not appear to favor any particular style of shawl. For household use and for sale, they made cotton or linen washcloths with simple striped or checked patterns. Round knit rugs and chair cushions were similar in feel to braided rugs. For one style of Shaker round rug and cushion, yarn was knit into tubes that were sewn together in a spiral. The Shaker Museum at Old Chatham includes late-nineteenth-century knit rugs. The Shaker sisters taught young girls to knit: In 1845, the caretaker for the Girl's Order, whose work she supervised, knit eleven pairs of stockings and twenty-two pairs of "footings."[115]

Separatists at Zoar knit the usual plain stockings, mittens, and shawls, although a more fanciful Zoarite knit these polka dot "looped" wool men's mittens, circa 1880. The loop surface was often seen in New England knitting. (Zoar Village State Memorial, The Ohio Historical Society)

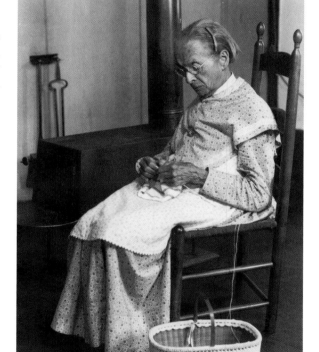

Eldress Fannie Estabrook at the Hancock Shaker village near Pittsfield, Massachusetts, in the 1930s. Superior craftsmanship distinguished Shaker knitting, made for their communities or to sell. (Library of Congress)

The sisters and children knit by hand for their own use during the early days, but most Shaker communities also owned and used knitting machines. Shaker sisters hand processed wool and linen fibers for weaving and knitting until carding and spinning mills were available. Knitting was an important source of income for Shaker communities. Although the sisters turned to commercial fabric and machinery for economy and time efficiency, they continued to make by hand — or by hand and machine — those textiles for outside markets. Certain of the sisters' shops gained a reputation for high-quality knit goods, some made using machines. The sweaters ("Shaker" knits) and

Schoolboys in Amana, Iowa, learn to knit — with mixed degrees of enthusiasm — at the *Strickschule* (knitting school), circa 1905. Knitting lessons were taught after school during communal times. (Amana Heritage Society)

Amana schoolgirls held knit stockings in progress and balanced knitting baskets on their laps as they posed for this photograph, circa 1905. (Amana Heritage Society)

stockings were finished by hand, however. The sisters hand-knit cuffs and edgings onto machine-knit sleeves and bodices of sweaters, and they hand-knit footings onto machine-knit tubes for stockings.[116] The collection at Canterbury Shaker Villages includes hand-knit gloves, rugs, and stockings dating from the 1790s to the 1820s. By the turn of the twentieth century, the Canterbury Shakers converted some rooms in their laundry building into knitting rooms, where they installed knitting machines to make bicycle stockings and varsity sweaters.[117]

Inspirationists of the Amana Colonies

Members of the Community of True Inspiration — founded in 1714 as part of the German Pietist movement — emigrated from Germany to escape religious persecution and settled on Iowa farmland in 1855. They called their colony Amana, "to remain faithful." Religion brought the Inspirationists together, but financial necessity led them to pool resources, build seven villages, and establish industries, all of which allowed them to live communally for more than eighty years. Knitting in early Amana began during childhood. All children, boys and girls alike, learned to knit stockings and mittens in *strickschule*, or knitting schools, as part of their daily curriculum. Sheep raised in Amana provided wool for yarn, typically dyed in shades of blue, black, or brown and

Historical Pattern
1880s Zoar Mittens

This pattern is taken from a pair of mittens in the Zoar collection (OHS #H9169). The mittens were donated to the Ohio Historical Society by a former member of the Zoar Society and likely date to the late-nineteenth century. The original mittens are in Zoar stored with the Zoar textile collection. This pattern interpretation is by Susan Goehring.

Pattern Size: Man's size medium (same as original mittens)

Materials: 2-ply sport weight wool yarn — one half skein each red, black, green, and blue; one set of five double-pointed needles, size 1.

Gauge: 24 sts = 2 inches

Cuff Lining: In scrap color (black, although original mittens use grey-blue) cast on 88 sts using stranded cast-on method. Divide sts evenly on four needles. K 15 rows in same color. K 2 rows in red.

Picot Fold Line: Row 1: In red k 1 * k 2 tog, YO *, repeat between *s, k 1.

Next row: In red, k into yarnovers as if they were normal stitches.

Cuff: K 12 rows in red. K 10 rows in black.

Mitten body: Rows 1–2: * k 2 red, k 2 black *.
Rows 2–4: * k 2 blue, k 2 Green *.
Repeat above 1 time.
Continue this color pattern for remainder of mitten.

Thumb Gusset: Row 1: k 2, place marker, inc 1 st in each of next 2 sts, place marker, knit around.

Rows 2–3: Knit around, slipping markers.

Row 4 (increase): Knit around, inc one st in the st after the 1st marker and in the last st before the 2nd marker (2 inc made).

Repeat last 3 rounds until there are 24 sts between markers.

Next row: K 2, remove marker, place thumb gusset sts (24) on stitch holder, remove marker, knit around.

In order to balance pairs of increases, you will want to make the increases lean to either the right or left of the section being increased.

Mitten Body, continued: K 2, cast on 20 sts. Knit around (total = 108 sts).

Continue knitting around on 108 sts until piece measures 61/2 to 7 inches above cuff or 11/2 to 2 inches less than desired finished length.

To Shape Tip: Row 1: * k 1, ssk, k to last 3 sts on 2nd needle, k 2 tog, k 1 *, repeat on needles 3 and 4.

Row 2: Knit around.

Repeat last 2 rows until 36 sts remain. Divide sts onto two needles and finish top with Kitchner stitch.

Thumb: Transfer stitches on holder and sts that were cast on at thumb opening to four needles. There should now be a total of 44 stitches for the thumb. Pick up an additional 2 sts at each end of thumb opening, making a total of 48 sts. Knit around for 2 to 21/2 inches or to 1 inch less than desired finished length. Shape thumb tip the same as mitten tip, following above instructions until 8 sts remain. Finish with Kitchner stitch.

Cuff Lining: Fold on picot fold line and stitch cast-on edge to inside mitten body.

A knitter among the Separatists at Zoar used nine colors of yarn to make these plaid mittens, circa 1880, a creative way to use odds and ends of leftover yarn. (Zoar Village State Memorial, The Ohio Historical Society)

Exceptionally fine lace
and bead knitting was
lavished on Amana baby
bonnets. (Amana
Heritage Society)

mill-spun at the Amana woolen mill or handspun by retired men. Coopers made their sets of five double-pointed wire needles. The boys knit mittens to sell in stores and at the woolen mill, and many girls knit for their hope chests. Traveler Charles Nordhoff observed children knitting from 9:30 A.M. until 11:00 A.M. Their teacher told him that knitting "kept them quiet, gave them habits of industry, and kept them off the streets and from rude plays."[118]

Marie Trumpold of Middle Amana describes how stockings were made when she was a young girl in the *strickschule* during the 1920s:

> The men's stockings were a mid-calf length worked in a knit two, purl two ribbing from the cuff to the toe. The ladies stocking was a bit more complicated. These were started on four needles, knitting in the round, beginning at the cuff, which fit just below the knee. It began with a knit two, purl two ribbing for about an inch or inch-and-a-half. Then it was straight knitting. This "knitting in the round" does not involve purl stitches, unless a texture is desired. At the end of every other round, a purl stitch was added, which created the look of a seam and aided in counting the number of rounds knitted. As the bottom of the calf was reached, decreases were added on each side of the "seam" to narrow the stocking to fit the ankles.

The heel was added next, then a gusset was created, and knitting continued until the correct length of the foot was reached. Then decreases were put in to shape the toe and the stocking was finished.[119]

Duplicate stitch initials were embroidered onto stockings in different letter styles with yarn in contrasting colors. Initials made matching easy in the communal laundries and were embroidered to face the stocking wearer.

Elders who led the communal villages "frowned on idleness, even during the evening hours."[120] Knitting, however, was an approved activity. Knitters elaborated on patterns they found in books brought from Germany or in magazines like *Needlecraft* and *Home Arts*. Lace knitting for doilies, tablecloths, and bedspreads was especially popular and was worked on very fine needles with crochet cotton. Knitting patterns were handed down or adapted, with each knitter finding ways to personalize the work. Amana mittens, for example, were similar to Scandinavian designs, but each knitter used a signature pattern: stripes on the cuffs, patterns for the palm, or designs with deer, "Iowa," or rosettes.[121]

People in Amana felt the intimate touch of knitting throughout their lives. From birth, babies in Amana wore exquisite hand-knit white cotton lace

Fancy knitting was also lavished on baby bootees and stockings in Amana. (Amana Heritage Society)

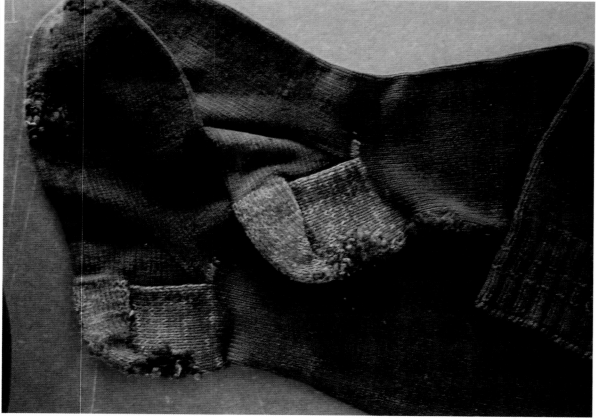

Amana knitters darned and mended what was perhaps a favorite pair of warm, comfortable, hand-knit stockings. (Amana Heritage Society)

Men's and women's hand-knit wool stockings, Amana, Iowa, circa 1900. The women's stockings feature lacy white knitting, whereas the men's are in solid colors. Initials stitched onto stocking tops simplified sorting into pairs in the communal laundry. Typically, initials faced the wearer. (Amana Heritage Society)

bonnets — some trimmed with pale pink or blue satin ribbons, others in fine bead knitting, and each with some variation of a star or spiral pattern knit into the back. No adult dared risk community disapproval by making and wearing anything so fancy, but for the *baby* everyone nodded approval. Doting parents or grandparents gave a little Amana girl her own hand-knit black version of this bonnet to cover her head when she began religious school. Knit coverlets and doilies softened the plain lines of Amana furniture, and room-sized rugs hand-knit from fabric strips gave new life to sewing scraps and old clothing. Amana knitters turned out untold numbers of practical, comfortable, warm stockings that were then darned and patched over time. Until the 1960s, each person was dressed for burial in traditional white clothing that included hand-knit white stockings and either a knit man's cap with a star pattern on top or a woman's bonnet with the star on the back, the latter remarkably similar to the baby bonnet. Useful from cradle to grave, knitting even accompanied the men and women of Amana into the afterlife.[122]

American utopian communities ended for reasons as distinct as their ideals. Bishop Hill Colony fell to pressures from the Civil War and financial mismanagement. Separatists of Zoar lasted eighty-one years until railroads brought the outside world to them.[123]

Amish and Mennonite Knitting

The Amish emigrated from Germany, the Alsace, and Switzerland in the early eighteenth century and settled in American farming communities where they could live simply and practice religious beliefs in freedom and privacy. Their descendents thrive in communities throughout the United States and Canada. "English" people (as outsiders are called) associate the Amish with driving a horse and buggy, wearing modest plain dress, and stitching quilts in unique colors and designs. Their knitting traditions are less well known to outsiders.

In the early days, Amish women knit shawls and capes, mittens and gloves, typically in solid dark colors consistent with the plain dark clothing worn by men and women. Between 1860 and 1920, Old Order Amish women in Lancaster County, Pennsylvania, knit colorful knee-length stockings, many with scalloped tops in vivid contrasting hues from purple, rose, and pink to brown, green, and blue. These stockings were part of private dress, as the long dresses and laced black boots hid their stockings. Sometimes these colorful stockings are called "wedding" stockings; only adult women wore them and perhaps as part of their wedding clothing. They may have knit and worn such stockings because the Lancaster County Amish lived near Germantown, Pennsylvania, home to mills that manufactured "Germantown" yarns. During the 1860s, these mills used the first synthetic, aniline dyes to create a much wider range of bright-colored yarns than were previously available. Amish life was private, but never closed to outside influences. Perhaps they used inexpensive mill ends of yarn for their stocking tops. Women knit their stockings to a gauge of about ten stitches per inch in the round from the top edge down using double-pointed needles, shaping the calf and toe with careful decreases and usually turning a round heel.[130]

The Amish began to buy their stockings and mittens during the first half of the twentieth century, though some knitters continued to make mittens and stockings for their families. Women also knit and crocheted rugs, placemats, and lamp mats to place beneath kerosene lamps. Leftover yarns were knit into lively and colorful combinations, with some

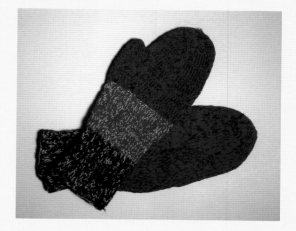

Amish mittens made in Lancaster County, Pennsylvania, circa 1930. (Heritage Center of Lancaster County)

Lancaster County Amish wedding stockings, one pair dated 1873, the other dated 1876. (Heritage Center of Lancaster County)

lamp mats knit and then embellished with crocheted flowers. Amish rug knitters usually worked with strips of torn fabric in garter stitch, some sewn together in patches that reflected Amish quilt designs. By the 1930s, hooked rugs had largely replaced knit rugs. Amish families, private collectors, and such institutions as the Heritage Center of Lancaster County in Lancaster, Pennsylvania, preserve the heritage of Amish knitters.[131]

Mennonites are another religious group that left Europe seeking religious freedom more than four hundred and fifty years ago. The Iowa Mennonite Museum in Kalona, Iowa, includes knit mittens and children's stockings, one dated around 1902. However, most of the shawls, caps, scarves, and mittens knit by family members are kept within Mennonite families.[132]

Shakers, a celibate sect that recruited new members through conversion, dwindled to two hundred by 1931, and only a small number remain today, all of whom live at Sabbathday Lake in New Gloucester, Maine. At the Amana Colonies, communalism ended in 1932, but the Inspirationists continue with separate arms for tending to religion and business (a healthy tourist trade). The Museum of Amana History preserves Amana knitting in its collection, and the Amana Arts Guild sells hand-knit woolen Amana mittens.

Indigenous Knitters: The Art of Acculturation

Westward expansion decimated Native American populations and cost the majority of Native American people their homelands. Pacific Northwest Indians had lost an estimated 95 percent of their original population by 1900. Survivors among Pacific Northwest tribes continued to knit into the twentieth century, perhaps taught by missionaries but as often learning from one another through the generations. Fran James of the Coast Salish Lummi people in Washington learned to knit at the age of nine from her grandmother, who knit and sold socks for 25¢ a pair.[124]

Coast Salish people in Washington are among the knitters of the Cowichan sweater, an exceptionally warm and wooly garment that takes its name from the Cowichan people of Vancouver. Some attribute the introduction of knitting among the Salish people to the Sisters of St. Ann, missionaries who arrived in the Cowichan Valley from Victoria in 1864 and taught among the Salish women to knit socks and mittens. However, many of the early white settlers were British fishermen, who brought their Gansey (or Guernsey) and Fair Isle knitting traditions. Creative beyond socks and mitts, the women began knitting sweaters and long johns, working in the round with five double-pointed needles. The earliest sweaters were one color, but over time Salish knitters began knitting with more colors, carrying yarn across the back of the work between color changes in the Fair Isle manner. Authentic Cowichan sweaters are hand-knit by Coast Salish people in one-ply, handspun, natural-colored sheep wool. Knit in the round with set-in sleeves and a characteristic shawl collar, no two sweaters are alike. Cowichan knitters create unique designs with geometric and pictorial motifs inspired by anything from a Chinese tea box to oak leaves or traditional Salish basket designs.[125]

Knitters were also found among the Pueblo, Hopi, and Navajo people of the Southwest, populations that survived somewhat better than most thanks in part to living in isolated homelands. Centuries before the Spanish arrival, Pueblo people built terraced adobe villages in regions that became New Mexico, Colorado, and Arizona. Presumably, Pueblo people learned knitting from Spanish settlers, who also introduced *churra* sheep for wool in the Southwest. Pueblo knitters, usually

The Cowichan Sweater

By Nika, 1936

Now praise the Indian sweater
In accents clear and bold!
No garment suits us better
For working in the cold.

While water pipes are frozen,
While wood-piles melt away,
That trusty garb is chosen
When buckling for the fray.

For, though it shows rotunder
The over-portly form
The sweater is a wonder
To make the blood run warm.

Oh, cherish, wear and guard it;
Refuse to have it washed;
All hints that we discard it
Indoors may too be squashed.

So thank you, woolly baa-lamb,
For yielding us your fleece.
Thank you, whoe'er you are, ma'am,
Who first removed the grease;

Who carded, span, and knitted,
With labour and with art,
Each sweater snuggly fitted
About a grateful heart.

From *The Cowichan Leader* newspaper in Duncan, B.C., Canada, February 20, 1936. Reprinted with kind permission of the *Cowichan News Leader*.

men, made leggings for everyday wear and for ceremonial dance costumes. Early in the twentieth century, Charles Francis Saunders observed Pueblo men knitting.[126] Hopi knitters also made long white leggings or shorter black ones as part of ceremonial dance costumes, knitting and traditions that continue today.

Among the Navajo people, the Franciscan Fathers of St. Michaels Catholic mission near Window Rock, Arizona, observed Navajo culture and language in exceptional detail — even recording Navajo words for the range of natural colors of Navajo sheep wool used for weaving and knitting. According to the Fathers, Navajo women owned the sheep and

processed the wool; Navajo men knit sturdy wool leggings and carrying bags.[127] In the Ramah region of the reservation, men fashioned wooden knitting needles about five inches long from hardwoods, like Fendlerbush or black greasewood, that could be polished to a smooth surface. Nineteenth-century Navajo knitters also used metal needles in sets of four, either obtained from the Zuni people or made from umbrella ribs broken into six- to eight-inch-long pieces. Needles were said to last a long time and were stored in a sack on the wall inside the hogan (the traditional Navajo dwelling). By 1910, Navajo knitters commonly purchased their steel needles from trading posts. One Navajo woman said she stopped knitting after she returned from internment at Fort Sumner in 1868, probably because she had no wool.[128]

Nineteenth-century observers in the Southwest mention Navajo knit leggings (also referred to as stockings) beginning in 1857. Early descriptions of Navajo knitting and knitters vary regionally and often conflict. According to one source, Navajo knitters said their people learned to knit from Puebloans after the Spanish introduced sheep. Others claimed knitting was introduced during internment at Fort Sumner. Most agreed that more Navajo men than women knit leggings, though one source claimed women were the knitters. Some observers said both men and women wore leggings, though others claimed only men wore them. According to the Franciscan Fathers, men were the usual knitters because they wore the leggings, although women began to wear them after 1910.

Cowichan sweater, circa 1925. Each warm, wooly Cowichan sweater knit by a member of the Coast Salish tribe has unique knit-in patterns. (Burke Museum of Natural History and Culture)

This set of five hand-carved knitting needles was used to knit Cowichan sweaters in the round with set-in sleeves. (Burke Museum of Natural History and Culture)

A Snohomish woman knits, her yarn held in a woven basket, in the couple's temporary summer house on Puget Sound, Washington, 1905. Their salmon catch hangs above the campfire to be smoked and cured for winter. (Photograph by Norman Edson, University of Washington Libraries)

Tulalip women card and spin wool on the porch of their cabin at Tulalip Indian Reservation in Washington state. Photographer Edward S. Curtis made this image in 1898. (Library of Congress)

Puyallup Indian Mary Hote knits in the round, crafting either a sleeve or stocking, circa 1900. Her knitting basket exemplifies the artistic quality of the Pacific Northwest basketry tradition. (Washington State Historical Society)

Descriptions of nineteenth-century Navajo leggings also vary. Some leggings were knit with feet, others without feet; some footless leggings were knit down to the toes, others had a narrow knit or plaited strap under the instep. Several observers described blue leggings knit in the round with purl-stitch ridges down the outside of each leg and at the top and bottom, probably for sturdier edges that resisted curling. In the Ramah region, leggings were dark blue or black, with no designs. However, in 1875, New Mexico Governor William Arny collected leggings with red-and-white zigzag designs on a blue background. Another observer claimed that old Navajo women wore white leggings and only men wore colors. Navajo men and women also knit mittens, usually in solid black, blue, or white yarn. Knitters said mittens were knit in one piece beginning at the wrist. Some left a hole for the thumb, knit separately and stitched to the mitten. Navajo-knit mittens, leggings, and carrying bags appear nearly lost to history.[129]

Native Alaskan Qiviut Lace Knitting

By Donna Druchunas

Donna Druchunas is the author of *Arctic Lace: Knitting Projects and Stories Inspired by Alaska's Native Knitters* (Fort Collins, CO: Nomad Press, 2006).

In isolated villages scattered around Alaska, Yup'ik and Inupiat women knit lightweight and luxurious accessories out of qiviut, the underdown of the arctic musk ox. These lacy scarves, shawls, and nachaq-hoods are sold by the Oomingmak Musk Ox Producers' Co-operative, owned and operated by more than two hundred Native Alaskan women and headquartered in Anchorage.

Although knitting was introduced to Alaska by missionaries and today many Native Alaskan women learn to knit from their mothers, grandmothers, aunts, and neighbors, there was no indigenous knitting tradition in Alaska prior to the 1960s. The impetus for this new knitting tradition began in the 1950s when John Teal, an anthropologist from Vermont, decided to experiment with domesticating musk oxen. Teal's goal was to launch a cottage industry in Alaska for the indigenous people to create products made from local resources.

Musk oxen became extinct in Alaska in the 1800s, but the species was reintroduced from Greenland in the 1930s. A decade of research ensued, as Teal experimented with breeding musk oxen and harvesting their qiviut. After deciding that it would be possible to maintain a herd of musk oxen in captivity, Teal recruited several women to help him develop a line of yarn and products. Dorothy Reade, a knitter and spinner from Oregon, handspun many samples of yarn and worked with Ann Lillian Schell and Helen Howard, both from Alaska, to design the co-op's first lace-knitting pattern, adapted from the carvings on an ancient ivory harpoon head. Because few of the Native Alaskan women spoke English, the knitting patterns were charted. To teach the knitters the lace pattern, Ann or Helen would sit behind each student, often on the floor, and point to a square on the chart, then make the corresponding knitting stitch.

At the first workshop in 1968, nine women completed the lessons and were ready to start knitting the Harpoon Scarf pattern. Since that time, workshops have been taught all over the state of Alaska, and a signature pattern — inspired by Yup'ik or Inupiat artwork and designed and knit by Native members of Oomingmak — has been developed for each of the original member villages. More recently, the co-op has added a line of colorwork patterns, knitted in natural taupe qiviut and white yarn that is a blend of qiviut, wool, and silk. Knitters in new villages joining the co-op today knit projects from this Tundra and Snow product line.

Although Oomingmak members are scattered all over Alaska, many of the knitters live in small villages of only a hundred or so residents in the Yukon–Kuskokwim River delta in southwest Alaska. Jobs here are scarce, and extra work in seasonal commercial fishing jobs gets snatched up quickly, mostly by men. (In other areas where work is more plentiful, many women prefer to work in higher-paying jobs and do not knit for money.) Packaged food is expensive, as it has to be brought in by plane or barge, and the selection in the local stores is meager. Because of this, many Native Alaskans rely on hunting, fishing, and berry picking for much of their diet. They follow the seasonal traditions of their ancestors, staying in their villages during the winter months and moving to fish camp for much of the spring and summer. Knitting provides women in these remote areas a way to make money without disrupting the routine of their traditional lifestyle. Since an ounce or two of qiviut and a pair of knitting needles is small and lightweight, and the accessories of the Oomingmak Co-op are small, the portable projects are a perfect fit for the mobile lifestyle of the knitters and allow them to retain control of where and how they live and raise their families.

Women learned to knit lace with qiviut yarn at the first knitting workshop. (Oomingmak Musk Ox Producers' Co-operative)

Knitters practice using qiviut during a workshop in Tununak, on Nelson Island. (Photograph by Bill Bacon, Oomingmak Musk Ox Producers' Co-operative)

The Nelson Island Diamond pattern was adapted from the trim on parkas and is knit by co-op members on and near Nelson Island. (Photograph by Bill Bacon, Oomingmak Musk Ox Producers' Co-operative)

THE SATURDAY EVENING POST

An Illustrated Weekly
Founded A.º D.º 1728 by Benj. Franklin

FEBRUARY 20, 1915   5cts. THE COPY

'ISH'S SPY—By Mary Roberts Rinehart

Chapter Five

Knitting for an Age of Optimism

The decades surrounding the turn of the twentieth century were good years, signaling a new Progressive Era and the arrival of an age of optimism. American society was changing. More Americans were moving to cities, where they enjoyed special expositions and celebrations. People were having fewer children — fertility had dropped by a third — and infant mortality had fallen dramatically thanks to better sanitation. Early in the century, the first motion picture was released, and the Wright Brothers made their first successful flight. By 1909, Henry Ford had sold thousands of Model T automobiles, and Alice Huyler Ramsey and her three female companions first drove coast to coast across the nation.

An image of the industrious knitter with an equally industrious kitten from a Corticelli Yarns catalog.

After the assassination of President McKinley in 1901, he was succeeded by Theodore Roosevelt. Under the Roosevelt administration, millions of acres of forests were secured for public use, the Panama Canal was built, and seeds were laid for America's subsequent role in the world. America seemed to run itself under presidents William Howard Taft and Woodrow Wilson. The war that began in Europe in 1914 seemed far away to most Americans.

Twenty-five million Europeans migrated to the United States between 1850 and 1915, whereas only 41 million citizens were native born. The rising tide of immigration, industrialization, and urbanization created pressing, even desperate, social needs. Although still denied the vote, women were at the forefront of social reform in health care, labor, education, suffrage, and an array of other welfare concerns. A new generation of women, including many single college graduates, dedicated remarkable amounts of time — many their entire lives — to social reform during the Progressive Era. In every state, reformers worked for the betterment of society.

Knitting played a role in certain social reform efforts. In 1914, three hundred and fifty Europeans were stranded at Ellis Island after World War I broke out in Europe. Concerned the "detained aliens"

Opposite page:
A young woman of the late Progressive Era appears to ponder the complexity of turning a heel on her hand-knit stocking on the cover of the *Saturday Evening Post*, February 20, 1915. The quiet pursuit of knitting at home was part of everyday life for many women.

"Listen to the Knocking at the Knitting Club" by *chanteuse* Adele Rowland was a hit of the 1910s. The lyrics described the day's fancy for knitting: "All the girls are going nutty knitting, knocking while they're knitting through the day, knitting in the parlor when they're sitting, knocking just to pass the time away, young and old are knitting nowadays, knitting is the universal craze!"

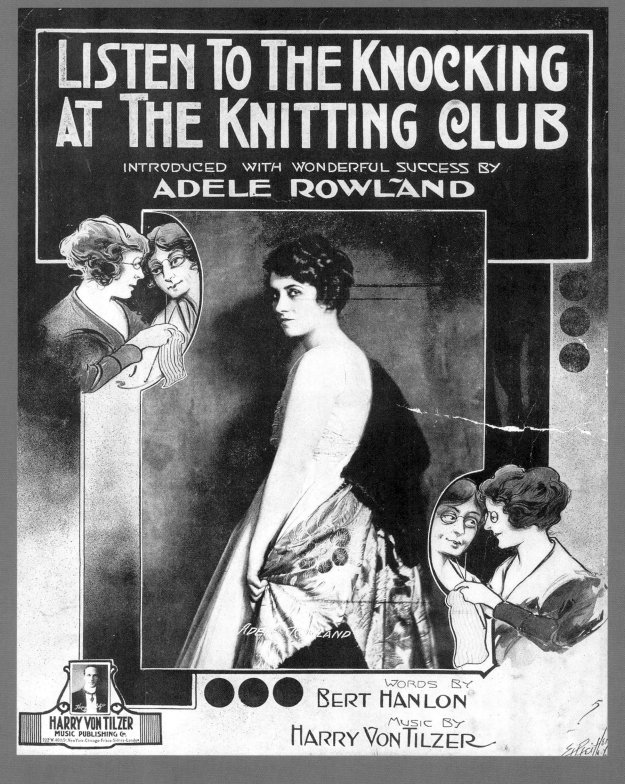

A group of orphans work on their knitting while the youngest play with toys at the Danish Lutheran Orphan Asylum in Chicago in 1906. (Chicago Historical Society)

had nothing to occupy their time, the commissioner of immigration conferred with the American Red Cross, YWCA, and Columbia University. Their solution: provide materials for the detainees to make handcrafts, including knitting, to contribute to the Red Cross. The Daughters of the American Revolution, founded in 1890, set up an Ellis Island committee to establish a workroom and gave detained immigrants small kits including knitting materials. This idea of occupying people with the constructive work of knitting spread to the prison system. In 1915, under the auspices of prison reformer Thomas Mott Osborne, convicts at Sing Sing and Great Meadows knit in classrooms and the prison yard while listening to a concert by the Prison Mandolin Club.[133]

The quiet pursuit of needlework, including knitting, was part of everyday life for many women. The popular magazine, the *Ladies' Home Journal*, informed readers that women's "dainty fingers" still practiced the "homely" art of knitting. Ida Saxton McKinley, America's first lady from 1897 to 1901, knit hundreds

Prisoners knit in a classroom at Sing Sing, Ossining, New York, 1915. Prison reformer Thomas Mott Osborne incorporated knitting lessons into reform measures at Sing Sing and Great Meadows prisons. (Library of Congress)

of slippers for charity auctions and, as a token of admiration, presented Mademoiselle Calve, an opera singer, with a pair of her hand-knit blue slippers.[134] In 1902, thousands of knitters across America entered 4,980 hand knits in Lion Brand Yarn's competition for the finest pieces. A knit bathrobe by Mrs. A. Clinton Knight of New York City earned the $200 first prize, while Mrs. A. H. Christ of Cooperstown, New York, won $10 for her hand-knit American flag. Others earned awards for knit slippers, shawls, gloves, afghans, jackets, socks, and opera capes.[135] Women who entered

This handcraft class for immigrant children at the Henry Street Settlement, 1910, included basketry and needlework that appears to be knitting or crochet. Social worker Lillian Wald founded the Henry Street Settlement in New York City's Lower East Side in 1895, intending to help new arrivals fit into American society. Although the original photograph is labeled as a knitting class, that is not the main activity. It is not unusual for photographs to be mislabeled, making research about hand knitting more difficult. (Library of Congress)

Historical Pattern
1910s Ladies' Cozy Jacket

This pattern comes from Art in Knitting *(Vol. 16), 1917.*

Pattern Size: 36-inch bust measure.

Material: 1 Pair No. 4 Amber Needles; 10 Skeins Maroon Zephyr 4-fold.

Instructions: Cast on 50 stitches. Knit plain for 56 ribs. Then cast on 50 and knit 56 ribs. Bind off. Knit 56 ribs. Bind off.

Sleeve: Cast on 48 stitches. Knit plain for 6 ribs. Then increase 1 stitch each rib until there are 68 stitches. Knit plain for 14 ribs or according to width of sleeve. Decrease 1 stitch each rib until there are 48 stitches. Knit 6 ribs. Bind off. Sew up sleeves. Sew jacket at under-arm. Sew in sleeves.

Edge: 1st R: Crochet ch 5; skip 2 ribs; 1 dc; * ch 2; skip 2 ribs; 1 dc; repeat from .

2nd R: 1 so over ch 2; S dc over next ch 2; 1 sc over next ch 2; repeat.

Sweaters with leg-of-mutton sleeves were popular during the 1890s and into the early twentieth century. The full part of the sleeve began with 120 cast-on stitches, although patterns of the time did not specify gauge. The knitter was advised to "use her own judgment" when selecting finer or coarser yarns and working the sweater in different sizes. *Fancy and Practical Knitting,* 1902.

---

the labor force and were active in progressive movements of the age appeared not to have given up their knitting — or perhaps they knit to relax and recuperate from the demands of working outside their homes. A Boston physician prescribed knitting for his recuperating patients who could not tolerate absolute idleness. Apparently, a stylish and lovely young woman knitting was not an unusual sight, for in 1915, Charles A. MacLellan painted a *Saturday Evening Post* cover illustration showing a knitter who puzzled over turning the heel on a sock she was knitting on four needles.[136]

Knit Fashions

Fashionable silhouettes for women changed dramatically during this time. The woman of the 1890s cinched her waist to a stylish hourglass shape, further exaggerated with enormous puffed sleeves and a skirt shaped like an inverted cone. From 1900 to 1908, the fashionable woman corseted her body into an S-shaped silhouette, with a high-boned collar, full blousy bosom, flat skirt front, and rounded back hipline that flared into yards of skirt fabric falling to the floor. Shirred and puffed sleeves perched above her tiny waist. Women's

BEAR BRAND BLUE BOOK

of YarnKraft

MANUAL OF WORSTED WORK

Volume 18

PRICE 25 CENTS

A young feminine knitter illustrated on the cover of Bear Brand Blue Books held her knitting needles more convincingly than the Woolco Girl. *Bear Brand Blue Book of Yarn Kraft,* 1916.

The Woolco Girl

Historical Pattern 1910s Knit Picot Stitch Shawl

Designer Helen Marvin touted the knit picot stitch as an "altogether happy discovery, bound to please even the woman who demands all grace and all practical value from the humble art of knitting."

This clever hand-knit apparel for women and girls comes from Woman's Home Companion.

Picot stitch instructions: Cast on 94 stitches and knit one row plain.

Second row: * knit together two stitches, and without slipping them from the needle, knit them together again upon the back thread. This gives two stitches upon the right needle for two stitches upon the left.

Repeat from * throughout the shawl.

magazines suggested pretty knit shawls that fit over the stylish silhouette. The *Ladies' Home Journal* recommended a three-cornered shawl, well suited for an elderly lady, knit in white wool with white crochet taffeta ribbon edging, or in warm red with matching fringe and ribbon if worn only in the house. Another shawl was knit in wide horizontal stripes of white, pale blue, and black and finished with eight-inch fringe. Knitting that alternated fine and coarse needles created a shirred striping effect on another three-cornered shawl considered "pretty for evening wear."[137] At the beginning of the century, according to *Woman's Home Companion,* patterns for knit scarf shawls called for plain garter stitch on large wooden needles. By 1905, knitters were advised to create an "improved and beautified" shawl with such loose, lacy openwork as the looped stitch, the herringbone stitch, or the "absolutely new shawl stitch" called the picot.[138]

After 1909, women's fashions settled into straighter silhouettes with a higher waistline and hobble skirt that fit tight around the ankles. Designer Helen Marvin published a pattern in *Woman's Home Companion* for a long, slender cape that complemented the new shape. Inspired by a popular London style, the cape was knit in two garter-stitch rectangles sewn together, lined with soft silk, and embellished with tassels front and back. In 1912, Marvin also designed beguiling patterns for a child's Saxony mittens and a loosely knit muff-and-collar lined in pale blue satin.

She combined knitting with crochet and sewing in a little girl's hat and coat knit in "brioche" stitch with white Shetland wool, lined in garter-stitch pink Shetland wool, and trimmed with flower-print fabric cuffs and buttons.[139]

Between 1890 and 1920, patterns for hand knits shifted from Victorian frou-frou to fashionable sweaters, scarves, caps, and mittens better suited to progressive American society. Nearly all the patterns in Butterick Publishing Company's *The Art of Knitting* (1897) were characteristic Victorian dainties for home and family, although a "Foot-Ball Sweater" for men and ladies' knitted sweater were harbingers of things to come for knitters. Fashion hand knits grew in popularity as more people, especially women, took up active sports. By 1902, Butterick's *Fancy and Practical Knitting* had "special departments devoted to garments and hosiery suitable for Golf, Cycling, Tennis, Rowing, the Gymnasium and Pastimes generally." Cycle and golf stockings for ladies or gentlemen were patterned with textured and colorful

Ladydown sweater, with knit-in neck wrap. *Bear Brand Blue Book of Yarn Kraft*, 1916.

Ladies' Bicycle Mitten, Cycle or Golf Stocking for Ladies or Gentlemen. *Fancy and Practical Knitting*, 1902. Hand knits were well suited for more active lives, and the change was especially evident for women of the Progressive Era.

Title page of *Corticelli Lessons in Knitting and Crochet*, 1917.

Right Top The Tennis, the Motor Girl, and the Regatta. Women wore fashionable knits with sports-conscious flair. *Bear Brand Blue Book of Yarn Kraft*, 1918.

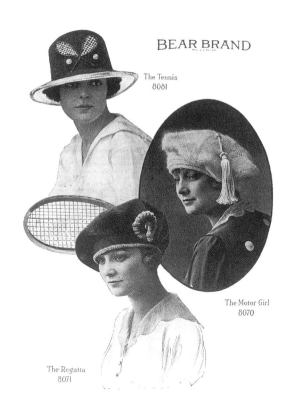

Helen Marvin published clever hand-knit apparel for women and girls in *Woman's Home Companion*.

Men's sweater fashions were long and austere, often knit in simple garter stitch. *Art in Knitting*, 1917.

stripes. In 1916, the *Woolco Knitting and Crocheting Manual* from F. W. Woolworth Company featured a Ladies' Athletic Sweater — the model wielding a tennis racket — and generously sized scarf-and-hat "sport sets" for women. The Woolco Girl showed that working with Woolco Yarns was "one of the most fascinating forms of recreation." In 1917 *Art in Knitting* by Novelty Art Studios, Chicago, included "sport" tams and sweaters for women, and *Corticelli Lessons in Knitting and Crochet Book* had sleeveless athletic pullover sweater vests. Motion picture star Irene Castle, who modeled a Corticelli vest in the pattern book, said that "For motoring, golf, or mountain resort this Sports Vest [Corticelli pattern] is ideal." In 1918, *Bear Brand Blue Book of Yarn Kraft* — one of Bucilla's Blue Book Library of Art Needlework Publications — named its knit and crochet hats for sports: the Tennis, the Regatta, and the Motor Girl. The new sport of automobile motoring, of course, required a new wardrobe with hand-knit automobile helmet and motor coat — extra-long with gores and a wide collar to snuggle into when motoring in open cars. There were plenty of patterns for long, comfy cardigans styled for men and women, plus knit boudoir jackets, leggings, gloves, mittens, hats, neckties, knee caps, comfy slippers, and socks.

Sweaters were high style. In 1917, the *Ladies' Home Journal* described the slipover sweater as a fashion craze and advised readers that sweaters were "an absolute necessity for almost every occasion." Corticelli Silk Mills assured knitters that all the sweaters in its pattern

books were the "latest models from our New York Department of Design, which is under the direction of Mrs. Addie Crandall Smith, an expert in knitting and crocheting." Smith informed knitters that long knit coats of brushed wool for town wear were all the fashion in London. She also advised, "Knitted scarfs, too, are somewhat lording it over the most costly fur, and, like the knitted coat, they have become more elaborate and attractive, and incidentally more voluminous, many of them being veritable shawls."[140] Bear Brand Yarns claimed its designers were "leaders in developing artistic and practical models" for sweaters. In 1918, *Bear Brand Blue Book* devoted five pages to patterns for military comfort garments, while patterns for women's sweaters warranted more than fifty pages. The Bear Brand patterns were knit as a single flat piece, then stitched on the sides and underarms.

Sweater fashions were worn long, many with knit belt and ribbed waistline, some in a kimono style, and others with ruffle and pleat variations that fell below the waistline. Angora lent a stylish flair to collars.[141] According to the *Ladies' Home Journal*, sweaters were just right for a shopping trip, for around the house on cold days, and for nearly all varieties of outings: "The forecast for autumn and winter shows no lessening in popularity of the sweater, which means that nothing more acceptable can be suggested for Christmas gifts, for the college girl's new outfit, the bride's honeymoon trunk or the stay-at-home young woman who plans wisely and well. Since all want to look their best on

Ladies' "Motor" Cap and Scarf. *Art in Knitting,* 1917.

Right Top: Bear Brand pattern designs were innovative and new; sweaters were knit flat and sewn up the sides or over the shoulders. *Bear Brand Blue Book of Yarn Kraft,* 1918.

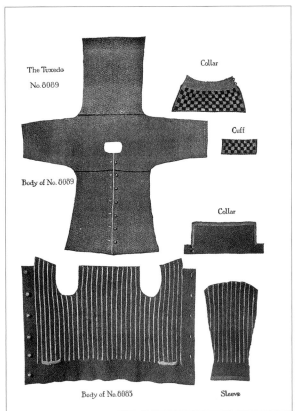

Several pattern manuals included knitting instructions for sweaters for the family dog, typically sized to fit a small terrier. *Bear Brand Blue Book of Yarn Kraft,* 1918.

Above and right: Pershing Coat and "Over the Top" Scotch Cap. Fashion knits with a bit of military authority may have appealed to women who had shifted to knitting for the "boys over there" during World War I. *Corticelli Yarn Book,* 1919.

every occasion, there are many times when a good-looking sweater fills the need."[142] The woman with a political agenda could make another kind of statement by knitting "The Suffrage" from *Bear Brand Blue Book of Yarn Kraft.* For the little folks, there were patterns for slipover and cardigan sweaters in a range of loose-fitting styles. Knitters could order booklets with working directions for these patterns from the *Ladies' Home Journal* for 15¢. Bear Brand Yarn Manufacturers also sold Yarnkraft pattern books with sweaters, hand knits for children, and stylish vests, tams, and scarves.[143] Most pattern books included instructions and close-up photographs of knitting techniques and pattern stitches.

After war broke out in Europe, military styles influenced the cut of popular women's clothing, sweaters in particular. Knitters who turned out sweater vests, stockings, and helmets (one-piece garments that covered head, neck, and chest) for soldiers certainly had the proficiency to make their own stylish sweaters. And, as the makers of Coricelli Yarn assured knitters, "Although so well employed in knitting for the soldiers, most women yet have time to make a few things for themselves or the members of their families."[144] Only four months after America entered the war, the *Ladies' Home Journal* published patterns for the "latest military sweater" with knit belt and tam for women and a slipover vest named "Navy Boy." In 1918, a

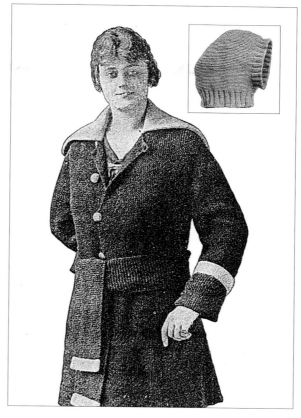

Knit Motor Coat. Knit in dark brown with light tan collar and cuffs, the motor coat had gores in the skirt that gave it "correct lines." More people bought automobiles, and wearing the right hand knits made driving more stylish, comfortable, and perhaps a bit warmer. *Corticelli Lessons in Knitting and Crochet*, 1917.

Inset: Automobile Helmet. This practical if not especially flattering cover-up for motoring was knit flat in garter stitch, shaped to the head, and sewn up the back. Women motorists wore large hats with protective veils. *Corticelli Yarn Book*, 1918.

woman's military-style sweater — brass buttons, epaulets, wide belt — graced the cover of *Corticelli Yarn Book*. The Pershing Coat knit in dark brown with tricorner pockets and an "Over the Top" Scotch Cap — a "military model effective in navy blue with tassel of red silk" — appeared the following year in *Corticelli Yarn Book*. *Fleisher's Knitting and Crocheting Manual* (Sixteenth Edition, 1918) had patterns for patriotic blankets: the Red Cross afghan with a large cross, the Liberty Blanket embellished with an American flag, and the Conservation Blanket knit with two pounds of scrap yarn.

Even more patterns for baby and children's clothing appeared in magazines and knitting manuals: baby sacques, bonnets, leggings, bootees, slippers, lacy veils, cardigans, pullovers, caps, tams, skirts, petticoats, and mittens. Many baby bootees, sacques, and bonnets were lace knit. Baby bootees and bonnets predominate in historical collections of children's knit clothing that date to the first decades of the twentieth century. Apparently knitters craved patterns for baby clothes. Lower birth and infant mortality rates invite images of doting relatives knitting for a smaller number of babies who were more likely to live. And all those hand knits were so practical for children's wear — a smock sweater suited an active five-year-old boy well indeed.[145] Even the family dog warranted its own sweater pattern in *Bear Brand Blue Book of Yarn Kraft* and in *Corticelli*

Left Top: Sweater fashions for women were long and often belted at the hip, some with brushed wool or angora that simulated fur trim. *Art in Knitting*, 1917.

Left Bottom: The Suffrage. A knitter could dress in a sweater that expressed her political agenda. The pattern specifies yellow and blue yarn. *Bear Brand Blue Book of Yarn Kraft*, 1918.

Pink Knit Baby's Bootees. Pink lace-knit baby's bootees from circa 1905–1915, one of countless labors of love that were saved and donated to historical collections. (Wisconsin Historical Society)

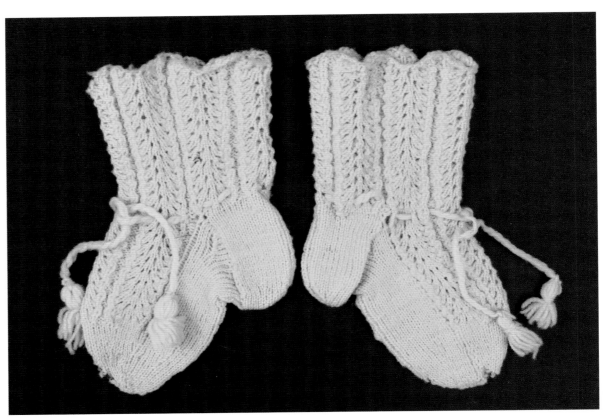

Bootees for the Babies. Knitters continued to lavish pretty and practical hand-knits on babies and children.

Knit with two contrasting colors against a white background, a child's cardigan sweater was practical and pretty.

Experts recommended wrapping newborns and infants with an abdominal band. In 1889's Hygiene of the Nursery, physician Louis Starr advised mothers knit her baby's band: "Any woman who is apt with her knitting needles can make one, and the product has the advantages of being readily applied and of keeping its position without the aid of either strings or pins." (Washington State Historical Society)

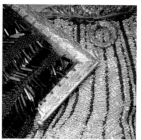

These evening bags from about 1915 were popular women's accessories. They were knit using glass beads and silk yarn. (Washington State Historical Society)

Yarn Book — sized to fit a fox terrier and knit with Corticelli Knitola Fingering Yarn.

Lace knitting patterns were a holdover from Victoriana frou-frou. Butterick's *The Art of Knitting* (1897) and *Fancy and Practical Knitting* (1902) included patterns for dozens of lace edgings, doilies, counterpanes, and other lace-knitted "useful and ornamental articles." One doily centerpiece had an 80-row repeat, and the pattern for a lace-knit cover for a whisk broom holder could be completed in 121 rows. For the home, *Needlecraft* printed a pattern for an exquisite knit lace luncheon set — "one of the novelties that will prove practical" — with instructions spelled out for each of 108 rounds and a 40-round edging. *Needlecraft* also offered a frilly slip-on sweater pattern, one of the "newest summer sweaters" knit on size 15 wooden needles with 12 ounces of Shetland knitting yarn. Fleisher Yarns advertised a new lace-stitch sweater in its Fleisher Crocheting and Knitting Books. Knit lace insertions and edging patterns appeared in *Needlecraft*. A counterpane pattern highlighted a lacy leaf-and-diamond pattern. Not for the timid knitter, the counterpane square had a 160-row repeat, and the matching border a 33-row repeat.[146]

KIMONOS

Asian design influenced architecture and apparel, including wrap-around sweaters dubbed the "kimono" style. Women wanted more comfortable clothing that fit active lifestyles, including working at jobs they were taking over for men who left for war. *Fleisher's Knitting & Crocheting Manual*, 1917.

"Diamond-wound" balls of yarn from Fleisher's Yarns eliminated the "old way" of winding skeins into balls, no doubt appealing to knitters who wanted the latest improvements in knitting technology. *The Ladies' Home Journal*, December 1917.

The star pattern often seen on the back of baby bonnets was adapted to a table cover — knit with 108 rounds and a 40-round edging. Instructions for the luncheon set doilies sized for plates and tumblers. For the plate-size doily, the knitter stopped after round 58, for the tumbler doily at round 19. *Needlecraft*, March 1917.

Patterns for Victorian frou-frou — like this whisk-broom cover created with 121 rows of lace knitting — carried over into the Progressive Era. *Fancy and Practical Knitting*, 1902.

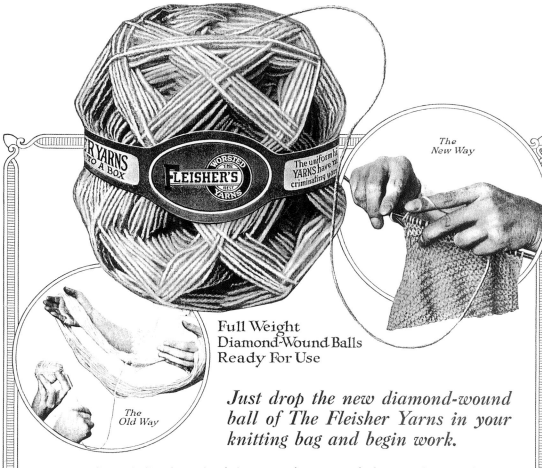

THE FLEISHER YARNS
IN DIAMOND WOUND BALLS READY FOR USE

The New Way

The Old Way

Full Weight Diamond-Wound Balls Ready For Use

Just drop the new diamond-wound ball of The Fleisher Yarns in your knitting bag and begin work.

No tedious winding from the skein, no tangles, no stretched yarn — the most pleasant, convenient and economical way to use yarns. Each ball is full weight, some contain one full ounce, some two full ounces — each box contains a full pound of yarn.

The softness and warmth, the fine finish and beautiful dyes, the unusual working qualities and great durability of The Fleisher Yarns make them the preference of discriminating yarn users everywhere.

Fleisher's Knitting Worsted	Fleisher's Ice Wool	Fleisher's Lustrous Teazelyarn
Fleisher's Saxony Yarn	Fleisher's Shetland Zephyr	Fleisher's Golf Yarn
Fleisher's Spanish Worsted	Fleisher's Cashmere Yarn	Fleisher's Vicuna Yarn
Fleisher's Shetland Floss	Fleisher's Highland Yarn	Fleisher's Aurora Vicuna Yarn
Fleisher's Germantown Zephyr, 4-Fold	Fleisher's Silkflake Yarn	Fleisher's Paradise Zephyr
Fleisher's Germantown Zephyr, 8-Fold	Fleisher's Silkanwool Yarn	

Use The Fleisher Yarns always — look for the trade-mark ticket on every ball.

Fleisher's Knitting and Crocheting Manual the standard instruction book and authoritative guide to fashions in garments made of yarns. It contains full directions for making the newest styles of sports wear, kimonos, shawls, babies' wear, afghans, etc. Price 25c.

Free booklet describing The Fleisher Yarns and their uses mailed on request

S. B. & B. W. FLEISHER, Dept. B, Philadelphia

Yarn and Needles

Knitters could "knit the new way" on circular needles, a distinct advantage over straight knitting needles for some knitting projects. With circular needles, knitters could knit in the round without four or five double-pointed needles that some found cumbersome. Circular needles also held hundreds of stitches securely on a single pair of needles. Britain's W. L. M. Clark Company advertised circular knitting needles at 10¢ to 40¢ each: "Insist on Clark Twin-Plex — accept no imitation." Twin-Plex needles accommodated either straight or circular knitting, and the springy celluloid guaranteed knitting points held at the correct knitting angle.[147] Frank L. Sessions appears to have filed the first American patent application for a circular knitting needle, awarded November 26, 1918. *Needlecraft* offered the gift of a pair of straight, amber-colored celluloid needles to any subscriber who signed up four new subscribers to the magazine. In 1902, Butterick's *Fancy and Practical Knitting* purposely omitted knitting needle size and yarn size and quantity because there were too many regional variations. By 1916, however, manufacturers took steps to standardize knitting needle sizes. Fleisher's system measured actual diameters of needles and hooks in millimeters, and Bucilla developed a printed gauge that showed exact diameters of needles and hooks.

Knitters selected among yarns from different manufacturers. F. W. Woolworth Company of Boston sold Woolco Knitting Worsted, Woolco Germantown Zephyr, and Woolco Shetland floss in a range of colors and each at 10¢ a skein.[148] The Nonotuck Silk Company made Corticelli Yarns in several varieties: Knitola Fingering (long staple wool), Tezola (brushed to a thick nap), Scotola (Scotch Fingering Yarn), Flosola ("high class"), Angola (blending wool with Angora goat fleece), Saxola ("better than the usual Saxony"), Yankola, and Cashmere. Bear Brand Yarns from the Bernhard Ulmann Company claimed high manufacturing quality: "A garment made of Bear Brand Yarns is never disappointing."[149] S. B. & B. W. Fleisher of Philadelphia produced yarn in "every color in the rainbow." Fleisher Yarns "are always [the] safest yarns for any fine knitting, therefore the most economic; because infinite pains are used to keep them *absolutely uniform* in size, weight and finish. And all women love the *fleeciness* of the Fleisher Yarns and the many, bewildering, beautiful Fleisher shades." Fleisher advertised its new Diamond Wound Balls already

Knitting needle manufacturers marketed newness to progressive knitters. "You can't drop stitches; and it's so much faster and easier! Knitting is a real pleasure when you use the CLARK TWIN-PLEX (Patent Pending)." The soldier and sailor serve as reminders that America had entered World War I one month before this advertisement appeared. *Needlecraft*, May 1918.

wound from skeins: "no tedious winding from the skein, no tangles, no stretched yarn."[150] Apparently sales were good; Fleisher even advertised on a neon billboard. The Fleisher Yarn Company was founded by Simon and Moyer Fleisher, sons of German Jewish immigrants. Younger brother Benjamin W. Fleisher joined the company after Moyer retired, and the name changed to S. B. & B. S. Fleisher Manufacturing. By 1917, Fleisher was a world leader in knitting yarns.[151]

Knitting at home assured the least expensive way to have the latest fashions, colors, and styles. Patriotism influenced personal knitting, too. In 1918, *The Delineator* magazine recommended that knitters make small, inexpensive gifts for a wartime Christmas: "This is to be a lucky Christmas, the first Christmas of our real participation in the great war. . . . At home we are pushing forward, too, giving up every unnecessary thing for the great necessity of winning the war. Our Christmas gifts this year will be small things that we can make ourselves."[152]

The fifteenth edition of *Fleisher's Knitting & Crocheting Manual,* 1917, introduced the new diamond-wound balls of yarn. Delighted with the popularity of sweater knitting, Fleisher's also added new vicuña and brushed yarns, plus patterns for "kimono" sweaters, designs obtained through "European connections."

The Vast Variety of Yarn from Sears Roebuck

HIGHEST GRADE KNITTING YARNS.

German Yarns.

No. 18K3900 German Knitting Worsted yarn, standard quality, four skeins to the pound, manufacturer's weight. Comes in the following colors: Cardinal, scarlet, medium and navy blue, purple, medium and seal brown, sheep's gray, black mixed, black or white. State color wanted.
Price, per pound 79c
If by mail, postage extra, per pound, 18 cents.

Fleisher's First Quality German Yarn.

No. 18K3902 German Knitting Worsted yarn, Fleisher's first quality, always runs smooth and always the same, four skeins to the pound, manufacturer's weight. Colors same as No. 18K3900. State color wanted.
Price, all colors, per skein $0.28
Per lb . . (Postage extra, per lb., 19c) . 1.07

No. 18K3904 German Knitting Yarn, our next quality high grade yarn, four skeins to the pound, manufacturer's weight. Colors same as No. 18K3900. For a good satisfactory yarn buy this first quality yarn. We recommend it as our best, which contains a long wool filling; and we guarantee every hank sold. State color wanted.
Price, all colors, per skein 25c
Per lb . . (Postage extra, per lb., 18c) . 96c

Saxony Wool Yarn.

No. 18K3906 Saxony Wool Yarn, imported. Made of the finest Australian wool; twenty skeins to the pound, manufacturer's weight. Colors, scarlet, cardinal, wine, pink, light, medium or navy blue, medium or seal brown, black or cream white. State color wanted.
Price, per skein 6½c
Per lb . . (Postage extra, per lb., 18c) $1.25

No. 18K3908 Spanish Knitting Worsted yarn, imported, eight skeins to the pound, manufacturer's weight. Colors, cardinal, navy blue, seal brown, black or cream white. State color wanted. Price, per skein $0.14
Per lb . . (Postage extra, per lb., 17c) 1.10

Crinkled Shetland Floss.

The Highest Grade, Best Quality Yarn.
No. 18K3910 Shetland Floss, fine grade imported wool, twelve skeins to the pound, manufacturer's weight. Colors, light blue, medium blue, light pink, dark pink, lemon, lilac, cardinal, dove, nile green, black, snow white or cream white. State color wanted.
Price, per skein, all colors 7c
Per lb . . (Postage extra, per lb., 15c) . 82c

Crown Knitting Cotton.

No. 18K3790 Crown White Knitting Cotton. Best quality, 4-thread, put up 10 balls to the pound, manufacturer's weight, and 2 pounds to the box. Nos. 6 to 24.
Price, PER ½ POUND (5 BALLS) . . . 23c
If by mail, postage extra, 5 balls, 10 cents.

No. 18K3794 Crown Navy Blue Knitting Cotton, same quality as above, Nos. 8 to 16. Price, PER ½ POUND (5 BALLS) . . . 23c
If by mail, postage extra, 5 balls, 10 cents.

No. 18K3798 Crown Blue and White Mixed Knitting Cotton, same quality as above, Nos. 8 to 16. Price, PER ½ POUND (5 BALLS) . . . 23c
If by mail, postage extra, 5 balls, 10 cents.

No. 18K3912 Coral Yarn, Imported, twelve skeins to the pound, manufacturer's weight. Colors, cardinal, light blue, pink, yellow, garnet, peacock blue, black or cream white. State color wanted.
Price, per pound, $1.40; per skein . . 13c
If by mail, postage extra, per skein, 16 cents.

No. 18K3914 Fairy Floss or Crinkled Yarn. Used for fancy knitting, twelve skeins to the pound, manufacturer's weight. Colors, black or white only. State color wanted.
Price, per pound, $1.10; per skein . . 10c
If by mail, postage extra, per skein, 16 cents.

Germantown Yarn.

No. 18K3916 Germantown Wool Yarn, imported. Sixteen skeins to the pound, manufacturer's weight. Colors, scarlet, cardinal, wine, light, medium or navy blue, pink, seal brown, yellow, green, purple, gray, black, white or cream. State color wanted.
Price, per pound, $1.30; per skein . . 8½c
If by mail, postage extra, per pound, 20 cents.

Imported Angora Wool.

No. 18K3918 Angora Wool, best quality imported yarn. Colors, black, white or gray. State color wanted. 16 balls to the box.
Price, per ball, $1.25; per ball 8c
If by mail, postage extra, per box, 7 cents.

Imported Angora Yarn
½-ounce Balls.

No. 18K3920 Angora Yarn. A superior quality put up 8 balls to the box and will knit full one-half ounce to the ball. One of these balls will knit as far as 4 balls of the ordinary Angora. This is an advantageous way of buying Angora yarn, as it does away with tying and knotting. Comes in white, gray, black, cardinal or brown. State color wanted.
Price, per ball $0.29
Price, per box of 8 balls 2.20
If by mail, postage extra, per box, 9 cents.

Imported Ice Wool.

No. 18K3922 Ice Wool, imported. 1-ounce balls, put up eight balls to the box. Colors, black, white, pink or light blue. Give color wanted.
Price, per ball 9c
Price, per box 70c
If by mail, postage extra, per box, 8 cents.

Zephyr Worsteds.

No. 18K3924 Zephyr Worsted, Imported. Berlin zephyr, 4-ply, called single. For working rug patterns, etc. Colors, scarlet, cardinal, garnet, wine, light pink, dark pink, light, medium and navy blue, nile, medium and dark green, olive, brown, tan, canary, orange, gray, purple, black or cream white. Forty laps to the pound, manufacturer's weight. Give color wanted. Price, per lap 3⅓c
12 laps for . . (Postage, per lap, 1c) . . 40c

No. 18K3926 Zephyr Worsted, Imported Berlin zephyr, 2-ply, called split zephyr. Colors, same as No. 18K3924. Give color wanted. Forty laps to the pound, manufacturer's weight. Price, per lap 3⅓c
12 laps for . . (Postage, per lap, 1c) . . 40c

Darning Cotton.

No. 18K3802 Best Fast Black Darning Cotton, 4-ply, diagonally wound, 34 yards on a spool. Absolutely fast color, will stand washing and boiling. Also comes in white, brown, tan or gray. State color wanted.
Price, PER DOZEN 23c
If by mail, postage extra, per dozen, 12 cents.

Mending Yarn.

No. 18K3806 H. B. Cashmere Mending Yarn. Manufactured from the very highest grade of scoured wool. 30 yards warranted. Once tried, you will use no other. Colors, brown, navy, tan, gray, black or white. State color wanted.
Price, PER DOZEN 24c
If by mail, postage extra, per dozen, 4 cents.

Sears Roebuck claimed to sell the "Highest Grade Knitting Yarns" in *Catalogue #117*, Sears Roebuck & Co., 1908.

Anywhere in the United States, knitters could order yarn from the Sears Roebuck & Co. catalog. In 1908, Sears sold a variety of yarn in an impressive number of colors. A glance at the yarns knitters could choose shows America's dependence on yarn imported from Germany, England, and Australia.

Yarn Colors Price (per pound)

German Knitting Worsted: Cardinal, scarlet, medium and navy blue, purple, medium brown, seal brown, sheep's gray, black mixed, black, white
$0.79

Fleisher's First Quality German Yarn: Cardinal, scarlet, medium and navy blue, purple, medium brown, seal brown, sheep's gray, black mixed, black, white
$1.07

Saxony Wool Yarn, Imported from Australia: Scarlet, cardinal, wine, pink, light blue, medium blue, navy blue, medium brown, seal brown, black or cream white
$1.10

Crown Knitting Cotton: Navy blue, blue and white mixed
$0.46

Crinkled Shetland Floss, Imported: Light blue, medium blue, light pink, dark pink, lemon, lilac, cardinal, dove, nile green, black, snow white, cream white
$0.82

Fairy Floss or Crinkled Yarn (used for fancy knitting): Black, white
$1.10

Imported Angora Wool: White, gray, black, cardinal, brown
$1.25

Imported Angora Yarn ("will knit as far as four balls of 'ordinary' Angora"): Black, white, gray
$4.40

Imported Ice Wool: Black, white, pink, light blue
$1.40

Berlin Zephyr Worsteds, Imported (for working rug patterns): Scarlet, cardinal, garnet, wine, light pink, dark pink, light green, olive, brown, tan, canary, orange, gray, purple, black, cream white
$1.30

You can help

AMERICAN RED CROSS

Chapter Six

The Knitting War

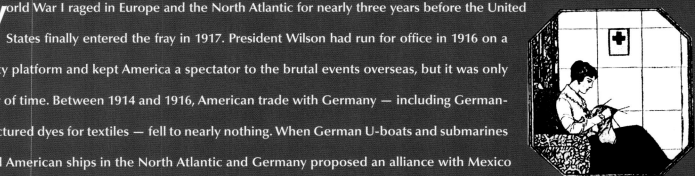

World War I raged in Europe and the North Atlantic for nearly three years before the United States finally entered the fray in 1917. President Wilson had run for office in 1916 on a neutrality platform and kept America a spectator to the brutal events overseas, but it was only a matter of time. Between 1914 and 1916, American trade with Germany — including German-manufactured dyes for textiles — fell to nearly nothing. When German U-boats and submarines attacked American ships in the North Atlantic and Germany proposed an alliance with Mexico — an offer that would return Texas to Mexico — Wilson finally asked Congress for a declaration of war. On April 6, 1917, Congress voted to enter the Great War. American knitters too took up their weapons to fight a knitting war.

A knitter works industriously for the Red Cross in this pattern-book illustration.

The World Knits for War

By the time America entered the war, knitters around the world were already sending hand-knit comforts to soldiers and refugees in Europe. In the far-flung British dominion of Australia, volunteer knitters turned out astounding numbers of socks.[153] Knitting often appeared in heart-wrenching poetry composed by those on the home front. Philadelphia N. Robertson penned her poem, "A Woman's Prayer:"

I am so placid as I sit
In train or tram and knit and knit;
Within the house I give due heed
To every duty, each one's need,
Sometimes the newsboys hurry by,
And then my needles seem to fly
And when the house has grown quite still,
I lean out on my window sill —
And Pray to god to see to it
That I keep sane enough to knit.[154]

Helen Bosanquet wrote in her "The Old Woman's War-Work" about a knitter who lost her own son to the war and now knit for the sons of others:

Opposite Page:
American Red Cross posters helped launch nationwide knitting campaigns to supply soldiers and civilians with warm clothing. This classic poster was created by artist Wladyslaw T. Benda. (Library of Congress)

91

With patriotic fervor, children knit for the Red Cross. (Library of Congress)

Her Boy *is* "Over There." The U.S. government tugged at Americans' heartstrings and pocketbooks with an advertisement showing a mother who has sent her son to war. She knits and dreams of his return home.

Steel knitting needles such as these were all that was available to knitters during World War I. The pins were notorious for leaving marks on yarn, so knitters resorted to using dark yarn.

Her Boy
is
**"Over
There"**

She has given her all. With a proud heart and a firm smile she has made the supreme sacrifice of motherhood — her son. Her patriotism, her loyalty cannot be measured by mere dollars — she has given of her heart's blood, of her very soul.

And you are but asked to lend! If you *gave* every dollar that you have and hope to have, your sacrifice would be as nothing to hers. But you are asked only to lend, to *invest* in the best security in the world.

U. S. GOV'T BONDS THIRD LIBERTY LOAN

Contributed through Division of Advertising   *United States Gov't. Comm. on Public Information*

This space contributed for the Winning of the War by

THE PUBLISHERS OF NEEDLECRAFT

I'll shape the toe and turn the heel,
And vary ribs and plains,
And hope some soldier-man may feel
The warmer for my pains.[155]

American knitters were caught up in the world's struggle and emotional pleas from allied nations to knit for soldiers and refugees. In Chicago, women knit for the Christmas Fund for French Children. Australian knitters invented a spiral sock pattern, knit without a heel, a style that soldiers praised for longevity and comfort. The American Fund for French Wounded teamed with the American Red Cross and asked needle-workers to make shawls for "thousands of suffering, destitute women" in France; Bear Brand Yarn sponsored the shawl advertisements. For wartime gift giving, knitters were advised to craft odds and ends of yarn into small, inexpensive gifts — hats, dolls, caps, slippers — and that meant more savings toward the war effort.[156]

Knit Your Bit for the Red Cross

Inspired by the International Red Cross Movement in Europe, Clara Barton and colleagues in Washington, D. C., founded the American Red Cross in 1881. Bolstered by a congressional charter in 1905, the mission of the Red Cross included assisting American

Young and old alike felt compelled to support the boys over there. Clerk Alice C. Burmester knits during a coffee break at work. (Chicago Historical Society)

The process of getting socks from knitters to soldiers was explained in this 1914 cartoon.

Mr. J. Leon Phillips holds yarn for his wife as she knits for the war effort in Palm Beach, Florida, March 1917. (Library of Congress)

Historical Pattern World War I Red Cross Soldiers' Wristlets

This pattern comes from Red Cross instructions reprinted in various publications during World War I.

Material: ½ Hank Knitting Yarn (1/8 lb.); 4 Red Cross Needles No. 1.

Instructions: Cast on 52 sts on 3 needles (16-16-20).

Knit 2, purl 2; for 8 inches.

To make opening for thumb, knit 2, purl 2 to end of 3rd needle. Turn. Knit and purl back to end of first needle, always slipping first st. Turn. Continue back and forth for 2 inches.

From this point continue as at first for 4 inches for the hand.

Bind off loosely and buttonhole thumb opening.

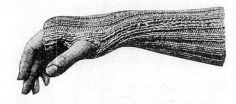

Red Cross Garments
For the Army and Navy
With official instructions by the American National Red Cross and Navy League of the United States

The official Red Cross wristlet for the U.S. Army and Navy was knit flat in rib stitch and the side sewn, leaving an opening for the thumb. *Art in Knitting*, 1917.

Patriotic songs such as "We'll Do Our Share (While You're Over There)" from 1918 were big hits during the war. (Library of Congress)

who in 1918 ran a Red Cross canteen in the capital's Union Station. Wearing her khaki uniform, she handed out newspapers, cigarettes, coffee, and sandwiches to soldiers on their way to army camps or battlefields. Doing Red Cross work made Roosevelt feel truly useful. "I loved it," she said later, a sentiment undoubtedly shared by millions of other Red Cross volunteers.[157] The American Red Cross had a long reach among knitters. Women who lived in major cities and isolated regions alike knit for war relief. Sewing and knitting committees of the Chicago Red Cross chapter were a major resource for the nation. American Indian women were knitters, and reservation women's clubs knit socks and sweaters for the Red Cross, including the Uintah and Ouray Indian Red Cross Auxiliary in Fort Duchesne, Utah. More than five thousand American Indian adults and thirty thousand American Indian students enrolled to help Red Cross war efforts.[158]

The Women's Bureau of the Red Cross was created in July 1917 as a way to direct the productivity and energy of those women who wanted to support the war effort but had no professional training. The Women's Bureau first director, Miss Florence Marshall, sent two Red Cross agents to England and France, and they reported back on military and refugee needs. Based on their report, consultations with the British, Canadian, and French Red Cross, and knitting experts from commercial mills and women's magazines, the Women's Bureau established needs and standards for knitting. The Women's Bureau issued five hundred thousand circulars with knitting directions for a set of four pieces most needed in France: an aviator's helmet, hot water bottle cover, wash rag, and a pair of bed socks. The Bureau of Standards and the supply service of the Red Cross selected four-ply gray and khaki wool for wartime knitting.[159]

Along with the Navy League, the American Red Cross supplied much of the yarn, patterns, needles, and instructions for knitting and set the standards for production and distribution of hand knits to the military. Yarn companies also published knitting patterns for military comforts for the soldiers and sailors in their pattern books. Novelty Art Studios in Chicago carried official instructions for Red Cross socks, a sleeveless sweater, and a helmet (one piece garment that covered head, neck, and chest). *Fleisher's Knitting and Crocheting*

armed forces and facilitating national and international disaster relief. The growth, mobilization, and organization of the American Red Cross accounted for the phenomenal quantity of wartime knitting. Though the Red Cross provided assistance during the Spanish-American War, the organization's growth during World War I was nothing short of extraordinary. Between 1914 and 1918, the number of local chapters grew from 107 to 3,864, and membership from 17,000 to more than 20 million. Among the volunteers was Eleanor Roosevelt,

Manual (Sixteenth Edition, 1918) had patterns for service sweaters, socks, caps, wristlets, and helmets, and *Bear Brand Blue Book* (Volume 18, 1918) featured a section of similar comfort garments for soldiers and sailors. Standardization was of critical importance for knit and sewn articles sent to soldiers. For example, in 1917, the Red Cross called for two million comfort kits for American soldiers in France and for the wounded convalescing in hospitals. The comfort kit was to include such necessities as a toothbrush, shaving brush, soap, khaki washcloths, and foot powder, and a selection of such niceties as pencils, writing paper, playing cards, tobacco, a pipe, and tobacco paper — plus a pair of heavy socks that could be hand-knit. The Red Cross standardized not only the contents but also the containers: All items were sewn in a standardized folding or drawstring bag.[160] The *Ladies' Home Journal* published articles that emphasized the importance of knitting *only* the articles officially approved by the Red Cross: wash cloth in white cotton, gray or khaki wool sleeveless sweater, muffler of a designated length, thumbless mittens, hot water bottle cover, helmet liners, bed socks, and the much-needed men's socks "evenly and firmly knitted so the finished article is without knots, lumps or ridges to blister the feet in marching." The Red Cross specified instructions for

each piece and supplied standard emblems to sew onto hand-sewn or hand-knit donations. Those people who were not active members of a local Red Cross unit could sew or knit simple, small items — knit wipes for surgical use, knit washcloth — and were allowed to hand embroider a red cross as a "bit of sentiment."[161]

Hand knitting for the troops could go awry if knitters failed to adhere to high standards set for production and distribution. Although American textile factories were at capacity, demand for knits exceeded production. America's European and Russian allies were in desperate need of socks. To avoid waste, knitters had to use regulation gray wool available at cost from the Red Cross' supply service offices, and no knitter was to begin without checking a list of needs kept by the Navy League or Red Cross. Too many independent organizations distributed supplies indiscriminately, so knitters had to trust the Navy League or Red Cross to send hand knits where they were needed. An army private writing from France in the *Stars and Stripes* military newspaper advised Americans to "donate your summer's knitting to the Red Cross and they will see that we are taken care of." Above all, knitters had to give up the notion they could hand-select recipients, such as the woman who insisted "nobody but a fighting Belgian is to wear her pair of bed-socks."[162]

A simple garter-stitch sweater vest knit up fast and kept the boys overseas warm through the winter. The vest was knit in the round with ribbon on the lower edge and two rows of single crochet around the neck and armhole openings. *Art in Knitting,* 1917.

Left: Knitters braved steamy New York City summer weather to knit wool helmets the troops would need in the winter. *The Woman Citizen,* October 6, 1917.

The American Junior Red Cross emerged from a partnership between the Red Cross and regional schools when the United States entered the war. By 1919, 11 million American youth had each paid 25¢ in membership dues, and they intended to support war victims. Junior Red Cross members raised money for war funds, donated clothing and hospital supplies for war victims, grew Victory Gardens, and prepared friendship boxes for war refugees overseas. The American Red Cross estimates the Junior Red Cross contributed an extraordinary $3,677,380 in funds during the war and an impressive 10 percent of all Red Cross products, including knitting. Schools across the nation remained open from three to five days a week for Red Cross work during summer break. Teachers worked with student groups that sewed and knit; children in Montana, Minnesota, and the Dakotas alone made more than fifty thousand garments and other supplies.[163]

The Knitting Image

The nation called on its women on the home front to conserve food supplies, work in industry, and volunteer for the war effort. Some men praised those women who knit to contribute. Essayist Richard Burton extolled knitting in *The Bellman* magazine in 1917 as a quiet, domestic virtue carried out by "stay-at-homes" who formed the "rear guard of the sisters of mercy [nurses] in the field." Burton raised knitting to mythic proportions, believing that "the emblem of the knitting needle is one of a trinity of which the other two members are the plowshare and the sword."[164] Another man wrote that women, driven by the "exigencies of war" had "quietly turned their backs on feminist movements . . . and set themselves to that least exciting, most old-fashion, most feminine of occupations, knitting." Wasn't it wonderful that wartime knitting led women to a "soul-satisfying reversion to type," as *Scribner's Magazine* claimed in January 1918. The image of a woman knitting took on an emotional charge. Knitting needles in a woman's hands illustrated the cover of patriotic sheet music, "We'll Do Our Share (While You're Over There)." A government advertisement for war bonds linked knitting with self-sacrifice, declaring to citizens that if they donated every dollar they ever earned to the war effort, their "sacrifice would be as nothing to hers."[165] An already proficient knitter whose output still fell short of the Red Cross quota could adopt the more patriotic and efficient "double knitting" method — knitting two sweaters or socks at one time on one pair of needles. Using this method, one sock progressed inside the other, with alternate stitches for outer and inner sock held on one pair of needles.[166]

Suffragists considered knitting for the war effort another kind of activism. Miss Helen Hill headed a knitting unit at the headquarters for the 27th Assembly District of the Suffrage Party in New York City. Hill's squadron of knitters invited all local

This Page and Opposite:
American Red Cross posters helped launch nationwide knitting campaigns to supply soldiers and civilians with warm clothing. (Library of Congress)

Postcard sentimentalizing the Red Cross knitter.

KNIT A BIT
FOR OUR FIRST LINE OF DEFENSE
WOOL, NEEDLES AND DIRECTIONS
Comforts Committee of the Navy League
OF THE UNITED STATES
509 FIFTH AVENUE, NEW YORK CITY

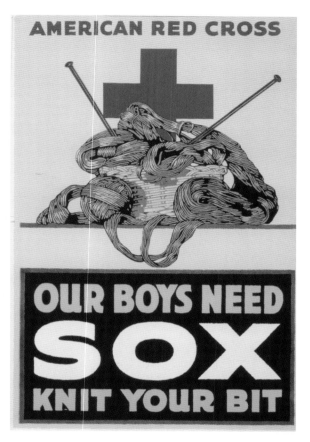

AMERICAN RED CROSS

OUR BOYS NEED SOX KNIT YOUR BIT

women's societies to knit or donate money for wool. She and her entourage printed circulars, which they handed out from table to table in restaurants and to neighbors sitting on city stoops. The nearby Hippodrome Girls' Knitting Club met at the 27th Assembly District's headquarters, conveniently located near the Great White Way theater district. A photographer marveled at their "flying fingers" that could produce a length of two-and-one-half inches in half an hour. The "Knitting 27th" turned out comfort hand knits for the Navy League, specifically 5 garments each for 712 sailors on the warship USS *Missouri*. Asked if the 3,560 hand knits would be ready in time, Hill replied: "Well, these are the same women who helped get the signatures of more than 500,000 women of New York City who want to vote. Women who did not let the grass grow under their feet until they had performed that arduous task are not likely to stop at a little thing like knitting winter garments for 712 sailor boys." The 27th Assembly District calculated the suffragists' wartime knitting pledge at 73,491,216 stitches, or some 40,828 hours of knitting. The women paid for their own wool — either donated or bought with cash donations — for an estimated savings to the nation of $6 million to $7.5 million.[167]

In Georgia, the Atlanta Equal Suffrage Association established Uncle Sam's Knitting Camp.

The Red Cross even sponsored knitting for "The Destitute Women of France," as shown in this 1918 *Needlecraft* advertisement from Bear Brand Yarns.

Knitting Ballet of the Hippodrome. The knitting club met at the nearby 27th Assembly District of the Suffrage Party in New York City, where a photographer marveled at their "flying fingers" as they knit for the war effort. Note the proud display of knitting bags. *The Woman Citizen*, October 6, 1917.

Miss Helen Hill, a leader in the 27th Assembly District of the Suffrage Party in New York City, exuded confidence that the same women who fought for the vote were up to the "arduous task" of knitting for hundreds of sailors as part of the Navy League's wartime support for the troops. *The Woman Citizen*, October 6, 1917.

Right: The Jeanne d'Arc Knitting Bag was the "bag of the hour" in 1918. A true badge of honor, the knitting bag had become a political statement. The black satin bag attached to a sterling silver bracelet for convenience while knitting in the car or on the trolley. *New York Times*, September 22, 1918.

Conservez les minutes
KNIT A STITCH EN ROUTE

Jeanne d'Arc
—the bag of the hour

Smart black Satin Bag, attached to sterling silver bracelet, a most convenient feature. From silver holder yarn unwinds freely — many extra stitches may be knit on motor or trolley. Just large enough to hold purse besides necessary sock needs— combining utility with its air distingue.

No. 2400 . . . . $2.00

Mrs. E. N. Gibbs was assigned the rank of major general for her knitting service and placed in command of the camp. Set up on a military model, five knitting companies served under Gibbs, each with a captain and two lieutenants supervising a squadron of workers, each of whom knit two finished articles and recruited two more knitters every month. There was also a Home Guard that included invalids and housewives who could not attend the camp. Companies were designated as Company 1 — Sweaters; Company 2 — Mufflers; Company 3 — Wristlets; Company 4 — Wool Sox; and Company 5 — Helmets.[168]

Ubiquitous Knitting

Knitting and knitting groups were part of a patriotic fervor — everywhere, everyone seemed to be knitting for the boys at the front. Society doyennes knit. The clergy sanctioned knitting during sermons. Young people promenaded city streets with oversized knitting bags, often carried with them to the theater. Young women

were said to stop their motorcars to flirt with young men, drop their hands from the steering wheel, and pick up knitting needles. Some knitters — those who had "come to the end of a perfect row" — found themselves absorbed by the process of knitting itself; as *Catholic World* magazine reported in 1918: "Knitting has become your food and drink; it nourishes you as completely as the finished article encloses the man. Sundays, week days, midnight, crack of dawn, street car, parlor, kitchen, all times and places are one. They exist only for knitting."[169]

The ubiquitous knitter no doubt inspired the inventors of the day who patented ingenious knitting devices.[170] In 1918 alone, Emma M. Veness patented knitting needles with shallow hooks on the working ends (a design intended to minimize dropped stitches); Karl W. P. Reece patented needles with a removable shaft to move knitting loops across a neck opening more easily; Frank L. Sessions was issued a patent for a circular knitting needle with different-size connecting cables (designed for knitting in the round without the

Mrs. Thomas H. Barry, the wife of the U.S. Army's General Barry, knits for the boys over there. Society doyennes were photographed doing their part for the war effort, presumably to encourage everyone to do their bit. (Chicago Historical Society)

Employees of the Chicago, Milwaukee & St. Paul Railroad freight office use their break time from work to knit for the troops. Each woman was well prepared with the ubiquitous, oversized knitting bag. (Chicago Historical Society)

cumbersome four- or five-needle process); and Alpha H. Metcalf invented a set of three telescoping knitting needles. The latter gave knitters a simple, compact way to assemble three different-size needles in a single unit; smaller-diameter needles slid one within the other into hollow needles, assisted by a spring mechanism. In 1919, William H. Brown patented circular knitting needles designed to knit small-diameter sleeves, mittens, and socks. Then in 1920, the improved knitting needles invented by Philadelphian Henrietta L. Kelsey addressed the dilemma of knitting in the dark. Her patent read:

> Knitting . . . is very much in vogue at the present time, and is extensively practiced under various conditions in public places, such as theaters, etc., which, during certain periods, are sparsely illuminated. In order to facilitate the use of these implements in darkness or semi-darkness, my invention has been directed to providing needles of this type with luminous points, which are plainly visible under such conditions.[171]

Kelsey applied luminous paint — no doubt laced with radium — to the needle points, protected against wear by an overlying transparent material.

Perhaps inventors manufactured these inventions and knitters found them useful, but the must-have knitting accessory was the knitting bag. The wartime knitting bag served as the knitter's badge of patriotism and an imposing fashion statement. The larger the size, and the bolder the fabric, the better the bag. One novice knitter, however, warned that knitting bags posed a "snare" for wartime dollars. Fancy department stores charged as much as $40 for just the right knitting bag.[172] The proficient knitter fashioned her own bag, like the Jeanne d'Arc knitting bag in black satin with a sterling silver bracelet combining "utility with its air distingué."[173] Knitting bags were at the forefront for women who descended on Albany, New York, demanding better labor standards for women and minors. The women believed that legislators, hardened to previous siege tactics of female workers, saw them for the first time as real people who represented thousands of other women with "innocent little knitting bags just like theirs." As *The Woman Citizen* magazine proclaimed, "Behind the knitting bags were knitters, and behind the knitters were ballots."[174]

Learning to Knit

Aspiring knitters faced a number of quandaries: How do I learn to knit? Where do I find wool? What do the

Historical Pattern
World War I
Simultaneous Socks

This pattern comes from The Delineator, *November, 1918.*

To speed up the process of Red Cross knitting socks for soldiers, knitters knit two socks at one time — one inside the other. Knitting with the standard four needles, the outside sock is knit "inside out," the American way, while the inside sock is knit "right side out," the Continental way. The technique of knitting two stockings (or even sweaters) at one time required the knitter to hold yarn for each piece and alternate knitting and purling the stitches.

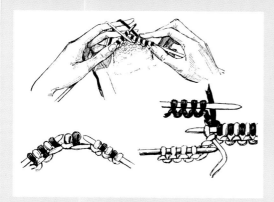

The technique for knitting two sweaters or stockings at one time.

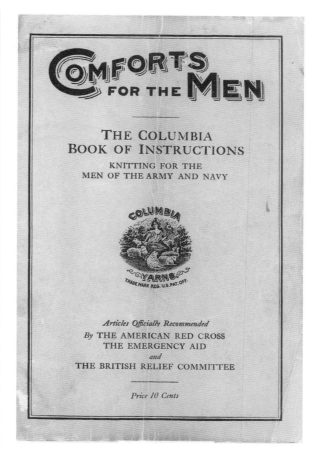

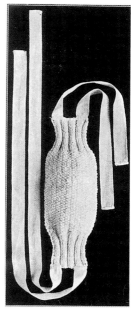

Comforts for the Men from 1917 included American Red Cross and British Relief Committee patterns, including directions to knit this eye bandage.

soldiers and sailors need? For some new knitters, Red Cross instructors and sympathetic mothers, aunts, and grandmothers were only too happy to oblige. On a different scale, however, eight hundred employees at the Butterick Building in New York City decided to learn to knit for the navy. Butterick employees were inspired by the thought that *their* work — a pair of knit woolen socks, gloves, or a sweater — could stand between frostbitten feet and cold sea spray for a sailor on watch in the North Atlantic. Few of the Butterick employees — mostly women and a few men ineligible for military service — knew how to knit, so the knitting organizers taught eight hundred people to knit in two half-hour lessons. Then they asked the navy for a knitting assignment. Tentatively, the Navy League offered the knitting required to outfit sailors aboard two destroyers. Within six weeks — half the anticipated time —

the Butterick knitters turned out a sweater, gloves, and two pairs of socks for each of 198 men on the destroyers, 792 garments in all.

Not enough, the Butterick force decided, and requisitioned knitting duties for the navy's largest battleship, the USS *Nevada*. A crew of 879 men needed sweaters, socks, and gloves twice annually for a total of 7,032 comfort hand knits. Learning that this work needed to be completed within two months, Butterick appealed to an estimated 1 million readers of its publication, *The Delineator*. Readers ordered knitting instructions and patterns, and men were asked to send money for wool. *The Delineator* article stated, "If you begin to knit, your six best girl friends will follow your lead." Knitters sent finished sweaters, socks, and gloves to Butterick, which assured quality and proper distribution.[175]

The Emancipation of Male Knitters
The ever-present patriotic wartime knitting led to lively arguments about the suitability of men for the work. Although Butterick employees expected men to buy wool for women to knit, some men were also knitters. Men were seen strolling into Red Cross headquarters to ask for knitting wool. At least one railroad conductor knit between stations.[176] Archibald Craig of Jersey City expressed strong feelings on the subject. To the editor of *The Woman Citizen*, Craig wrote that he

A Red Cross knitting teacher instructs a novice knitter who was an experienced fireman. Men who were not at the front often knit during the war, some insisting that any man who loved his country would refuse to be idle during times of crisis. (Minnesota Historical Society)

learned to knit just two months earlier and could already knit socks faster than his wife. "Men who love their country and who believe in sex equality should be ashamed to be idle when this leisure occupation is of the greatest practical use to the nation," he proclaimed. Still worked up on the subject two months later, Craig wrote again that "it is as easy for a man to learn as for a woman."[177]

An anonymous gentleman wrote to *The Atlantic Monthly* in 1919 equating freedom to knit with masculine emancipation and asked, "Now, why shouldn't a man knit?" Women considered themselves emancipated into business, the professions, and the arts that were considered masculine, and some men now felt pushed into a back row. Men who practiced traditionally feminine pursuits — embroidery, sewing, darning socks, knitting — believed they had to work in secret. Times needed to change if the emancipation of men was in sight, as the anonymous writer stated: "We shall come into our own. Ere long we shall take our knitting

and our crocheting with us on the train, and practice these manual arts, with which we have long been secretly familiar, openly and without criticism. . . . Instead of rushing out between acts at the theatre to smoke a hasty cigar or to fill our stomachs with some unnecessary drink or reflect, we shall knit a few rounds on a sock for Sammy."[178] The World War I soldier was nicknamed Sammy (from "Uncle Sam").

To Knit or Not to Knit

The national fervor for knitting generated more controversy than simply the question of whether men should knit. Reports surfaced that soldiers used hand-knit sweaters, helmets, and wristlets to rub down horses or swab gun barrels. Furthermore, some speculated whether those scratchy wool socks really were comfortable for soldiers on the march. The most strident anti-knitting critic was perhaps Samuel S. Dale, who wrote in *Literary Digest* in 1918, "For God's sake, wake up and stop the hand-knitting." The road to

As part of the Red Cross Auxiliary, Native American Uinta (Ute) women knit for the war effort in Fort Duchesne, Utah, 1918. (Denver Public Library Western History/Genealogy Department)

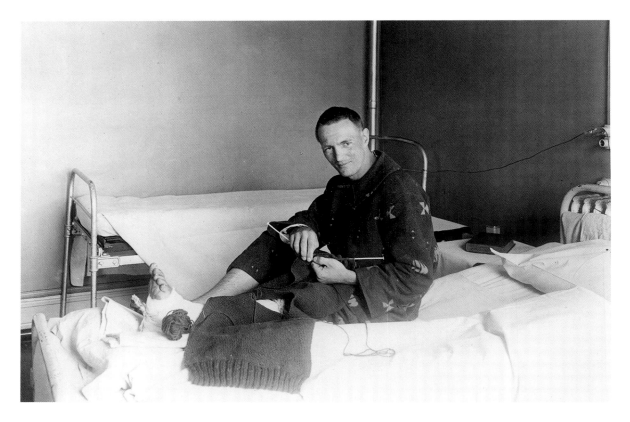

knitting for the military was paved with good intentions, Dale believed, but hand knitters were wool wasters. Dale's arguments, and he believed "there is no reason why any intelligent person should not understand them," were that the United States did not produce enough wool for military usage, so wool was imported, thereby further wasting energy on transport. In addition, he complained that knitters used expensive new wool and that hand-knit socks did not wear as well as their industrial knit counterparts.[179]

Dale's anti-knitting stance drew a flood of replies — some quite rude — from aggravated Red Cross officials, knitters, and non-knitters alike. Some dismissed his opinion after they learned he was employed in the textile industry. A Red Cross division manager took apart the errors in Dale's calculations about the nation's wool supply and produced firsthand reports from soldiers who gratefully wore hand-knit sweaters through bitter winters in France and Flanders. As for durability, the Red Cross claimed machine-made socks lasted a third as long as hand-knit ones. In his appeal for hand knits for France, Central Committee Chairman William Howard Taft said the answer to the question whether or not to knit was "emphatically, KNIT!"[180]

Rumors of a knitting needle shortage at the beginning of the war turned out to be nothing more than unequal distribution that simulated a shortage.[181] The wool-supply issue was truly problematic, however; by mid-1918, the Red Cross was reluctant to issue an appeal for women to knit as much as possible. Attempting to solve this problem, Red Cross and War Industries Board officials set priorities for wool usage:

1) Army and navy received all the wool needed for uniforms and other military uses;

2) American Red Cross received wool chiefly for yarn; and

3) the public got whatever was left.

At the heart of the wool-supply question lay the War Industries Board inability to gauge precisely how much wool was available. Therefore, the Red Cross never knew exactly how much wool would be available for yarn, although it did know there was none to waste.

Nevertheless, knitters soldiered on with yarn and needles. The Red Cross remained convinced of the value of hand knitting for the war effort: "It may be true that better knitting can be done by machinery, but there is not that sense of intimacy or sentiment in a garment made by a machine, given to a soldier in wartime, which a garment made by the hands of some patriotic woman possesses."[182]

Historical Pattern
World War I Red Cross Soldiers' Socks

This pattern comes from Red Cross instructions reprinted in various publications during World War I.

Material: 2 Pair No. 1 Red Cross Steel Needles; 1½ Hanks (3/8 lb.) Knitting Yarn.

Instructions: Set up 60 sts (20 on each of 3 needles). Knit 2 plain and purl 2 for 35 rows (4½ inches).

36th R: Knit 4 plain sts; knit 2 together. Repeat until the round is completed. There are now 53 sts on the needles. Knit 50 rows plain until leg measures 11 inches (6½ inches of plain knitting). Take half the number of sts (25) on first needle for the heel (leaving 12 and 13 sts on the second and third needles for the instep). On the 25 sts knit 1 row; purl 1 row alternately 26 times (3 inches). Always slip the first st.

Begin to turn heel on the wrong side. Slip 1; Purl 13; purl 2 together; purl 1. Turn work over. Slip 1; knit 4; slip 1; knit 1. Pass it over slipped st. Knit 1; turn; slip 1; purl 5; purl 2 together; purl 1. Turn; slip 1; knit 6; slip 1; knit 1. Pass it over slipped st. Knit 1. Continue working toward the sides of the heel in this manner, leaving 1 more st between decreases on every row until all sts are worked in. There should be 15 sts on the needle.

Pick up 13 sts on side of heel; knit the 25 sts on 2nd and 3rd needle onto one needle, which becomes your second needle.

With your 3rd needle pick up the 13 sts on other side of heel and knit 7 sts off your 1st needle so that you will now have 21 sts on the 1st needle; 25 sts on the 2nd needle; and 20 sts on the 3rd needle.

1st needle (a) knit to within 3 sts of end; knit 2 together; knit 1.

2nd needle (b) knit plain.

3rd needle (c) knit 1; slip 1; knit 1; pass slipped st over; knit plain to end of needle. Knit around plain (d).

Repeat (a), (b), (c), and (d) until you have 13 sts on 1st needle, 25 sts on 2nd, and 12 sts on the 3rd. Knit plain for 4½ inches.

1st needle (e) knit 10 sts; knit 2 together; knit 1.

2nd needle (f) knit 1; slip 1; knit 1; pass slipped st over; knit 19 sts. Knit 2 together; knit 1.

The official Red Cross sock measured 11 inches from heel to toe and 14 inches from tip of heel to top of leg ribbing. *Art in Knitting*, 1917.

3rd needle (g) knit 1; slip 1; knit 1; pass slipped st over; knit 9 sts; knit 2 rows plain (h).

Repeat (e), (f) , (g) , and (h) 5 times. Then narrow every other row until you have 5 sts on your 1st needle, 9 sts on your 2nd needle, and 4 sts on the 3rd. Knit the 5 sts on your 1st needle on to your 3rd. Your work is now all on 2 needles opposite each other.

Break off yarn, leaving a 12-inch end. Thread into worsted needle and proceed to weave the front and back together, thus: * Pass worsted needle through 1st st of front knitting needle as if knitting and slip st off. Pass through 2nd st as if purling — leave st on. Pull thread through 1st st of back needle as if purling; slip st off; purl thread through 2nd st of back needle as if knitting — leave st on. Repeat from * until all the sts are off the needle.

When finished the sock should measure; (foot) 11 inches from tip of heel to tip of toe; (leg) 14 inches from tip of heel to tip of leg.

Chapter Seven
The Knitting Doldrums of the 1920s

Prosperity soared and Americans were in the mood to celebrate after World War I ended. Newly affluent Americans in the laissez-faire nation of President Calvin Coolidge could afford homes, insurance, shares in the stock market, and even overseas travel. Americans bought newly affordable automobiles — by 1929 there was one car for every five Americans — plus radios, telephones, cosmetics, and the latest electrical home appliances. With the promise of the American dream in sight, more families moved from farms to cities, especially to exuberant California. Newfound wealth also supported higher education and culture. Publishing, bookstores, literature, and theater thrived. The Museum of Modern Art opened in New York, and the Literary Guild and Book of the Month Club were founded. New technology — employing electricity in particular — spurred the success of motion pictures and radio.

An image of the classy knitters of the 1920s.

Yet times were not rosy for all. Prosperity for farmers fell far short of that enjoyed by business, and postwar fears slowed immigration to a trickle. The U.S. government enacted a quota system for immigrants, except for Asians who were barred outright. In addition, the passage of the Eighteenth Amendment in 1919 banned production, transport, and sale of alcoholic beverages, opening the door to the clandestine speakeasy and notorious social catastrophes due to Prohibition.

Women at last won the vote in 1920, and they did not look back. Architect Julia Morgan exemplified the "new woman of the 1920s" — confident, daring, trying on new roles for women. The flapper broke standards of the past: She bobbed her hair and wore short skirts, makeup, and even trousers. The growing passion for sports made stars of women athletes.

Opposite page: The era of patriotic wartime knitting behind them, knitters seemed to retreat into their homes during the 1920s. Yarn companies tried to entice knitters with the promise of the latest fashions in knitting patterns and plenty of new yarns — silk, wool, rayon, angora, and camel's hair. *Fleisher's Knitting & Crocheting Manual,* 1920.

Right: Actress Mary Pickford knit a sweater between scenes for the 1926 movie *Sparrows*. She donated the sweater to the American Red Cross for a disabled veteran. (Library of Congress)

Designer Emma L. Boardman used lively designs in contrasting colors to bring out the sporty look in men's golf stockings. *Needlecraft,* January 1922.

Knitting designer Emma L. Boardman crafted this pair of women's bedroom slippers — "a delightful gift" — finished with a ribbon tie and flower embroidery. *Needlecraft,* January 1922.

The Knitters Not So Much in Evidence . . .

Knitting appeared destined to languish during the 1920s. In *Needlecraft* magazine, poet W. Livingston Larned, for one, fretted about the apparent demise of knitting in America:

> What if all the ones who knit should never knit again?
> What if busy needles stopped, the busy world around?
> What if those who wear the weaves should ask for them in vain?
> What if not in one wee home we heard that clicking sound?

Larned warned that mothers and grandmothers must continue to knit:

> From cradle, onward to the grave, they play such noble part
> That we should raise the work they do to some sublime estate.[183]

Had the millions of stitches knit into hundreds of thousands of wartime stockings and bandages exhausted America's knitters? Did knitting hold too many sad memories for those who had knit during the war? Did millions of fervent wartime knitters lay aside their needles and yarn when the war ended?

Fortune magazine reported a postwar knitting boom peaked in 1922, driven by millions of women who had knit for soldiers. Sales of knitting wool topped 10 million pounds.[184] "Hands freed from war work will now turn to the fashioning of beautiful knitted and crocheted garments," read an optimistic note in *Bear Brand Blue Book of Yarnkraft* (Vol. 20, 1919). Articles about knitting dwindled through the decade, however, and few knit pieces in museum collections appear to date to the 1920s. Consumers could buy commercially knit sweaters, gloves, and socks at the burgeoning numbers of department chain stores and catalogs, so the need for hand knitting was certainly not so great. But perhaps 1920s knitters were more reserved than their wartime counterparts for whom knitting in public had been a patriotic statement. *Literary Digest* observed that the "knitter is not so much in public evidence as during the war, but in private we may assume that she — and occasionally he — still carries on her, or his, useful work." Grace Coolidge, America's first lady from 1923 to 1929, attracted a bit of attention after she entered her knitting in a New England competition and when she knit on the porch of their family lodge in Vermont, perhaps working on the famed Coolidge counterpane bedspread. Movie star Mary Pickford was photographed in a serene moment on a movie set knitting an American Red Cross sweater for a disabled veteran.[185]

Knitting Designs of the Twenties

Women's magazines and yarn manufacturers still found a market for patterns that whet the knitter's appetite for yarn. *Needlecraft* ran patterns for nearly anything that could be made with yarn and needles, from baby bootees to a cloche hat, bedroom slippers to neckties, lacy edgings to counterpane, and cardigan and pullover sweaters for children and adults. The number of knitting patterns dwindled, however, as the decade progressed, and by May 1927 *Needlecraft* had no patterns for knitting, although sewing, quilting, and embroidery were well represented. The *Ladies' Home Journal* published patterns ranging from knit tassels and lace insertions to golf stockings with striped or herringbone design cuffs — perfect with golf knickers. Claiming that "every child needs a sweater," a *Ladies' Home Journal* pattern for a little pullover with diminutive ducks on the pockets was written in graduated sizes to fit one- to six-year-olds. The home was not forgotten in the knitter's repertoire. Knitters could find patterns for a knit scrap rug and leaf-design afghan.[186]

Sweaters drove much of the fashion interest in knitting during the 1920s. Long, slender sweaters reflecting Art Deco verticality were the mainstay of the flapper wardrobe. The brilliant and influential fashion designer Gabrielle "Coco" Chanel introduced softer minimal shapes for women, replacing severe corsets, and sweaters followed this fashion style. "These adaptable garments, it seems, have come to stay," cheered *Ladies' Home Journal,* claiming its bright red Iceland

110

Grace Coolidge, first lady from 1923 to 1929, was known for her knitting expertise. Following the traditions of her New England heritage, Coolidge entered her knitting in county fairs. (Library of Congress)

Handmade Sweaters and Hats Are Smartest

By MURIEL MUNSON
and
ETHEL M. McCUNN

No. 3267 N (Left). An imported hat bought from one of the exclusive shops! It surely looks so, but it can be made by anyone who understands only the simplest crochet-stitches. A fine straw is sold for the purpose, and costs only about a tenth as much as the finest crocheted hats sold in the stores

No. 3268 N (Center). Two shades of brown with just a little orange made this attractive hat which is crocheted of paper twist, though sweater-silk or any similar material may be used. A transparent wax brushed over these hats greatly increases the wearing qualities

No. 3269 N (Below). Two shades of the same color are used for this prettily striped sweater with its matching crocheted posy. Worked entirely in stockinette-stitch, there are no pitfalls for the inexperienced worker

No. 3270 N (Above). Hemstitching, fagoting, and other open stitches are quite as fashionable on sweaters as on silk dresses

canvas, 27 inches wide (about 12 squares to the inch), 1 yard grosgrain ribbon, 2 inches wide.

Gauge: Nine rounds equal 1 inch; 8 stitches equal 1 inch.

Chain 3, join.

1. Work 6 d c in the ring.
2. Two d c in each st.
3. * Two d c in 1st st, 1 d c in next st; repeat from *
4. * One d c in first 2 st, 2 d c in next st. Repeat from *, making 24 st in all.

Continue to increase 6 st (or just sufficient number to keep work stretched flat) in different places so that they do not come directly over those of the preceding round.

5. Begin "polka-dot" pattern as follows: Over, insert hook in st, directly below on 2d round (skipping 2 rounds), repeat once, take off all 5 loops, ch 1, skip 2 sts on round and fasten in next st, 4 d c, increasing where necessary, and repeat dot to end of round.

Next two rounds plain, increasing as before. Repeat dots, working them between those of the 5th round. As crown increases, it will be necessary sometimes to make 2 dots between those of the preceding rounds in order that they may be spaced about equal distances apart. Work thus until top of crown is eight inches in diameter, about 216 stitches. Work four rounds without increasing. On next round decrease 6 times, at equal distances apart, and repeat every eighth round 3 times, so that decreases do not come over one another.

BAND: Cut canvas correct length for desired head-size (22 inches is medium head-size). Fold double 1¾ inches wide. Seam and sew to hat, holding in or stretching crochet-work, if necessary.

BRIM: 1. Work a d c through double mesh of canvas, skipping every 3d mesh. (If the hook will not go through canvas, a blanket-stitch may be embroidered on edge in every 2d square, then work 2 d c in 1st st, 1 d c in next st.)

2. Increase every 8th st, 1 round even.
3. Increase every 15th st, so that increases do not come directly over those of the preceding round. Begin dot pattern. Work 3 more rounds, repeating dot on last round, and increasing 8 times if a full brim is desired. Turn; work last round in opposite direction. Fasten off.

Concluded on page 16

Hand-crocheted hats and knitted sweaters are fashion's latest edict. Plaits, folds and creases also help in forming the hats of the season, giving individuality and an appearance of having been molded on the head. For the woman who likes to crochet her own, there are various materials on the market, such as straw, paper twist, or any of the silks, rayons, or mercerized cottons used for making sweaters.

These same plaits, folds, etc., are a wonderful boon, as they can be so arranged as to make a hat of almost any shape, provided, of course, that it is not too small, becoming to almost any person. Crowns are not so high, but must possess at least one fold.

The smart sweaters shown here are splendid examples of the handmade sweaters being worn. They are both in stockinette-stitch and follow the lines considered chic for sports-wear, no matter what the fabric may be.

Crocheted Hat, No. 3267 N

Material required: Straw, or silk, etc., steel crochet-hook No. 8, 4 inches of

Historical Pattern
1920s Knit Thread Lace

This pattern comes from Needlecraft *magazine, August 1924.*

Pattern has a simple 6-row repeat over 6 stitches:
1. Fagot (that is, over twice and purl 2 together, or purl-narrow), knit 2, over twice, knit 2.
2. Knit 3, purl 1, knit 2, fagot.
3. Fagot, knit 2, over twice, narrow, over twice, knit 2.
4. Knit 3, (purl 1, knit 2) twice, fagot.
5. Fagot, knit 9.
6. Bind off 5, knit 3, fagot.
Repeat from 1st row.

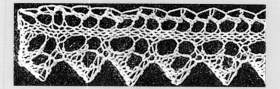

"Laces, knitted of thread, is a form of needlecraft that has become increasingly popular," according to needlework editor Mary Sue McClanahan.

wool, lace-knit slipover sweater "embodied all the best and newest developments of sweater fashions."[187] In response, *Fleisher's Knitting and Crocheting Manual* of 1920 featured dozens of slipover and cardigan patterns for men, women, and children's sweaters — plus accessories like scarves, stockings, gloves, and baby layettes. Fleisher's and Bear Brand patterns included measurements for gauge.

Sportswomen of the 1920s chose smart new sweaters suited for active lives. At San Moritz, women who went in for "ski-shooting" wore heavy sweaters knit with white yarn. *Fleisher's Knitting & Crocheting Manual*, 1920.

In the world of high fashion, a hand-knit sweater catapulted designer Elsa Schiaparelli into the *haute couture* spotlight. Schiaparelli took the 1927 Paris fashion scene by storm with her cravat sweater — a *trompe l'oeil* white bow knit to simulate a tied scarf on a simple black pullover. An instant success, her design linked fashion with humor and fine art — surrealism in particular. A knitter from the Paris Armenian community had knit Schiaparelli's cravat concept using a traditional stitch worked with three needles. *Trompe l'oeil* knitwear became signature pieces within Schiaparelli's revolutionary collections: sweaters knit to simulate a man's tie, a handkerchief in a pocket, a crossword puzzle, and even a skeleton X-ray.[188]

Selling Yarn to Knitters

No longer hostage to the urgency of war, yarn companies marketed fashion knitting. Makers of yarn survived the languish in knitting by selling yarn to rug hookers until instruction books promoted stylish knitting patterns.[189] Fleischer Yarns sold lavish pattern manuals, while Bear Brand Yarns offered free directions for a "beautiful modish Navajo Sweater." The American Southwest entranced tourists during the 1920s, and designers responded by adapting "Indian" patterns to clothing. The H. K. H. Silk Company advertised artificial silk (rayon) yarn for their "newest from Paris" coat-sweater — knit in Heminway Texto yarn trimmed with "monkey fur." Collingbourne Mills in Elgin, Illinois, marketed artificial silk yarn for sweaters and ties in Virginia Snow's pattern

The Trianon Bedjacket. The not-so-sports-minded knitter could choose a soft, comfy bedjacket pattern. *Fleisher's Knitting & Crocheting Manual*, 1920.

113

According to manufacturers' advertisements, women could turn out stockings with a knitting machine in a fraction of the time required to knit by hand. Despite the wide availability of knitting machines, hand knitting continued throughout the 1920s.

The Devos scarf sweater was a novelty design with a scarf, knit separately, sewn to the sweater neckline. *Fleisher's Knitting & Crocheting Manual*, 1920.

The York Sweater. Knitting patterns showed sweaters worn for active sports like ice skating, golf, and tennis. *Fleisher's Knitting & Crocheting Manual*, 1920.

How They Make Money in Their Own Homes

One woman has averaged $70.00 a month for three years in spare time, besides taking care of her home and family. Thousands are turning odd moments into dollars

HAVEN'T you often wished for some practical way of making money right in your own home? Of course you have—and you have felt sure that there must be some steady home occupation that would bring you, not just "pin money" but many extra dollars in return for your spare hours. Well, there is just such a spare time money plan—and it is called "AUTO KNITTING."

Let us tell you how you can use this plan to make your "extra money" wish come true—without interfering with your household duties or regular daily work. But first listen to the remarkable story of Mrs. Frank Unger—one of the ambitious and energetic home earners who make money Auto Knitting.

Mrs. Unger's Own Story

"When we were first married," says Mrs. Unger of New York, "there was plenty of cash to meet the bills, but by and by we began to notice that there wasn't any surplus.

"Our expenses were steadily increasing. My husband's wages were hardly enough to meet the household accounts, to say nothing of clothing. And so things ran along for months with us pinching and skimping and trying desperately to break even.

"I began wondering what I could do to help. To go out and work was impossible, because I had a four months old baby to care for. I must find some sort of home work that would pay good wages.

"I began looking in the magazines and newspapers for some sort of paying home work, but no one seemed to have any work to offer me.

"Then one day I opened the paper to look for work as usual. And on one of the pages this headline caught my eye: 'How To Make Money Right At Home.' Of course I started to read, and soon I was real excited. It was about a woman whose husband got a small salary—hardly enough for them to live on. She wanted to make extra money just as badly as I did. But she had two little children, so she couldn't do any paying work unless she could find something to do at home. It was my situation exactly.

"Then it went on to tell how at last she did find home work—making socks on a hand-knitting machine, and how the company paid her for making them, and furnished replacement yarn for each lot of standard socks she sent in. The name of the firm was The Auto Knitter Hosiery Company and they were located at Buffalo, N. Y. So I wrote a letter to the company, asking for free information. In just a few days I had a reply telling me all about the machine and the details of their home work proposition. And then I was more enthusiastic than ever and sent for an Auto Knitter.

How I Made Money

"In a short time my knitter arrived. At first I was a little bit afraid, because I didn't know anything about machines, but finally, with a little patience and the aid of the clearly written instruction book, I completely mastered the operation of the Auto Knitter.

"Then I started to work in real earnest, putting in every minute I could spare from my housework. And all the while checks from the Auto Knitter Hosiery Company kept coming in for each lot of standard socks I sent them. I love my work more each week."

That is Mrs. Unger's story in her own words. In 37 months she made $2,538.50—averaging $70.00 a month for more than three full years! She made all this in wages under her Work Purchase Contract, and in addition sold part of her work to her own private trade at good prices.

She did this in a home where there are her husband and children to look after and the usual housework to do.

"And now we are realizing the dream of a lifetime" concludes Mrs. Unger in her letter. "A little cottage of our own. Our Auto Knitter has helped to make it possible. To those who want to make extra money at home in their spare time, I heartily recommend the Auto Knitter. There is nothing like it."

How You, Too, Can Make Money at Home

Mrs. Unger has told you in her own words what she has accomplished through Auto Knitting. Her earnings for a period of more than three years, have averaged $70.00 a month and the best part of it is that she still has her Auto Knitter which can be used to earn more money as the months roll round.

Of course, Mrs. Unger is a skillful and ambitious worker. But before she got her Auto Knitter, her skill and ambition did not bring in the money she wanted. The rapid Auto Knitter gave her the opportunity to turn her ability to financial advantage.

And, Mrs. Unger is not the only one—thousands of home-earners are turning spare hours into dollars with the Auto Knitter. The Auto Knitter is indeed the World's Champion Money Maker.

No hand-knitting machine operator, working under any Work Purchase Contract, has ever earned as much with any hand-knitter as has been earned by one individual operating the Auto Knitter, the World's Champion hand-knitting machine.

This marvelous machine has to its credit the payment of the largest total amount of wages in cash to workers, this sum now amounting to nearly half a million dollars paid out under the Work Purchase Contract. When you link up with the Auto Knitter, you link up with a proved success.

Find Out Today About The Champion Auto Knitter!

Clearly and briefly, here is our proposition: The Auto Knitter Hosiery Company enters into an agreement to buy all the standard socks you knit on the Auto Knitter and send in to them, paying a fixed guaranteed price. This wage-rate has never been greater than it is today. Besides the cash wages the company has a wonderful exclusive Double Value Plan which gives you valuable merchandise rewards and actually doubles the value of every hour devoted to Auto Knitting. Checks and replacement yarn are sent promptly for each lot of work you send in. Previous experience in either hand or machine knitting is not essential. With the World's Champion Auto Knitter and the Auto Knitter Self-Instructor, the ambitious Home Earner readily learns to turn out standard Olde Tyme Wool Socks.

ALL INFORMATION FREE

Of course you want to know more about the marvelous machine that has helped Mrs. Unger and so many thousands of people all over the country. Send right away for the company's free literature and read about the happy experiences of other Auto Knitter owners. Find out about the money-making opportunity offered you. Remember that Mrs. Unger lost no time in getting the facts. You are in her position today. Will you follow her example? Just write your name and address in the space below. Full details will go forward to you at once. THE AUTO KNITTER HOSIERY COMPANY, INC., Dept 711, 630-638 Genesee Street, Buffalo, N. Y.

Pioneers in Home Knitting Industry—Sole Manufacturers of the genuine Auto Knitter—No Connection with any other Concern.

Mrs. Frank Unger

Made $308.64 in Spare Time
"It had been just one year since I sent my first shipment to the company, and during that time they have paid me in checks $308.64. I only work a part of the time but I could hardly have seen my way out had it not been for my little Auto Knitter."
Mrs. O. F. Ladd, Arkansas (No. 12)

Has Made $600.00 Knitting
"I have already sent to the company 118 shipments of socks and have received either a check or yarn for each and have always received my replacement yarn in good shape. I have received my knitter nearly all the time until the last month. I have received the best of treatment from the company and found they do all they promise and even more."
Walter Huie, Missouri (No. 11)

Earned $472 With Her Auto Knitter
Mrs. A. L. Heggen is the wife of a Minnesota farmer. She does all her own housework and cares for her two boys, aged two and four. "Yet with all this," she writes, "I have found time to make 1,320 pairs of socks, for which I have received $472.35."

Operates Three Machines
"I bought my first Auto Knitter from you about two years ago and since then have had no other employment that that of knitting. Since the first year I knit and sent the company 1128 pairs of men's hose with never a pair rejected. Friends saw the work and orders began to come in. Can't give all the figures but have made $1600 out of this specialty besides all other hose."
Theo. S. Kellog, Utah (No. 1)

Has Knit 20,000 Pairs
"All the work I have done has been pleasant and easy and without annuity. I have now knit 20,000 pairs of men's socks and women's and children's hosiery. The Auto Knitter Hosiery Co., will give you a square deal at all times and they are prompt in sending their checks, also replacement yarn."
Mrs. W. E. Straub, Pennsylvania (No. 2)

The World's Champion Auto Knitter

The perfected hand-knitter that knits the famous Olde Tyme Socks—known the country over as the "Proud Product of America Home Industry." Successful Auto Knitter Home Earners take pride in this product and insist on maintaining the standard which has made Olde Tyme the most popular wool socks in America. On sale by thousands of stores from coast to coast.

Auto Knitter Earnings Now Worth Double
You must find out all about the New Auto Knitter Double Value Plan which doubles the value of every hour devoted to Auto Knitting. Under this exclusive Auto Knitter feature Mrs. Unger's earnings for 37 consecutive months would have a value of over $5,000. Send the coupon now—and full details of the new plan will come by return mail.

THE AUTO KNITTER HOSIERY CO., Inc.
Dept. 711, 630-638 Genesee Street
BUFFALO, N. Y.

Send me full particulars about the Champion Money-Maker, I want to know exactly how I can earn money at home in my spare time with the Auto Knitter. I enclose 2 cents postage to cover cost of mailing. It's understood that this does not obligate me in any way.

Name...
Street and Number.................... Post Office.............. State........
Needlecraft 11-24

books, the sweaters embellished with fringe and tassels.[190] For $2 worth of yarn from Peace Dale Mills in New York City, a knitter could make the latest long sweater striped in orange and dark green from its 25¢ "Remarkable Knitting Book" featuring forty-two designs like those sold in the "best New York shops." Allies Yarn from Eaton Rapids Woolen Mills in Michigan mailed free color samples of wool yarn for knitting stylish sport sweaters, Tam-O'Shanters, and warm things for babies, all at "modest cost." A number of women set up needlecraft shops and sold yarn in their homes; Mrs. L. H. B. of Massachusetts offered business advice in *Needlecraft* for a home shop.[191] Even though few inventors patented new knitting devices, in 1920 W. C. Rhodes patented a way to secure knitting needles to knitting using safety pins and short cylinders, and David Genese received a patent in 1925 for a holder that secured the tips of knitting needles together.

Historical Pattern
1920s The Imogene Scarf

*This pattern comes from Needlecraft maga-
zine, November 1924.*

The Imogene sweater — in clove brown,
medium blue, light red, and yellow — was
knit in stockinette with garter-stitch bands
plus a double row of lace knit. A simple
openwork stitch knit over 60 stitches set off
the coordinating Imogene scarf.

Pattern stitch for scarf:
1. Knit 1, over twice, repeat, ending with
   knit 1.
2. Knit back, dropping the over-twice
   loops.
3, 4. Knit plain.
5, 6. Like 9th and 10th rows.
7 to 10. Knit plain.

The Imogene Sweater. Sweater fashions
promised comfort and good looks.

Cover illustrations show the knitting
woman as youthful and active.
*Fleisher's Knitting & Crocheting
Manual,* 1920.

Perfect for novices, the Babbette Jacket was knit in one piece using garter stitch and shaped with increases and decreases. A row of crochet worked in every ridge around the jacket stabilized the shape. *Fleisher's Knitting & Crocheting Manual*, 1920.

The Harrow Sweater combined warmth with freedom of movement, perfect for children. *Fleisher's Knitting & Crocheting Manual*, 1920.

The Daisy Sweater, ideal for little girls who liked dainty yet warm and comfy sweaters. *Fleisher's Knitting & Crocheting Manual*, 1920.

Historical Pattern
1920s Baby Bunting Set

The "particular mother" welcomed patterns for knit garments that held an important place in the wardrobe of her little ones. *Fleisher's Knitting & Crocheting Manual*, 1920.

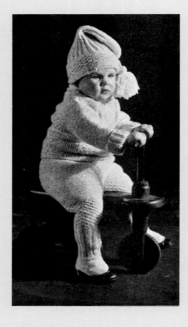

This pattern comes from Fleisher's Knitting & Crocheting Manual *(17th Edition), 1920.*

Material: Fleisher's Germantown Zephyr, 4-fold, 15 balls white.

Needles: 1 pair No. 4.

Sweater
Patterns:

1st and 2nd Rows: * Knit 2, purl 2. *

3rd and 4th Rows: * Purl 2, knit 2. *

Cast on 60 stitches, work pattern even 3 times. Keep lower edge even. Knit 6 rows even. At end of 6th row cast on 10 stitches. Knit 10 rows even. Work 3 patterns. Knit plain 10 rows. Bind off 22 stitches, knit 10 rows. Cast on 22 stitches, knit 8 rows even. Work 3 patterns. Work 50 rows even. Work 3 patterns, knit 8 rows even. Bind off 22 stitches. Knit 10 rows even. Cast on 22 stitches, knit 10 rows even. Knit 3 patterns, knit 10 rows. Bind off 10 stitches. Knit 14 rows even. Bind off. Sew up shoulder seams.

Sleeves: Cast on 50 stitches. Decrease 1 stitch each edge every 8th row 10 times. Knit even until sleeve measures 8 inches.

Knit 2, purl 2 for 2 inches, bind off loosely.

Sew up seams, place seams to center of under arm.

Collar: Cast on 56 stitches, knit 12 rows even. Purl 1 row. Knit 6 rows.

Next Row: Knit 1, * knit 2 together, * knit 1.

2nd Row: Knit 1, * over, knit 1, * knit 1, knit 6 rows even.

Make 1 pattern. Knit 2 rows. Bind off loosely. Place center of collar to center of back. Sew to sweater. Make a slip stitch on right front, making buttonholes 1 1/2 inches apart. Slip stitch across pattern.

Drawers

1st and 2nd Rows: Knit 2, purl 2.

3rd and 4th Rows: Purl 2, knit 2.

6 stitches = 1 inch. 11 rows = 1 inch.

Cast on 72 stitches. Knit 2, purl 2 for 4 rows.

5th Row: * Knit 2, purl 2, knit 1, over twice, knit 2 together, purl 1. * Repeat between *'s.

6th Row: * Knit 2, purl 2, knit 1 stitch, drop next loop.* Work 8 rows even. Knit 2, purl 2.

Plain Knitting: Work 8 stitches, turn, knit 8, turn, knit 16, turn, knit 16, turn, knit 24. Work in this way until all stitches have been worked off.

Knit 64 rows even.

Pattern: 1 pattern even. Then decrease 1 stitch at beginning of every row until there are 44 stitches. Knit 2, purl 2 for 36 rows. Knit 6 rows plain. Knit 28 stitches, turn, knit 12 stitches. On these knit 12 rows even.

13th Row: Decrease by knitting the 6th and 7th stitches together. 1 row even.

15th Row: Same as 13th row.

Pick up stitches around the foot and instep. Knit 12 rows even. Bind off. This is one half of leggings. Work other half the same. Sew up seams.

Gusset: Cast on 12 stitches. Knit 26 rows even. Bind off. Sew on.

Cap
Pattern: Same as sweater.

Cast on 72 stitches. Knit 6 rows. Knit 1 1/2 patterns. Knit 6 rows. Purl 1 row. Knit 1 row, increasing 1 stitch at end of row.

Then for cap, slip 1, knit 1, * over, slip 1 as though to purl. Keep thread front, knit 2 together, * knit 2. Repeat between *'s for 7 inches. Then * knit 1, purl , * for 3 inches, decreasing 1 stitch at beginning of every row. Bind off tightly. Sew up seam. Draw end together. Sew to cap even with border.

Tassel: Wrap yarn 50 times around a 5-inch piece of cardboard. Tie one end and tie again about 1 inch from end.

The Knittin'est Woman

In 1926 poet and educator Ann Cobb wrote this dialect poem about a steady, home-loving knitter. Miss Cobb was an early teacher at the Hindman Settlement School in Appalachia and was dearly loved. This poem was published in *Kinfolks and Other Selected Poems by the Hindman Settlement School* (2003) and is reproduced courtesy of the Hindman Settlement School, Hindman, Kentucky.

Knittin'est woman ever I seed!
Quare how that runs around in my head?
The burying's gone like a sorry dream,
Now that I'm left alone with my dead.
Grands and greats she knitted their hose,
Seemly and stout of heel and knee.
And many's the pair our soldier lads
Battled in, over the old salt sea.
'Times, she'd take hit to bed with her
and throw out a sock in the lonesome night.
I've wakened and watched it flickering
Back and forth in the fire-log's light.
Preacher told of her steady faith,
And orderly walking all her days.
But living together for sixty years,
A man's remembrance holds little ways.

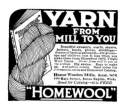

Knitters bought major brands of yarn sold in department store needlework shops and all manner of yarns sold directly from the mills.

Knitting had its thrifty, domestic side beyond the party world of fashion and flappers. Some young girls filled hope chests with handmade linens, including hand knits needed for housekeeping. Cost-conscious knitters could knit for two-thirds less when they bought direct from Home Woolen Mills of Eaton Rapids, Michigan, or they could buy a pound of yarn from Concord Worsted Mills of New Hampshire for $2, a four-ounce skein for 50¢.[192] Columbia Yarns used the nostalgic, sentimental aspect of knitting to mark its products. Their ads urged the knitter to follow in grandmother's footsteps: "Centuries old but always new, thus is the art of knitting. . . . Out of the ages that History has forgotten, it comes. But through woman's ingenuity, woman's love of beauty and woman's will to serve, on each new day it is born again. . . . Centuries old but always new, thus is the art of knitting."[193]

The United States would soon count itself fortunate to have its steady knitters. The bull stock market of the 1920s slid down an ominous decline and crashed in October 1929, throwing the nation into the tragic and stubbornly persistent Great Depression. Although the nation's party mood was over, American knitting was poised for a comeback.

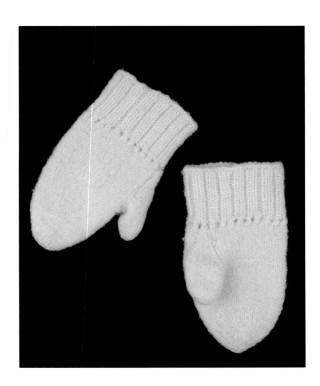

Left: Wool Baby's Mittens, circa 1920s. (Wisconsin Historical Society)

Homemade knitting-book folder, with wood covers, canvas binding, and hand-painted image.

Convent Tuxedo Sweater for Morning, Afternoon and Evening. Miss Virginia Snow designed a ladies' sweater embellished with pockets and a long collar with tassels. *Virginia Snow's Sweater Book*, 1924.

Some knitters first learned to make knit-like fabric using spool-knitting kits. The tubes knit using a spool knitter could be sewn or braided into ties and bands or used to make small, simple pieces like doll clothes.

Virginia Snow's SWEATER BOOK

SCARFS

NECKTIES

Virginia Snow Studios
ELGIN, ILL.

1924 EDITION   BOOK № 28   TEN CENTS

Historical Pattern
1920s Knit Tie

This pattern comes from Needlecraft *magazine, August 1924.*

Cast on 48 stitches and always slip the first stitch in every row.

1. Knit plain.
2. Purl.
3. Slip 1, knit 1, then knit 2 together all along the row until only 2 stitches are left; knit these plain.
4. Slip 1, knit 1, * pick up and knit the thread that lies between the stitch just knitted and the following stitch, knit the next stitch plain, repeat from * to within 2 stitches of the end of the row, knit these plain.
5. Knit plain.
6. Purl.
7. Same as the third row.
8. Slip 1, knit 2; pick up 1 and knit 1 alternatively to within 2 stitches of the end of the row, pick up 1, knit 2.

Repeat these 8 rows until 13 inches are worked. Then decrease 1 stitch at the end of every row until there are 24 stitches. Work for 13 inches and then increase at the end of every row until there are 48 stitches. Work for 10 inches and bind off.

Sew the long edges together, place the seam at the back of the work and sew up the ends. Press lightly, so that the pattern may not be spoiled.

Fancy patterns for ties knit with "artificial silk" (rayon) appealed to knitters. Ties looked best — and resisted stretching — when knit flat, folded, and seamed up the center back. With no gauge given, knitters were advised to knit a small sample and then "rearrange" the number of stitches required for the desired width. *Needlecraft*, August 1924.

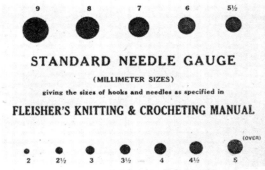

Knitters could order free directions for a "modish Navajo sweater" knit with Bear Brand Yarns. Tourists had discovered the American Southwest and adapted traditional Navajo and Hopi designs into knit patterns. *Needlecraft*, November 1921.

By the 1920s, certain knitting manuals had added gauge measurements to pattern instructions, and manufacturers sold knitting accessories that were more standardized. The Fleisher Gauge — white celluloid insured "practical indestructiblity" — helped knitters measure the sizes of knitting needles and crochet hooks.

Chapter Eight

Back to the Knitting Needles in the 1930s

Millions of Americans lost not only fortunes in the 1929 stock market crash, but also jobs, homes, and life savings. Farmers suffered as floods and dust storms devastated the Midwest. People struck like snakes at newly elected president Herbert Hoover, blaming him for America's misfortunes. The economy hit a low point in 1933 when national income fell to half that in 1929 and unemployment topped 30 percent. The birth rate also plummeted to its lowest level in American history. In 1932, the nation elected a new president, Franklin Delano Roosevelt, remembered today for his grand public works policies intended to stimulate economic recovery. Not everyone fell into poverty, however. Those who had kept their wealth indulged in luxury travel and *haute couture.*

"Back to the Knitting Needle"

During the thirties, knitting was back — with a passion! "All over the country needles continue to click, and justifiably so, for styles in knitting become better looking all the time," according to Virginia Pope, fashion columnist for *The New York Times*. An estimated 10 million Americans — one-twelfth of the population — picked up their knitting needles and turned around the postwar knitting doldrums of the 1920s. In 1933, *Needlework*'s editor wrote, "NEVER since the period of the World War has the art of knitting — that simple, wholesome occupation of our grandmothers' day — been so popular as at the present." According to *Good Housekeeping*'s needlework editor Anne Orr, "To knit or not to knit is no longer the question — we *do* knit."[194]

KNITTING

BY JULIANA STEIBLE

I darn, and sew, keep house, and go
  In every kind of weather,
I like to cook, or read a book
  Bound in paper, cloth, or leather.

Although I've tried to put aside
  THIS hobby so bewitching,
To hear the click of needles quick
  Sets my fingers fairly itching!

The poem, "Knitting," appeared in the November 1935 *Needlecraft.*

Opposite page: Obsessed with knitting! *Home Arts,* cover by Ralph Pallen Coleman.

From 1934 to 1935, yarn companies produced 40 to 45 percent more yarn, and Chicago's Boye Needle Company sold 50 percent more knitting needles. Boye sold 75 percent of the 10 million needles purchased in 1934, circular needles dominating sales. By 1935, Boye was manufacturing one hundred thousand circular knitting needles every month and still lagged three months behind orders. Demand led to innovation: Boye announced the "breathtaking" invention of the first knitting needle improvement since Pompeii: knitting needles with rounded points and a concave taper. Presumably, knitters appreciated such improvements.[195]

Everywhere you looked, someone was knitting. Americans knit on subways, trains, ships, planes, in restaurants, during class, at the movies, and on front porches. Lou Henry Hoover, America's first lady from 1929 to 1933, was photographed knitting in the White House Oval Drawing Room. A woman's college survey described the typical college girl as a healthy seventeen-year-old who liked to knit.[196] There were celebrity knitters, among them author and avid knitting advocate M. F. K. Fisher. First Lady Eleanor Roosevelt carried her knitting bag everywhere and was also designated America's "First Knitter." Motion picture stars were knitting: Clara Blandick and Doris Hill in *Men Are Like That* (1930), Annabella in *Dinner at the Ritz* (1937), Sylvia Sidney in *Dead End* (1937), and Glenda Farrell in *Stolen Heaven* (1938). In *A Tale of Two Cities* (1935), Blanche Yurka knit as Madame Defarge. In *The Women* (1939), knitter Lucile Watson played wise adviser to Norma Shearer, a young wife whose husband was attracted to Joan Crawford's character. Women were knitting "for husbands or for children, for nephews, occasionally for themselves, or for money, or for the poor."[197]

The U. S. Supreme Court Justices, however, drew the line when they spotted a woman knitting in their courtroom as they handed down decisions. A court attendant "whispered into her ear and her needles disappeared."[198]

Knitting and the Great Depression

Similar to Depression-era movies that ignored the bleak economy, women's magazines of the 1930s only hinted at hardships and make-do practices of the Great Depression. A 1935 feature article in *The New York Times Magazine* concluded: "In periods of worry and uncertainty not only do we need relief from tension and a new channel for pent-up energy but we need to see concrete results from our own efforts. Needlework has filled the need for women every age since Penelope sat at her web. Crocheting a scarf, knitting a dress slip one, knit two, thread over the needle, making something — women are proving its value every day."[199]

Opposite Page:
The theme of obsessed knitters was a common one in the 1930s, as this *Home Arts* cover illustration depicts.

123

Knitters were often featured on magazine covers during the 1930s.

Depression-era needlework magazines supplied patterns for practical hand knits like this ribbed bonnet that knit up quickly and stayed in place on the baby. *Needlecraft*, March 1933.

Influential needlework editor Anne Orr praised knitting for fun, but she added that knitters made useful things for their homes, inexpensively. Down-to-earth women's magazines printed patterns for such economical necessities as knitted wool baby panties or "soakers" that saved the expense of rubber pants.[200] Many knitting patterns in *Needlework* during the 1930s emphasized simple, useful projects: a baby bonnet, socks, scarves, a child's pullover sweater.

The otherwise sunny disposition presented in women's magazines was marred by occasional mentions of hardship or philanthropy. A 1933 *Needlework* editorial praised those who knit stockings, sweaters, and other warm things for the unemployed. *The Parents' Magazine* addressed the problem of young girls who needed new clothes, recommending they learn to make some of their own wardrobes: "To the girl clever with her fingers, who wants a bit of pick-up work for odd moments, knitting, crocheting and embroidery are all fun." Newspapers reported a knitting contest winner who supported his invalid wife in part with his knitting and who helped his mother supply his brothers with stockings. Hundreds of sweaters entered in another 1935 sweater-knitting contest all were donated to charity.[201]

The stress of economic hardship also lurked between lines that extolled the psychological advantages of knitting, which apparently helped cut down on smoking, too. The Knit Shop at Zahn's Department Store in Racine, Wisconsin, forbade smoking and observed that women who smoked when they first came to the shop invariably forgot about stopping for a few puffs after they became involved in their knitting.[202] Psychiatrists swore by the healing power of knitting for their patients, including a young woman who was "saved by knitting":

To this girl, her mind wandering in day-dreams and fantasy, a little knitted square of colored wool was the first hold on reality. The knitting grew and her interest with it. Vaguely it was intended for a scarf. The day she decided it was going to be a sweater was a day of real progress toward recovery. It was a problem for the instructor, for it would have been fatal to unravel a stitch. It taxed all her ingenuity, but somehow, the patient cooperating with zest, that shapeless scarf was manoeuvred into a sweater. Triumphantly it was completed and the patient began to get well.[203]

Knitting for Fashion

The use of therapeutic knitting to soothe nerves paled in comparison with the popularity of knitting for fashion. Yarn companies pinpointed fashion knitting as their road to survival during the Depression and created clever ways to sell yarn to knitters.[204] They advertised, printed pattern books, promoted fashion shows, sponsored knitting contests, devised new yarns and colors, and trained knitting instructors. Some companies hired high-powered publicists. New York's Bernhard Ulmann Company, for example, hired the Claire Wolff Agency to channel hundreds of thousands of dollars into a knitting promotion blitz. Wolff persuaded the Duke of Windsor to be photographed knitting, convinced Paris designers to focus on hand knits, staged lavish fashion shows for art needlework buyers, and posed Hollywood movie stars in hand-knit sweaters. Paris fashions featured hand knits in the collections of Schiaparelli, Kostio de War, and Lucien Lelong.[205] "More distinguished designers are taking a hand in planning and working out beautiful garments for women who knit," stated

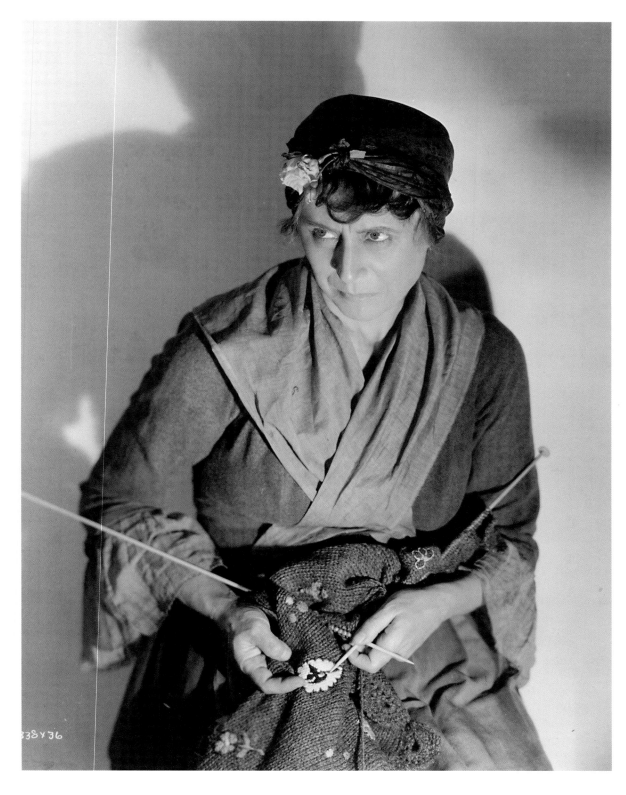

Actress Blanch Yurka played the famous literary knitter, Madame Thérèse Defarge, in 1935's film adaptation of Charles Dickens' *A Tale of Two Cities*. Madame Defarge, wife of a wine shop keeper with revolutionary leanings, calmly knits a registry of the names and crimes of those among the aristocracy whose heads should go under the guillotine. Knitting "with the steadfastness of fate," she's among those who storm Paris' Bastille, her knitting set aside and a knife tucked in her girdle. As her husband says of her — with more than a bit of wariness in his voice, perhaps — "It would be easier for the weakest poltroon that lives, to erase himself from existence, than to erase one letter of his name or crimes from the knitted register of Madame Defarge." (Photofest)

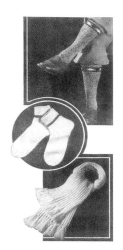

Practical stocking and scarf patterns, knit to a gauge of 17 stitches to 2 inches, show a sports-minded flair. *Needlecraft*, September 1934.

A little girl and her doll
could both enjoy stylish
hand-knit sweaters.
Designer Julia C. Averill
styled these matching
sweaters and berets in
pink Shetland wool for a
little girl and her doll.
Duplicate stitch cats
decorated the sweaters.
Needlecraft, June 1933.

The New York Times fashion editor Virginia Pope. The *Times* sold mail-order knitting instructions for the latest styles, including a suit jacket with square shoulders ("very Schiaparelli") and Vionnet sleeves or a sporty cape-and-skirt outfit. A lavender dress with "dignity and charm" was recommended for the older knitter. The Tyrolean look was popular, so Lanz of Salzburg designed two sweaters for the *Times,* each embroidered with peasant color schemes.[206] The DMC Corporation published knitting patterns in *The Encyclopedia of Needlework,* which included *Knitting* (Fourth Series) — an album with fifty-one patterns devoted to knitting.

Machine-made knits were expensive, and styles changed rapidly throughout the decade, two reasons women knit their own clothing. The boyish look of the 1920s gave way to the more voluptuous female silhouette of the 1930s. Knitting was perfect for figure-hugging sweaters and suits in vogue during the 1930s. By 1933, the fine, close-knit sweater styles were slightly bloused over waistbands, and collars varied from turtlenecks to large circular ribs. In 1936, the blousy shape went out of fashion, replaced by a two- to three-inch lower band. Many sweaters had lacy knit stitches, and pullover and cardigan twin sets were popular. Actress Lana Turner filled out her sweater especially well in *They Won't Forget,* a movie made in 1937 — known as the year of the "sweater girl." Boleros came into style, too. Toward the end of the decade, some

sweaters had coarse, nubby textures and there were colorful ski and skating sweaters.[207] Boucle was a popular yarn during the 1930s. Bouclette yarn, Columbia's boucle brand, was featured in more than twenty dress and suit patterns — many in lace knit or geometric designs — in the *Columbia Book of Misses' and Women's Bouclette Suits* (Volume 43). Instructions did not include gauge and, for a typical skirt pattern, began, "Cast on 402 stitches."[208]

Women's magazines encouraged knitting for a smart look at an economical price. *The Woman's World Book of Needlework for 1936* featured economical kits with yarn and patterns for children's sweaters and women's suits. The *Ladies' Home Journal* promoted fashion knitting from London, Paris, and the Riviera, and claimed it whisked such exclusive patterns as knit rompers for toddlers straight to America from the Riviera.[209] College girls in particular seemed smitten with fashion knitting. "I'm just in love with this work — all of us are," said one young woman, "and the things we knit are so much smarter than those you can buy at the shops." *Needlework* praised the patterns they printed for women's hand knits as "chic" and "modish." Knitters could whip up a knit blouse in "the latest mode" for mid-summer; a "modish cardigan" in a lacy stitch; an "extra-smart" beret, sweater, and scarf set; or an "especially charming" jumper suit. The sportswear patterns in *Fleisher's Classic Hand Knits for Men and*

Historical Pattern
1930s Baby Soaker

Reprinted from The Farmer's Wife, *March 1939.*

Both mothers and babies like these simply-made knitted wool panties. Mothers like them because they are easy to make and wash and they are adequate protection when the baby goes partying afternoons. The baby likes them because they are porous and so allow ventilation.

This is how they are made:

Materials: 1 (2 oz.) ball sport yarn — used for bathing suits, hosiery, etc.

2 (No. 4) needles.

Pattern: Cast on 130 stitches.

Knit 2, purl 2 for 1 inch.

Knit 1, y. o. (yarn over), knit 1; purl 2; knit 1, y. o., knit 1; purl 2; continue across row.

Knit 1, knit the y. o. and the next knit stitch together (to get rid of the extra "yarn over" stitch); purl 2; knit 1, knit the y. o. and the knit stitch together, purl 2. Continue across row. (This again gives you a "knit 2, purl 2 set-up.") This makes the heading.

Knit 2, purl 2 for ½ inch more.

Knit 1 plain row.

Knit garter stitch (knit hack and forth across garment, making every row a knit row — no purling, for rest of garment.

Knit *each* row to the last 3 stitches — then knit 3rd and 2nd st. together and knit last stitch.

This forms the garment into a V shape. Continue until no stitches remain.

Bring edges of top border together and sew down 3½ inches from top. Sew peak into place. Crochet a draw string, knotted at ends, 30 inches long of double thread, and run through heading at top.

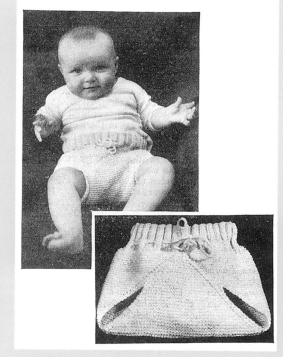

Mothers — and their babies — liked practical, economical hand-knit wool baby pants or "soakers." Soakers provided adequate protection and were porous enough for good ventilation. "Does he like his knitted pants? What do you think?" *The Farmer's Wife*, March 1939.

A Stunning Suit for Any Small Boy

"A Sweater for Babykins, A Stunning suit for Any Small Boy." Economical knits for children could also have good design. "Could there possibly be anything sweeter than the tiny white sweater, with its border decoration of rambler roses?" asked designer Clara E. Herlitzius. She praised the little sweater and knickers set as "the most intriguing little ensemble ever." *Needlecraft*, October 1930.

Women (Volume 43, 1936) included men's wool cardigans, cabled pullovers, vests, socks, sport gloves, and mittens. For women, there were twin sweater sets and simple pullovers — in Fleisher wool, angora, or cashmere — that fell just below the natural waistline. Styles were exactly right for sports and leisure, and patterns included gauge measurements.[210]

Knitting for the home often conformed to the popular Colonial Revival movement with roots in a distant past that valued old-fashioned styles. knit-lace edgings and insertions on pillowcases and table linens suited the look. An occasional knit-lace doily pattern challenged experienced knitters. The most famous knit for the home was perhaps the counterpane pattern known as the Coolidge bedspread, knit by Mrs. Coolidge. She allowed *Good Housekeeping* to reprint the pattern for the bedspread, knit in squares, in pattern book number 37, available on order for 28¢.[211]

More Yarns, More Knitting Needles
Hand knitting proved one of the few Depression-resistant industries during the 1930s. Knitters bought yarn from department stores or by mail order. The number of yarn manufacturers swelled from about ten to an estimated one hundred and fifty. Among the major players were Fleisher Yarn Company, James Lees & Sons, Bernhard Ulmann, Emile Bernat & Sons, and William H. Horstmann. In September 1936, Britain's Coats & Clark first sold wool knitting yarn — Red Heart — in the United States. Previously,

Coats & Clark sold only cotton threads to American handcrafters, but thanks to the knitting craze, manufacturing wool yarn in the United States became profitable. The Spool Cotton Company marketed Red Heart yarn, driving sales with pattern books for fashionable projects.[212]

Yarn companies enticed knitters with new yarns in new colors, backed by hundreds of thousands of promotional dollars poured into advertising. Bernat alone marketed an estimated sixty yarns, each in fifty different colors. One yarn shop alone offered 135 varieties of yarn in all manner of textures, from chunky yarns knit on large needles to delicate silks, textural tweeds, and rayon boucles.[213] McCutcheon on Fifth Avenue in New York City advertised in *The New York Times* that its special purchase of English viyella yarn for sweater and skirt ensembles would "supply the constant demand" of its customers.[214] Even the down-to-earth 1936 Sears, Roebuck & Company Golden Jubilee Catalog offered eighteen varieties of wool, angora, and rayon yarns in as many as twenty-five colors.

Yarn and knitting needle companies also reaped rewards in knitting accessories. In addition to celluloid, steel, and bone needles, *Fortune* magazine listed a variety of devices: "knitting gauges, stitch counters, one-armed chairs for knitters, and knitting bags that, when opened, unfold legs to stand on."[215] Inventors patented new knitting needles: straight needles with grooves behind the points that prevented yarn from slipping off (1938); and circular needles with detachable points (1935); with a rawhide connecting piece (1937); and with point ends that plugged together when not in use (1937). Nan Gilpin patented a knitting method that incorporated elastic yarns to prevent sagging (1936). In 1940, H. S. Kohler received a patent for knitting needles marked in inches to measure knitting length, and in 1941 C. G. Albino patented a knitting needle with a hook that swiveled out to pull up dropped stitches.

Men Who Knit
Women could not claim exclusive rights on knitting during the 1930s. All sixty salesmen at the Boye Needle Company were said to have mastered knitting fundamentals.[216] Across America, newspapers carried stories about men and boys who knit, influenced perhaps by photographs of the Prince of Wales and Prince George of England wielding knitting needles.

At Columbia University, the Knita Nata Nu fraternity posed knitting for a newspaper photo, and Dudley McCully of Pittsburgh won a $10 prize for his hand-knit dress. A former hockey star opened a needlework shop in Massachusetts and taught knitting lessons.[217] A sixteen-year-old boy placed fourteenth among three thousand entries in a New York City knitting competition. On the Boston Common, a man

College co-eds favored twin sets — here knit in angora — and slipovers finely knit in cashmere yarn and paired with hand-knit skirts that were still worn quite long in 1936. *Fleisher's Classic Hand Knits for Men and Women*, 1936.

Bucilla sold jiffy-knit sweater kits in different sizes to knit for children. Choice of colors: white, self-blue, navy, salmon-rose, and maize. *Needle Arts*, 1936.

Columbia Bouclette Suit No. 300. The collar and cardigan are a *trompe l'oeil* effect knit with bouclé yarn, the small dots in orange. The pattern does not specify gauge but calls for casting on 124 stitches for the back of the sweater, 410 stitches for the skirt. Columbia assured readers that, for a few dollars, the average woman could knit a garment that she could not purchase ready-made for less than $100. "Columbia Bouclette and Columbia Instructions are as nearly perfect as it is humanly possible to make them." *Misses' and Women's Bouclette Suits*, 1932.

Right: "New Needle a Boon to Knitters." Bucilla patented its Sure Fit Circular Steel Knitting Needle with an exclusive new feature used to measure knitting at any stage. The knitter slipped work in progress off the needle onto a flexible cord stored within the needle, measured the fit, and then put the stitches back onto the needles. *Needle Arts*, 1936.

Mending yarn, 1930s.

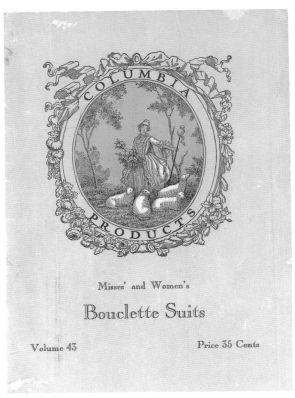

Misses' and Women's

Bouclette Suits

Volume 43   Price 35 Cents

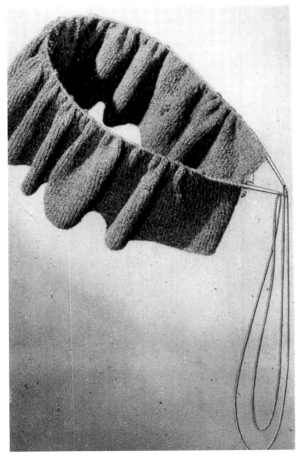

"outknitted 100 perspiring women" while they all knitted and purled away on a giant flag. The two star knitters in Francelia Dockstader's Salvation Army knitting class were both men; Elmer Hartin took his knitting everywhere, and Aagie Hensen saw no reason men should not knit. And a knitter identified only as a "genial, big-hearted man" worked on his fourth sweater to donate to the unemployed to wear while hunting for a job out in the cold. Both boys and girls attended knitting classes at one department store in the South. The knitting instructor reported that boys took as much interest as the girls and, in fact, found that boys were "not distracted from their knitting as often as a girl and will have the patience to finish the garment."[218]

Fashion Revues, Sales, and Contests
The knitting fashion show was the darling of yarn marketing strategies during the decade. Yarn manufacturers sponsored and organized fashion shows,

Historical Pattern
1930s Daphne Scarf

This pattern comes from Needlecraft magazine, August 1934.

1. Slip the 1st stitch, * knit 2 together; repeat from * across row.
2. Knit the 1st stitch, * take up the loop which lies between the stitch just knitted and the next one, pass the wool twice around the needle and draw through the stitch as if for knitting in the usual way, work a double twist in the same way in the next stitch on the needle, * and repeat from * to * all across, knitting the last stitch in the usual way in order to produce a tight border.
3. Knit across, taking the long loop and dropping the smaller one all across row. You will now have the correct number of stitches on the needle again.
4. Purl across.

The Daphne Sports Ensemble included a sleeveless sweater, beret, and triangular scarf in a fancy stitch.

Knitted Finger Bowl Doilies. Depression-era knitters could spruce up their homes with new sets of doilies. *Needlecraft,* April 1934.

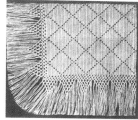

The knitter not up to the more complex Coolidge bedspread could settle for a simpler counterpane knit in strips of garter or stockinette stitch, designed by Christine Ferry and Flora Deuschle. *Needlecraft,* March 1935.

Left: Everyone seemed to be knitting bedspreads that suited the popular Colonial Revival style. Mrs. Grace Coolidge allowed *Good Housekeeping* magazine to copy her famous bedspread pattern, knit in squares and sewn together. *Good Housekeeping,* September 1936.

complete with models, designers, and hand-knit fashions, that toured the nation and sold yarn as well.[219] Rankin's of Santa Ana, California, held a fashion revue right on the floor of their needlework department, with two knitting instructors on hand. Well before the show, the instructors invited their top ten knitting customers to model their own knit dresses and later displayed the outfits in the store's windows. Gordon Cizek, buyer for Rankin's needlework department, reported a "spurt in yarn sales" that was "gratifying, indeed."[220] The New York Store in Moline, Illinois, presented a fashion revue of knit garments once a day for an entire week. "Store girls" were models, directed by a fashion stylist provided by the yarn manufacturer. The New York Store's advertising manager considered fashion revues the main reason that knitting and yarn sales continued to grow "with absolutely no sign of waning interest."[221]

A cabled white sweater suited the college man look. *Fleisher's Classic Hand Knits for Men and Women*, 1936.

The Emporium in Jackson, Mississippi, held knitting fashion revues twice annually in its knitting studio, attended by the yarn manufacturer's representative. Inevitably, fashion shows featured more knit dresses than sweaters; a knit dress required twenty-eight to thirty skeins of yarn, while a sweater only needed six or seven skeins.[222]

Advertised sales and special displays also spurred yarn sales. The Kresge Department Store in Newark, New Jersey, sold nearly five thousand balls of mill-end yarn at 16¢ each during a special advertised event. At Rhodes Department Store in Tacoma, Washington, the needlework department grabbed customers with what appeared to be a huge ball of yarn, two feet in diameter, and oversized knitting needles, each four feet long. The display manager had wound soft rope into a huge ball, painted it blue, speared the ball with two wooden stakes painted silver, and suspended it from the ceiling by "substantial chains." Department stores also showcased yarns and fashionable hand knits in coveted window display spaces, each intended to make the customer want to knit. The display manager at Rich's in Atlanta, Georgia, wrote "We're Stringing You" in clothesline rope against an electric blue background in a window display of hand-knit dresses, sweaters, and suits.[223]

Knitting contests meant free entertainment and fabulous prizes for Depression-era knitters. And the contests were free publicity for the knitting industry. The *St. Louis Globe-Democrat* reported a contest in which 698 hand-knit sweaters competed for 175 prizes, including an all-expenses-paid airliner trip to California (first place), a two-season hat wardrobe (tenth place), and kits for making a knitting bag (forty-eighth to one hundred and fiftieth places). In another contest, society grande dames served as prestigious jurors. Mrs. James Roosevelt, Grand Duchess Marie of Russia, and a *Women's Wear Daily* fashion editor selected winners from among three thousand hand-knit dresses sent to judging headquarters in New York's Waldorf-Astoria Hotel. First prize was a round-trip, all-expenses-paid railroad vacation to Hollywood. Other prizes included fur coats, perfume, Maidenform undergarments, and jewelry. In Tacoma, Rhodes Department Store invited each knitter who purchased yarn to enter its needlework department's knitting contest. More than one hundred knitters entered coats, suits, and dresses in the contest juried by faculty from a local college, and seven knitters were awarded yarn as prizes. Miss Catherine Ewing, Rhodes needlework buyer, reported that the "knitting vogue . . . shows no real sign of waning."[224]

Knitting Instructors

Needlework departments across the nation relied on staff knitting instructors to teach novice and expert

FLEISHER'S

Classic Hand Knits

VOL·43   FOR MEN AND WOMEN   20¢ (IN U.S.A)

Yarn manufacturers published knitting manuals with patterns tailored to suit every yarn texture and taste in clothing style. *Fleisher's Classic Hand Knits for Men and Women*, 1936.

knitters, adapt patterns, and sell yarn. Instruction from the kindly knitting advisor was free with yarn purchase. Knitting instructors helped prevent the badly knit dress or dreaded sweater failures — the worst possible advertisements for knitting and yarn.[225] Major yarn companies brought instructors to cities for specialized training. The graduation ceremony for new Bachelors of Knitting and Crocheting amazed one observer:

> Nearly a thousand super-knitters and high-powered crocheters recently went home from schools in New York, Chicago and San Francisco, carrying the very last word in knitting and purling to a breathless world. Right this minute in a thousand towns they are revealing the secrets of moss stitch and shell stitch, of the tricky — but not too tricky — cable stitch for sport sweaters, the widely adaptable stockinette rib and the knitted raglan sleeve. . . . No wonder the national demand for knitting instruction is a clamorous bass to the busy clicking of needles you hear when you put your ear to the ground."[226]

At Zahn's Department Store, Mrs. Gluck instructed neophytes and expert knitters alike: "When you buy the makings of a sweater, knitted dress or suit, you submit your measurements and Mrs. Gluck will make up complete instructions for you, so it's bound to fit, much to your surprise. A wide selection of colors and yarns at various prices." Advertising manager

Not *everyone* who picked up needles and yarn during the 1930s fell in love with knitting. Cover illustration by Mary Highsmith. *Home Arts Needlecraft*, February 1928.

"Top Rank in Smart Styling." A "jiffy-made" suit for the less-patient knitter called for larger needles and yarn knitting to a gauge of 6 stitches to the inch. *Needlecraft*, November 1935.

Swagger Frocks for Hand Knitting

NEW MODELS
BECOMING STYLES

"Swagger Frocks for Hand Knitting." Yarn companies organized fashion shows with hand knits, inevitably with more suits and dresses than sweaters. A knit dress or suit required considerably more yarn than a sweater — especially the longer skirts still in style in 1936. These suits were knit in a popular Bear Brand Twinkle Crepe, Angele Crepe, and fine Bucilla Shetland floss. *Needle Arts*, 1936.

Mr. Beacham of the Emporium believed the knitting instructor "is the biggest single factor of all. She must have a fine personality and know the ins and outs of knitting thoroughly." Similarly, Bernice Facer, knitting instructor for the W. H. Wright & Sons Company of Ogden, Utah, attributed the 45 percent gain in yarn sales achieved in just four months to good teaching: "Proper instruction is the big thing, and I attend the knitting school offered by the manufacturer of yarns we sell at every opportunity. When I started, I don't believe there were four women in Ogden interested in knitting, but I attended the manufacturer's school, found out how to give instructions and interest immediately increased."[227] Demand for knitting instruction was so great at one Southern store that the needlework department built a half-round table seating twenty-four students; this arrangement saved steps for the weary knitting teachers. Some college girls unable to find jobs during the Depression became knitting instructors or coordinated knitting style shows around the country.[228]

Throughout the unprecedented prosperity of the 1920s and the depth of the Great Depression during the 1930s, Americans kept knitting. The U.S. economy as a whole would not truly begin to recover until September 1939, when Europe once again plunged into war. Knitting would soar again to the forefront of society when the United States entered World War II.

The Naomi E. Cleaves School of Knitting in Hollywood, California, promised that after ten easy lessons in its Home Study Knitting Course a knitter could make anything from gloves to suits. Graduates were in demand for demonstrations at department stores and fashion studios. Enrollees also received a free Screen Star and Studio Fashion Bulletin. *Needlecraft*, November 1924.

The Knit-Pick was ideal for 1930s knitters on the go.

Knit-Pick
the ideal gadget for all crocheting and knitting fans.

Chapter Nine
An Army of Knitters

Most Americans, including President Franklin Roosevelt, hoped to avoid entering World War II. Painfully aware of German, Italian, and Japanese military expansion, the United States sent aid to Britain with its lonely stand against Nazi Germany. The Japanese airborne strike against Pearl Harbor on December 7, 1941, rested the decision, and America declared war within the week. The United States' entry into the war initiated a mobilization of all American resources as never before. A sense of urgency and national purpose led to extraordinary military and civilian productivity. The numbers were stunning. The American military built its forces from 800,000 to 9 million between December 1940 and June 1943, with forces peaking at 12.3 million in 1945. The labor force shortage brought on by the war turned Depression-era unemployment

Life magazine told Americans to knit when they asked what they could do for the war effort. The knitter pictured was Peggy Tippett, who learned to knit while at Notre Dame College in Baltimore. She was now knitting a V-neck sweater for the Citizens Committee for the Army and Navy.

on its head. Domestic war industries added millions of civilian workers needed to equip the military and sustain the home front. Civilians built 296,000 planes, 102,000 tanks, and 88,000 ships, and their efficiency only increased as the war progressed. The first Liberty ship built took 196 days to deliver; that time was cut to 27 days by 1943.

Women supported the war effort in the military and on the home front. Nearly four hundred thousand women served in the newly founded branches of the armed forces, including the army (Women's Army Corp, WAC), navy (Women Accepted for Voluntary Emergency Service, WAVES), coast guard (*Semper Paratus*, Always Ready, Women's Reserve, SPARS), air force (Women's Air Force Service Pilots, WASP), and marines (Women's Reserves), plus the army and navy Nurse Corps. Jobs for women ranged from clerical workers to photographers, from air traffic controllers to mechanics, and from medical technicians to flight instructors. Women saw active duty on the American continent and overseas.

Opposite Page: America's knitting army rallies on the sidewalk on Manhattan's East Side. Mrs. Paulie Wetstein, center, and Mrs. Sadie Schatt were making sweaters for the Red Cross while talking with Mrs. Wetstein's daughter, Ray Flicker, and admiring her new babe.

Young and old alike were knitting for the soldiers. Mrs. Myrtle Orsbee of East Montpelier, Vermont, knit sweaters in her front-porch rocking chair in 1942. Meanwhile in Moreno Valley, New Mexico, a rancher's daughter puzzled over casting on stitches for her knitting, 1943. (Office of War Information, Library of Congress)

Alwena Evans encouraged American knitters to make hand-knit comforts for children in Wales. Even before the United States entered the war, knitters felt called to relieve suffering among refugees. *The American Home*, January 1942.

On the home front, women were defense workers, service wives, farmers, mothers, homemakers, and knitters — most women shouldered several wartime roles at once.[229] Together they counted rationing coupons and strived toward victory. Civilians turned over scraps of metal, rubber, paper, and rags to salvage committees under the Salvage for Victory Program to keep war factories running. Even old golf balls, football bladders, and rubber toys could keep trucks and tanks in action, as did carrying home shopping instead of using store delivery. Americans saved every bit of oil and fat from cooking to donate toward nitroglycerin for explosives. They raised Victory Gardens and shared canning equipment after manufacturers stopped making pressure cookers. Americans conserved their precious wartime woolens in light of wartime wool shortages.[230] And throughout the war, Americans kept knitting.

The U.S. Knits Again

In November 1941, knitting made the cover of *Life* magazine: "To the great American question 'What can I do to help the war effort? The commonest answer yet found is 'Knit.'" *Life* printed knitting instructions and a regulation military sweater pattern. Why hand knitting for the war effort? Hand knits spared the expense and deterioration of industrial textile machinery, and knitters claimed hand-knit socks wore better than machine-knit socks. Knitting was also considered therapeutic at the front lines and on the home front, as *The New York Times* reported: "The propaganda effect of hand knitting cannot be estimated in terms of hard cash, but it is considerable. A sweater for a bluejacket. A helmet for a flying cadet, made by some devoted women in a small town far from the war, is sure to arouse interest in the navy or air force among the friends of the woman doing the knitting. And she herself feels that she has an active part in this vast conflict; she is not useless, although she can do nothing else to help win the war."[231]

"All I said was, 'Why don't you do something about the war, too, mother?'"

Knitting symbolized support for the American war effort, and knitters seemed to appear everywhere. *Business Week* noted: "Hardly a woman — from the Park Avenue debutant sunning herself at Palm Beach to the hard-working farmer's wife in her Iowa kitchen — feels really comfortable about sitting down for a few minutes without an R.A.F. [Royal Air Force] helmet or a refugee's sweater to work on." In New York City, Alwena Evans rallied families of Welsh descent to join a knitting club called "Handknits for the Children in Wales." Within a few months, forty-one branches sprang up around the country. Assembly lines of knitters made sweaters, caps, mittens, socks, underwear, and blankets for the British War Relief Society to ship to Wales.[232] Claire Trevor wore a Red Cross uniform and posed with her knitting in a promotional photo. Ginger Rogers knit between scenes on a movie set, and popular movies showed stars knitting, among them Risë Stevens in *The Chocolate Soldier* (1941).

Photographs in the Office of War Information Photograph Collection include knitters. John Collier photographed young girls knitting in Fort Kent, Maine, and a rancher's daughter knitting during a poker party at George Turner's ranch. Lee Russell captured a picture of a Tulare County, California, girl scout knitting at a farm workers' camp. Helen Fritz photographed Mrs. Myrtle Ormsbee, widowed mother of farmer Charles Ormsbee, knitting sweaters for the Red Cross in East Montpelier, Vermont. A poster featuring knitting needles and yarn — "Remember Pearl Harbor/Purl Harder" — won a place in the Works Progress Administration (WPA)

remember
PEARL
HARBOR

PURL
HARDER

Posters rallied Americans to wartime causes. Artists who worked for the government-sponsored Works Progress Administration (WPA) pioneered silkscreen printing techniques that streamlined color poster production. (Library of Congress)

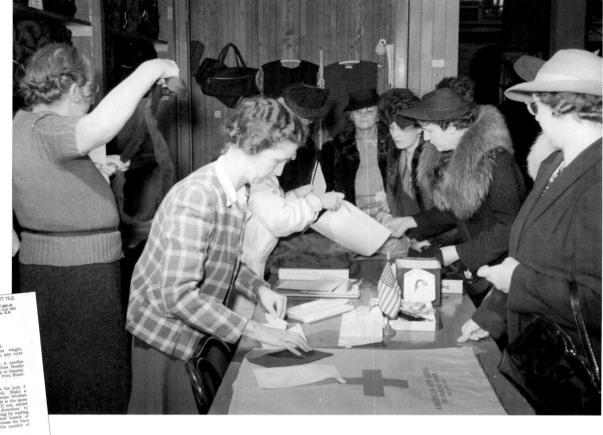

Red Cross volunteers distribute knitting supplies in San Francisco in December 1941. (Library of Congress)

CHILDREN'S MITTENS
(Sweater-weight yarn).

Equipment Needed:
Yarn — Sweater weight, 4/8, 1 to 2 ounces, any color not too bright.
Needles—Use 4. needles to fit the Red Cross Needle Gauge for mittens or beanies. Gauges available from Headquarters.
Scale.
6 stitches to the inch. 8 rows to the inch. Make a sample to determine whether or not your scale is the same as that given. If not, adjust the knitting directions to your own knitting by casting on fewer or more stitches, depending on whether you knit loosely or tightly. The sample of your knitting is also necessary in the number of may vary slightly, making adjustments necessary in the number of stitches cast on.
General Instructions:
Always join new yarn at end of row. Never knot or splice yarn in

These official American Red Cross instructions for children' mittens, knit in three sizes, was one of many patterns for soldiers and refugees.

Knitters were supplied with these Red Cross tags to sew onto their knit items during World War II.

1942 war poster competition. Knitters appeared in advertisements for everything from Cannon percale sheets, General Motors insurance, Solo hair accessories, Philip Morris cigarettes, and Cone Velvelette flannel, to Quaker Oats, *McCall's* magazine, Gripper Fasteners, and Listerine antiseptic for dandruff.[233] The knitter had become a patriotic icon that showed advertisers supported the war effort.

Two notable patents for innovative knitting needles were intended to enhance the knitter's efficiency. In 1944, Samuel Shapiro of Brooklyn, New York, received a patent for his illuminated knitting needle intended for use during black-outs or in dim light. The light from a tiny bulb housed in a special unit at the blunt end of the needle was transmitted through a Lucite shaft and out the tapered working tip. In 1945 Henrietta Fosse, Jean Palou, and Louis Lacombe of France patented a transparent knitting needle marked with gauge measurements.

Rules of Knitting Etiquette
Although knitting meant patriotism, knitting in public generated a degree of controversy — perhaps due to the sheer number of knitters. In response to a reader annoyed with ever-present knitters, etiquette guru Emily Post addressed the "thoughtless [who] may have assumed that problems of etiquette are held in abeyance in wartime." Mrs. Post's rules:

- Do not wave long or shiny needles about in the air.
- Do not flap your elbows "as thought you were a bird learning to fly." (This is very bad form: shun it like the wrong fork in the fish course.)
- Do not leave your wool in a bag at your feet and keep hauling it up every so often with arm thrust up higher than your head.[234]

To the reader who complained about women who knit during a lecture, she recommended that a knitter ask permission from the speaker beforehand. A *New York Times* columnist who considered this conflict between knitting etiquette and wartime need suggested that the "question that should have been put, perhaps, is whether any speaking should be permitted while women are knitting."[235]

First Lady, First Knitter
Eleanor Roosevelt had loved working in a canteen for the Red Cross during World War I, but she was not allowed to travel to Europe and help with refugee relief. By 1940, however, she was the first lady and had four sons in the military. Yet she yearned to be more useful. She wanted to work with Red Cross refugee relief efforts in Western European nations overrun by German troops. She longed to serve hot meals to refugee children and hand out medical supplies and warm clothing to survivors in Europe's war-ridden

Regional Knitting on the Home Front: Washington State

By Paula Becker

Paula Becker is a staff historian for www.historylink.org, the online encyclopedia of Washington state history. She has written extensively on social history, including war-effort knitting in Washington. Excerpt from historylink.org. reprinted with permission.

Around the nation, Red Cross auxiliary groups vied with each other to prove who could knit the most, the fastest. Washington knitters were among those who quickly jumped to action. Less than a month after Pearl Harbor, Seattle's Ravenna/Green Lake/Roosevelt neighborhoods alone had fifteen different groups churning out knitwear. Numbers were similar across the city.

Church basements, school lunchrooms, and members-only societies throughout Washington all had knitters busily clicking their needles. The *Bellevue American* opined on January 8, 1942, "Red Cross sewing and knitting should be part of every woman's life." Anyone who took home Red Cross yarn and then procrastinated was quickly brought into line. "Red Cross Knitting Must Be Turned In Now," trumpeted the *Vashon News-Record* on March 2, 1944.

Like meat, fats, sugar, and other goods, wool was in short supply. The Seattle Red Cross responded to this challenge ingeniously; as *The Seattle Times* reported on June 3, 1942: "Red Cross leaders are being trained . . . in the old-fashioned arts of carding and spinning yarn from wool . . . enabling the workers to produce articles for the fighting forces at a savings of more than $3.00 a pound in original cost of wool. Arts and Crafts leaders from the Works Projects Administration . . . are teaching the Red Cross workers the technique of spinning."

The output of these groups was prodigious: In the town of Enumclaw, a group of knitters met from one to four o'clock each Tuesday afternoon. After fortifying themselves with light refreshments they picked up their needles. Between January 1, 1943, and March 9, 1944, this group knitted 65 sleeveless army vests, 19 women's service sweaters, 25 army helmets, 3 navy helmets, 1 navy vest, 4 army scarves, 10 heavy coat sweaters, 4 afghans, 56 children's sweaters, 8 turtleneck sweaters, 5 pairs navy gloves, and 1 navy scarf.

The Burien newspaper reported that Three Tree Point Knitters in Seattle had "thirty knitters knitting all the time." In three months this group made 244 knitted garments, representing 4,290 work hours. *The Seattle Times* interviewed Mrs. Ella V. Martin, an eighty-seven-year-old Seattle knitter, and noted she was "one of the champion knitters in the University Presbyterian Church Red Cross group, having completed 64 sweaters and 17 pairs of socks since the beginning of the Second World War. . . . She is knitting because she has a nephew in the Seabees, and because of 'all the boys out there fighting.'"

By 1943, Fort Lewis Station Hospital near Tacoma was the largest army hospital in the United States, with beds to accommodate 3,806 patients. Thirty-six thousand wounded soldiers a month were being shipped back from overseas, many destined for Fort Lewis. Local Red Cross chapters supplied knitted comfort items for these soldiers, who were also encouraged to knit as occupational therapy.

Puget Sound knitters also knit wool helmets that fit under army-issue hard-shelled helmets worn by the soldiers who manned anti-aircraft guns installed at high points throughout the Puget Sound region. These guns, on sandbagged platforms ringed with powerful listening devices, were maintained around the clock throughout the war. "Can You Knit?" asked Seattle's *Northwest Veteran Newsletter* on January 3, 1942. "There are two thousand knitted helmets that are waiting to be made to cover the heads and ears of the many gallant soldiers who are guarding Seattle these cold nights from enemy planes and sabotage, *while you and you* are sleeping in warm beds . . . they are needed *now* not tomorrow. If these soldiers put off the task of guarding Seattle, how long would we last?" The prospect of cold-eared soldiers dropping their anti-aircraft guns for want of wool helmets may have been exaggerated, but Seattle's vulnerable coastal position created palpable fear of imminent attack among local residents.

A long woolen thread of hope, prayer, fear, and patriotism linked Washington home front knitters with the soldiers who received their handiwork. These knit goods, imbued with anxious good wishes, were also fated to suffer with the men who wore them. Home front knitters could not help knowing that their carefully crafted socks and sweaters might be part of a soldier's final uniform and end with him, bloodstained, far from home.

Lorraine crepe yarn, 1940s.

cities. Red Cross President Norman Cross informed her the times were too dangerous for the first lady to travel in Europe. In 1942, after two years of pleading, Franklin Roosevelt agreed to send her to England on an extended inspection tour. Characteristically, Eleanor was eager to be out among the people. At the Red Cross Club in London she met hundreds of American soldiers who complained they had no warm woolen socks, only thin cotton socks that blistered their feet. The following day Eleanor inquired about socks to General Eisenhower, whose quartermaster located and distributed 2.5 million pairs of wool socks. Whether or not they were hand-knit socks is lost to history.[236]

An inveterate knitter, Mrs. Roosevelt launched Red Cross knitting for war support at a Knit for Defense tea held at the Waldorf-Astoria in New York City on September 31, 1941. Americans designated her "First Knitter" in addition to first lady. Roosevelt carried her ubiquitous knitting bag with her during the war, while serving as a tireless advocate for Japanese-Americans, blacks in the military, and women in industrial war work.

Knitting for the Red Cross

Following in the footsteps of America's first lady, an army of civilian volunteers knit their bit and donated staggering numbers of hand-knit clothing and bandages. Before Pearl Harbor, knitters were already making men's sweaters for Bundles for Britain and for Russian and European refugee relief. In 1940, Honolulu firefighters knit sweaters, socks, and mittens for soldiers on the European front.[237] Under War Production Board designation, the American Red Cross supplied wool and knitting patterns suited to the U.S. military, its allies, and civilian war victims. Knitters turned out regulation garb like scarves, mufflers, hats, vests, socks, mittens, sweaters, helmet liners, and fingerless gloves for firing rifles — acceptable *only* in olive drab or navy blue yarn — and also knit walking cast toe socks, caps for bandaged heads, and men's coat sweaters for injured, convalescing soldiers.[238] Knitters also made fifteen- to twenty-foot-long bandages in garter stitch, rolled and sterilized for medical use.

Military uniforms took priority for wool, one of many products the War Production Board meted out under strict quotas during wartime. The Red Cross, however, was a top priority and was reported to have bought $2.225 million of yarn in 1941. Knitters could also buy yarn for a regulation military sweater at stores

Groups of school children were prolific knitters during the war. Bill Dickman, Jack Rosen, Melvin Sinykin, Leonard Strouse, and Arvin Zaikaner knit at Groveland School in St. Paul, Minnesota, in 1941. (Minnesota Historical Society)

for a discounted price of $1.85. Knitters could ply patriotic red, white, and blue knitting needles supplied by the Red Cross and other relief organizations, perhaps to the tune of one of many wartime songs about knitting: "Each Stitch Is a Thought of You, Dear," "Pick Up Your Knitting," "Knit, Knit, Knit," "Knit One Purl Two," "Knit, Sister, Knit," and "Knit a Kiss, Purl a Prayer." Many women knit for their husbands first, though, and then for the Red Cross.[239]

Knitting chapters large and small generated impressive quantities of hand knits. In 1941, the Department of Recreation in Manitowoc, Wisconsin, encouraged a dozen or so children, ages seven to fifteen, to knit for the Red Cross. After activities director Lucille O'Connell introduced knitting needles and instructions, the little girls turned fifty-seven skeins of donated Red Cross yarn into twenty-four sweaters during the first two weeks. The boys rolled yarn into balls and braided cords that tied sweaters at the neck. The Red Cross found all the children's first sweaters acceptable, and their pace picked up as their knitting skills improved with practice. The numbers of hand knits added up from individuals and small groups alike; in 1941 the Citizen Committee for the army and navy asked for, and received, 1 million standard khaki army sweaters. By March 1944, eighty-seven-year-old Seattle resident Ella V. Martin had knit sixty-four sweaters and seventeen pairs of socks.[240] Co-eds also knit for the war, among them the Ladies' Auxiliary for Red Cross Service (LARCS) members at the University of Washington and sorority sisters at the University of Arizona.

Yarn manufacturers published knitting manuals with patriotic themes to encourage knitting — and boost yarn sales.

Standardized knitting patterns, such as this balaclava, assured their usefulness for soldiers, airmen, and sailors.

When the United States entered the war, not everyone knew how to knit. Knitting instructors were critically important to the success of wartime knitting, as in this needlework class in Winona, Minnesota, in 1940. (Minnesota Historical Society)

"Don't Let Them Say: 'We are Forgotten Men!'" — a common theme of World War II pattern books, such as this 1941 book from Wonoco Yarn Co.

sumed vast quantities of yarn for war knitting, manufacturing companies' profits dwindled; they sold yarn to relief agencies and stores at deeply discounted prices. Retailers were forced to sell at further discounts to compete with free or at-cost yarn distributed by relief agencies. Still, business saw opportunity knock and knew that "knitting-wool manufacturers must feel like the pick-and-shovel prospector who struck the mother lode," as *Business Week* reported.[241]

Yarn manufacturers poured money into the promotion of non-war knitting. The Bernhard Ulmann Company sold more than half the branded knitting yarns in the country: Fleisher, Bear Brand, and Bucilla yarns. Ulmann's publicity consultant Claire Wolff now traveled to Hollywood, photographed movie stars in hand-knit sweaters, and jumpstarted the fad of knitting for men. Ulmann assured retailers of an impending "gold rush" in yarn sales; Ulmann, with seventy-seven years of experience in wartime and postwar yarn sales, was positioned to provide the yarn. Lily Mills Company of Shelby, North Carolina, offered free direction leaflets for sweaters and household items with purchase of its new cotton yarn that knit like wool. The American Thread Company of New York promoted yarn sales with *Star Variety Show* pattern books featuring the latest original designs for charm-

Selling Yarn

Women with wartime defense jobs had money to spend, and many had long hours to fill while husbands served overseas. Millions of women occupied their time knitting for war relief. Yarn manufacturers and retailers looked at the impressive numbers of freshly minted knitters and saw new customers for non-war yarn, needles, and patterns. Although knitters coning knit gifts by Cecilia Vanek. Similarly, in 1941 the James Lees and Sons Company of Pennsylvania published *Hand Knits for Men in the Service*, with patterns for cardigan and pullover sweaters, stockings, wristlets, gloves, mittens, helmets, vests, and caps.[242] Also in 1941 the Spool Cotton Company of New York published new pattern books to help sell yarn. *Knit for Defense* included directions patterned after regulation specifications for service men's sweaters and wool accessories.[243] The *Learn How Book* had illustrated knitting instructions and patterns for a classic pullover, cardigan, rib stitch hat, mittens, and anklets to knit with Chadwick's Red Heart knitting worsted, Germantown, wool floss, or baby wool.[244] The Royal Society, Inc., of New York distributed Patons and Baldwins Beehive knitting wool and knitting manuals with practical patterns for home and family. Department stores, the primary retailers of knitting yarn at this time, welcomed the publicity sent out by the manufacturers.

Department stores sold knitting yarn using familiar strategies learned during the 1930s knitting craze: fashion shows, knitting contests, new yarns and patterns, and especially free instruction with yarn purchase. One department store capitalized on the growing popularity of knitting in 1941 with quick turnovers of yarn, therefore nothing in the store for more than six months.[245] In 1944, stores in military regions learned that wives of service men were good knitting customers. The J. A. Kirven Company of Columbus, Georgia, launched a publicity campaign to attract military wives to knit for themselves, their husbands, and — ever more frequently with the ensuing baby boom — the "anticipated bundle from Heaven." The prospective mother was an especially good customer, given the shortages of layette items in the baby department. Kirven's attracted new moms with advertising copy that read, "Since the doctor said yes, your next step is Kirven's knitting department . . . there to select the softest, loveliest yarn and begin knitting for the new arrival."[246] With rubber for waterproof baby pants rationed, new mothers knit wool baby "soakers" by the score. A 1943 *Bucilla Wonder-Knit* knitting manual provided patterns for soakers and many other practical projects for only 10¢.[247]

Knitting instructors held a prominent role in keeping yarn departments profitable. In 1941, the art needlework section at P. A. Bergner's in Peoria, Illinois, hired a year-round knitting instructor to give free lessons, in particular for women involved in the Bundles for Britain movement. Bergner's buyer and knitting instructor Miss Pittard welcomed all ages, from the high school girl knitting herself a sweater to older women wanting to keep their hands busy. In 1945, Pittard was still actively recruiting new knitters with displays of knit garments and new patterns, plus

In spite of clothing restrictions under the dictate of L-85, women remained fashion conscious during the war. Knitters could order patterns and purchase pattern books for the popular close-fitting styles with squared shoulder lines. *The Ladies' Home Journal*, November 1942.

Wartime music such as "Knit One Purl Two" encouraged knitting to show patriotism on the home front.

a large table where women received free instruction.[248] The Oneonta Department Store of Oneonta, New York, arranged a comfy knitting corner where customers could sit and knit while receiving free instruction. At the Oneonta, the needlework department was situated near areas with kitchen gadgets and gifts, which attracted more customers to the knitting wool.[249] In 1942, the Evansville Dry Goods Company of Evansville, Indiana, recognized America's need to knit for the "fighting forces" and did its part to teach knitting by opening a large knitting shop on the balcony of its store. Under the guidance of Mrs. Louise Bibb, who had fourteen years experience, novices learned fundamentals and experienced knitters tackled more difficult problems of advanced techniques.[250]

Knitters offset clothing shortages by knitting their own practical bibs and jackets when babies arrived. Soakers in particular substituted for rubber and elastic. *Bucilla Wonder-knit*, 1943.

Knitwear designer Polly Rosenthal emigrated to the United States and was one of many who created new civilian fashions that stimulated the market for yarn and knitting. *Life* magazine stated, "The call for 1,000,000 Army sweaters is responsible for only part of the knitting boom." *Life*, 1941.

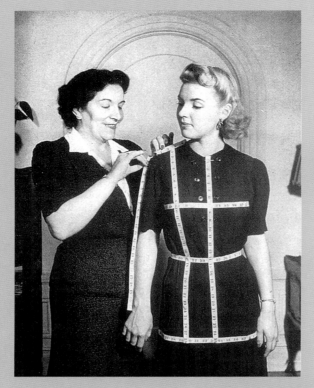

Right: A Mid-Riff Sweater in Red, White, and Blue. The youthful knitter could express her patriotism by knitting sportswear in patriotic colors.

Dress styles with padded shoulders and shorter skirts were "frozen" by the war.

with instructions for teaching needlework, especially knitting, to their students.[251] Teenage girls liked to knit for their boyfriends, *Good Housekeeping* reported. Virginia Bellamy's daughter learned to knit in school, but only knit little sample squares, and she wanted to knit doll clothes. Mrs. Bellamy designed patterns to make outfits for her daughter's dolls from the knit squares and sold directions (6¢) through the *Woman's Home Companion* Service Bureau in New York City. At Stix, Baer and Fuller in St. Louis, Missouri, knitting instructor Elmeda Brown taught a group of forty-five nine- to sixteen-year-olds to knit during Saturday morning classes throughout the summer. She reported that 99 percent of her students completed their knit sweaters by autumn.[252]

Knitting for Fashion and Warmth

Women were fashion conscious during the war, despite shortages and rationing. On March 8, 1942, President Roosevelt established the War Production Board, which issued the L-85 regulations. Manufactured clothing had to conform to codes restricting the use of nylon, rubber, silk, leather, and other materials needed by the military. Civilian clothing used less fabric in styles with shorter hemlines, close-fitting jackets, and plain dresses. Flourishes like trouser cuffs, double-breasted jackets, and extra pockets were considered wasteful and unpatriotic. Government regulations meant basic clothing styles changed little during the war. Hand-knit fashions were one way women could still create fashion in their wardrobes.

Many yarn companies published knitting manuals with patterns for hand-knit socks.

Yarn manufacturers and retailers alike targeted youth as future knitters. The Educational Bureau of the Spool Cotton Company claimed credit for 1.25 million elementary school children who learned to knit in school one year. The Bureau sent monthly news bulletins to thirty thousand home economics teachers

Hollywood movie stars modeled hand-knit sweaters to help yarn companies convince knitters that they, too, could dress like stars.

American households conserved and reused as much as possible, including "reclaimed wool" for children's knit sweaters and caps. Reclaimed wool was a broad term that described either reused or reprocessed wool under the U.S. Wool Products Labeling Act of 1939. *The American Home,* August 1942.

Civilian clothing adopted military touches during the war. This ribbed slip-on sweater was paired with a crocheted cap with "lots of military snap" down to its brass buttons. *The American Home,* February 1943.

Yarn companies, department store retailers, magazines, and designers alike promoted hand knits as elegant, fashionable must-haves for women's wardrobes.[253] "The wardrobe of the smartly dressed woman is not complete unless it includes at least *one* two-piece knitted dress," according to the *Wonoco Journal of Knitting.* The Bernhard Ulmann Company resurrected the glamorous Hollywood/hand knitting connection in a new pattern book, *Movie Star Hand Knits for Men,* in which popular Hollywood stars modeled hand-knit sweaters. A number of influential hand-knit designers fled Europe for the United States, though the rate of immigration had slowed to a crawl — only some twenty-three thousand immigrants arrived during the early 1940s and thirty-eight thousand in 1945. The creativity of designers Polly Rosenthal, Maria Krum, Erica de Menron, and Gizi Alton among others inspired "hand-knit sweaters, caps, gloves, dresses, socks [that] are the latest craze."[254] The Wonoco Yarn Company advised, "America's leading stylists are agreed that the well-dressed woman of today must include hand-knitted clothes in her wardrobe if it is to be complete." Wonoco designated itself America's largest distributor of wool and novelty yarns, and its patterns ran the gamut from women's fashions and baby clothes to afghans for the home and sweaters for the service man. As a bonus, Wonoco "instructresses" would write custom directions for individual measurements — free of charge — for any knitter who purchased any of the "Famous Quality Wonoco Yarns." The *F & K Style Book* advertised styles of "chic new knit wear" for women, free with yarn purchase, and all yarns were made in the United States. An especially helpful company, F & K provided free knitting help from "instructresses" and would reserve yarn for knitters pressed for cash: "If your budget won't allow for all the yarn necessary for a garment, send only money enough for the yarn you need . . . we will save the balance for 30 days until you send for it."[255]

Knitting had its practical side, too. In New Jersey, Elizabeth Ward knit dozens of pairs of mittens while she carpooled to her job in a wartime airplane factory, although she met with mixed success teaching a fellow commuter to knit. Her student, who knit a looser gauge, produced mittens of "heroic proportions."[256] Especially proficient knitters could win prize money for skillful knitting. In 1943, *Woman's Day* magazine sponsored a contest, extolling the versatility of knitting everything from filmy lace to sturdy sweaters. Mrs. D. J. Evans of Dallas, Texas, took home the $100 top prize for her raised-leaf stitch bedspread knit in creamy cotton yarn. The $50 second prize went to Mrs. Alfred Knudtsen of Baltimore for her blue-and-white wool Scandinavian-style cardigan, knit with $4.75 worth of wool yarn.[257]

Knitting was also practical because wooly hand knits warmed youngsters in homes kept cool during winter to conserve heating resources. Pattern books often targeted knitting for babies and small children. Bootees, undershirts, jackets, buntings, caps, and lacy blankets were popular for babies, as were knit dresses and shorts sets for toddler girls and boys. In 1942, the *Ladies' Home Journal* published patterns for "easy-to-knit things that young war brides, expecting their first babies and knitting for the first time, can make. Designed to be practical and beguiling."[258] The many pattern books for socks suggested that hand-knit socks were a popular way to keep feet toasty at home during the war. Pattern books from Botany Woolen Mills, the Jack Frost Yarn Company, and Fleisher's Yarn Company included socks, along with a variety of hand knits for men and boys. Among the multitude of children's woolies knit during wartime, some knitters — and lucky recipients — cared enough about simple mittens to donate them to a collection. In Kenosha, Wisconsin, a maternal grandmother knit mittens before the donor's birth and added the pink after she was born in 1942.

Military needs took priority in the textile industry, which meant shortages of civilian clothing. The *Ladies' Home Journal* recommended schoolgirls take responsibility for their own warm winter wardrobes. "Along with my regular war work, I'm knitting a complete group of accessories for school," said the *Ladies' Home Journal*'s teen advisor. She was knitting matching gloves and hats, plus monogrammed "Sister and I" sweaters that were the "*smartest* (and warmest) accessories in town!"[259] Some magazines printed knitting patterns that promoted judicious use of knitting wool, while others conserved wool by substituting patterns intended for cotton or rayon. Knitters ordered patterns designed to use small amounts of yarn for such practical items as slippers, hats, mittens, and baby clothes. Other patterns used odds and ends of wool in different colors (and even yarn unraveled from sweaters) for

Historical Pattern
World War II U.S. Navy Iceland Sweater

This pattern for a ribbed pull-over with turtle-neck comes from the official U.S. Navy publication, ARC-3F Code AF-60 of May 1942, as approved by the American Red Cross. No photograph of the sweater accompanied the pattern.

Equipment Needed: Yarn: 36 ozs. 4/4 sweater yarn, dark navy blue, for body. 6 ozs. 4/8 sweater yarn, dark navy blue, for ribbing.
Needles: One pair No. 8 needles for body. One pair No. 4 needles for ribbing.

Instructions for Making
Front: Using No. 4 needles and light wool, cast on 96 stitches.

K 1, P 1 for 5½ inches.

Tie in extra heavy wool and change to No. 8 needles.

First row: * K 1, P 1 for 8 sts., K 2 together. Repeat from * to last 2 stitches. K 2 together. (86 sts. now on needle.)

Note: Keep pattern of ribbing even though sometimes in knitting 2 together it brings two knitted or two purled stitches together. Do this throughout the sweater in spite of increasings or decreasings.

Second row: P 1, K 1.

Third row: K 1, P 1.

Fourth row: P 1, K 1. (This gives a "popcorn" border.)

Next row: K 1, P 1.

Repeat this row until work measures 12½ inches from beginning of heavy wool.

Cast off 3 sts. at beginning of next two rows for armholes.

Decrease 1 st. each end of needle every other row three times (74 sts. now on needle).

Work without shaping for 22 rows.

First Shoulder: K 1, P 1 for 30 sts. Turn. Work back and forth on these 30 sts. as follows:

First row: K 1, P 1 across,

Second row: K 1, P 1 to last 3 sts, P 2 together. P 1.

Third row: K 1, P 2 together. Work in pattern to end of row.

Fourth row: K 1, P 1 to last 3 sts. P2 together. P 1.

Fifth row: K 1, P 2 together. Work in pattern to end of row.

Sixth row: K 1, P 1 to last 3 sts. K 2 together. P 1.

Seventh row: Work across in pattern without decreasing.

Eighth row: K 1, P 1 to last 3 sts. K 2 together. P 1.

Work 3 rows without shaping. Bind off these 24 stitches.

Slip first 14 sts. of remaining 44 onto stitch holder or spare needle for front of neck.

Second Shoulder: Join in wool and work on remaining 30 sts. as follows:

First row: K 1, P 1.

Second row: K 1, P 1.

Third row: K 1, P 2 together. Work in pattern to end of row.

Fourth row: Work in pattern to last 3 sts. K 2 together. P 1.

Fifth row: K 1, P 2 together. Work in pattern to end of row,

Sixth row: Work in pattern to last 3 sts. K 2 together. P 1.

Seventh row: K 1, P 2 together. Work in pattern to end of row.

Eighth row: Work in pattern across row.

Ninth row: K 1, P 2 together. Work in pattern to end of row.

Work two rows without shaping. Bind off these 24 stitches.

Back: Work the same as for front until all narrowing after casting off for armholes is completed.

Work without shaping for 6½ inches. Bind off 26 sts. K 1, P 1 for 22 sts.

Bind off remaining 26 sts.

Sleeves: Using No. 4 needles and light wool, cast on 48 stitches. K 1, P 1 for 5½ inches. Tie in heavy wool and using No. 8 needles proceed as follows: Knit 4 *.

Increase once in next stitch, knit 7. Repeat from * to last 4 sts., increase once in next stitch, K 3. (54 sts. now on needle.)

Proceed as follows:

First row: P 1, K 1.

Second row: K 1, P 1.

Third row: P 1, K 1.

Fourth row: K 1, P 1.

Repeat the 4th row, increasing one stitch at each end of needle in the following 6th row and every 6th row thereafter until there are 74 stitches on the needle.

Be especially careful to keep pattern when increasing.

Continue in ribbing (K 1, P 1) without increasing until work measures 20 inches, including cuff. Knit 2 together at each end of every row until 60 sts remain, then cast off 2 sts. at the beginning of every row until 24 sts. remain, then cast off these 24 sts. Work another sleeve in the same manner.

With a damp cloth and warm iron press *carefully*. Sew up right *shoulder seam only*.

Collar: Using No. 4 needles and light wool, with right side of work facing, join in wool and knit up 24 sts. along the left side of neck, K 1, P 1 across the 14 sts. of the front (previously left on stitch holder).

Knit up 24 sts. Along the right side of neck and K 1, P 1 across 22 sts. of the back (left on needle) (84 sts.)

K 1, P 1 on the 84 sts. for 5½ inches.

Bind off *loosely* with a large needle, knitting the knit stitches and purling the purled stitches.

Sew up other shoulder and collar. Sew in sleeves, matching armholes. Sew up sleeves and sides.

Chapter Label should be sewed inside the back at neck of sweater.

Do not start another garment with left-over yarn.

Please return all unused yarn to Chapter.

Wartime Fashions Knit by Hand

Hand-knit dresses and suits dating to the early 1940s. An unknown knitter made these masterful garments. (Courtesy of the Textile Museum, Lowell, Massachusetts.)

Exhibition of knit garments from Mrs. Helen Sakurai's knitting class at the Poston, Arizona, Japanese-American internment camp. Women occupied countless hours knitting during internment. (Gift of William Hiroshi and Helen Shizu Sakurai — Richard, James, Helen, Fred and Florence Block 220-2AB Poston Camp II, Japanese-American National Museum)

patchwork, striped, and argyle designs, an idea perhaps adapted from British knitters. Consumers had less choice in ready-made clothing, and some women knit their own underwear and swimsuits.[260]

Japanese-American Knitters

Photographs of Japanese and Japanese-American knitters during World War II indicate a darker side of wartime knitting. An estimated one hundred and twenty-seven thousand Americans of Japanese descent lived in the United States before the war, generally clustered in California and the Pacific Northwest. Perhaps because many tended to maintain their Japanese cultural heritage, other Americans suspected they were more loyal to Japan than the United States. Bolstered by public fear of sabotage after Pearl Harbor, more than one hundred and ten thousand Americans of Japanese ancestry — two-thirds of them American citizens — were removed from their homes beginning in February 1942. The War Relocation Authority was given jurisdiction over the relocation of Japanese and Japanese-Americans. Forced to abandon or sell their worldly goods, evacuees were taken to internment centers scattered throughout isolated regions of the West.

Unlike other Americans who generally lived comfortably during the war, Japanese-Americans spent as long as three years confined in isolation knowing they had lost their homes and businesses. The typical camp housed thousands of people in rows of barracks surrounded by barbed wire and armed guards. Internees showed remarkable ingenuity in fashioning barracks into homes and desert land into gardens. Men and older people in particular grew depressed, bored, and restless living monotonous routines and deprived of freedom. Camp directors organized many different activities as distractions: movies, church services,

scouts, field trips, and handcrafts. At Heart Mountain in Wyoming, the scheduling department's forty-two instructors developed twenty-seven activities in which about six thousand internees participated each week. Some activities expressed traditional Japanese culture: the game of go, calligraphy, haiku writing, and bonsai tending. Official policy of the Heart Mountain administration, however, encouraged pursuits considered more "American" in content, including wood carving, and sewing and knitting lessons.

War Relocation Authority photographs — the official U.S. documentation of Japanese-American camps — cast a favorable light on the camps, showing a comfortable, somewhat cheerful depiction of domestic life. In several photos, Japanese-American women are knitting. In Utah's Topaz Relocation Center in 1942, a mother wearing a white sun bonnet knits in the round on four needles either a sleeve or stocking. At Heart Mountain in 1943, Mrs. S. Nako and Mrs. William Hosokawa smile during an afternoon of knitting in a barracks living room, a room that began as a bare barracks room ingeniously remade into a comfortable living space with hand-built furniture. Dorothea Lange's June 1942 photo captured a different tone showing Mr. Konda and his daughter in a barracks apartment, where he lived in two rooms with his two sons, married daughter, and her husband in San Bruno, California. He was a farmer who had raised his family in Centerville, Alameda County. Konda's daughter sits behind him, knitting. The Nakamura family was relocated to an apartment in one wing of St. Anthony's Hospital, Rockford, Illinois, after removal from Santa Cruz, California. A photographer captured the two Nakamura daughters in their living room with their mother, who is knitting.[261]

Perhaps these women of Japanese descent brought their knitting skills with them to the camps, or perhaps they learned to knit in classes offered by instructors. At least some Japanese-American women were already knitters before internment. In *Farewell to Manzanar*, a memoir of childhood in a relocation camp, Jeanne Wakatsuki Houston describes the rust-colored turtleneck sweater her mother knit for her father before the war, the same sweater he wore when his fishing boat was called back to shore in California after the bombing of Pearl Harbor. The sweater reappears toward the end of her story, reconnecting parents estranged during life in the camps:

Papa put an arm around her, needing her support. He was wearing the rust-colored turtleneck sweater he used to take on fishing trips, the one she had knit for him before the war. Now, as she talked, the fingers of one hand played over its yarn, as if inspecting her own workmanship. While the late sun turned this rusty sweater dark

shades of orange, they stood there in the great expanse of the firebreak, far out from the rows of barracks, weeping with relief and happiness, talking quietly, just the two of them.[262]

Whether they were knitters before the war or new knitters taught by camp instructors, some interned Japanese-American women kept their hands busy by knitting clothing for themselves and their families. While interned at the camp in Poston, Arizona, Mrs. Shohara learned to sew, knit, and alter dresses and skirts at the camp's School of Tailoring, which had about one hundred graduates in 1945. Her hand-knit jacket and skirt were donated to the collection of the Hirasaki National Resource Center collection at the Japanese American National Museum in Los Angeles. Shohara knit the straight skirt and V-neck jacket with a dark chartreuse yarn using a zigzag pattern, both fully lined with white satin.[263] A photo in the museum's collection shows a women's knitting class posing together at the Minidoka camp in Hunt, Idaho, about 1943. Another photo records a display of knit sweaters at the Poston camp and documents a knitting instructor with a Japanese surname, presumably a fellow internee. The dedication written on the reverse of the photo reads: "Poston, Arizona, May 28, 1945. To Mrs. Helen Sakurai, our beloved knitting instructor. May this recall the sweet memories of your students [*sic*] beautiful work through your untiring effort. Adult Education Dept. Unit II, Knitted garment exhibition January 12–13, 1945. West Side View of the 210 mess hall. Kazue Kozeni."

Perhaps the most poignant knit piece in the collection is the green wool sleeveless sweater vest knit by George Fujino's mother and sister while they were interned at Manzanar. They knit the vest from green wool to match George's uniform and mailed it to George who was serving in the military.[264] The army was one of the few ways out of a camp like Manzanar for young Japanese-American men, after the government formed an all-Nisei combat regiment. Jeanne Wakatsuki Houston explains the rationale for enlistment: "The most effective way Japanese Americans could combat the attitudes that put them in places like Manzanar was to shed their blood on the battlefield. The all-Nisei 442nd Regimental Combat Team was the most decorated American unit in World War II; it also suffered the highest percentage of casualties and deaths."[265] No evidence of organized knitting to support the war effort appeared in six months of issues from the 1943 Poston camp newspaper. Yet how many other interned Japanese-American mothers, sisters, and wives occupied their minds and hands by knitting for their men who enlisted in the 442nd Regimental Combat Team?

On May 7, 1945, Germany surrendered and the surrender of Japan followed on August 15, 1945. The war had ended, as had knitting olive drab and navy blue regulation military patterns. Millions of people had learned to knit, however, and yarn manufacturers and retailers predicted that fashion knitting would lead their industry into a postwar boom. Women who had been busy with defense jobs would return home, they believed. Postwar American women would "refuse to be at leisure" and would turn to needlework to keep their hands busy.[266]

Chapter Ten

The Family that Knits Together . . .

Exuberant Americans emerged from World War II anticipating a future as an unchallenged world power and the arbiter of peace and cooperation. The war that claimed the lives of 14 million military and perhaps as many civilians ended with German surrender on May 8, followed by the August 14 surrender of Japan after the atomic devastation of Hiroshima and Nagasaki. More than three hundred and twenty-two thousand Americans had died, with another eight hundred thousand injured. Yet the American homeland remained unscarred by war, unlike other world regions. Within a few months in 1945, 7 million men left the U.S. armed forces, eager to begin families, buy homes, get educations, and find good jobs.

But the conversion to peacetime would not prove easy. Labor unrest coupled with postwar inflation — at times reaching 25 percent — threatened to create economic chaos during the first two years after war's end. The rural population, lagging in prosperity and often lacking even indoor plumbing, continued to shift toward towns and cities. President Harry Truman's administration instigated Fair Deal social reforms that tried to level the American playing field through civil rights and higher wages. Still, American industry was geared for economic expansion, and American families were poised and ready to indulge in consumer frenzy for products rationed or unavailable during wartime: houses, cars, appliances, clothing, nylon, meat, sugar, and so much more. American factories that were geared for military demand, however, needed to shift production to meet civilian needs. Despite unprecedented economic growth, shortages — including shortages of yarn and clothing — would frustrate Americans for at least two years after the war ended.

Postwar Women Stick to Their Knitting

Yarn companies and department stores, where many knitters bought their yarn and learned to knit, predicted dramatic postwar demand for yarn. War-relief knitting had forced women to postpone their

Yarn companies and department stores were only too happy to teach knitting basics to anyone who had not learned to knit during the war.

Opposite Page: Wartime knitters who had supplied hand-knit comforts to the armed forces turned to knitting for themselves and their families during peacetime. This 1950s calendar image was entitled "Busy Little Body," which summed up many knitters of the era.

WOO HER...

and she's yours for life

"Woo her and she's yours for life." Many men who had returned from war sought wives with whom to settle down in postwar bungalows. Similarly, yarn manufacturers encouraged department stores to woo the growing numbers of women who, they predicted, would fill their leisure time with knitting. *Dry Goods Journal,* August 1946.

personal knitting, so their reasoning went, and given time and yarn, women would return to knit for their families.[267] In 1944, the Bernhard Ulmann Company had observed the wartime female labor force and asked, "Can these hands stop working?" Doubtful indeed. Ulmann predicted a knitting, crocheting, and embroidery boom — preferably fueled by plenty of Bucilla, Bear Brand, and Fleisher's yarns distributed by Ulmann. "And it's a sure bet that when women are no longer needed to weld ships, rivet planes, or sew parachutes, they'll refuse to be left at leisure. Their creative hands will want to keep working . . . and needlework will be the outlet for millions," read Ulmann advertising copy aimed at needlework stores. Ulmann cited the 262 percent jump in business between 1914 and 1918 — and the "snowballing" growth after the end of World War I.[268]

As predicted, many frenetic wartime knitters continued to ply knitting needles during peacetime. Elizabeth Kaiser Graber knit one hundred sweaters for British soldiers before Pearl Harbor and a pair of socks every day for the Red Cross during World War II. After the war she maintained her "reputation as a champion knitter" and knit clothing for twenty dolls for a church fair just two months before her death at age eighty-six.[269] A substantial number of women, including married women, continued to work outside their homes and also continued to knit. Knitters popped up among a number of high-profile working women. Author Dorothy Parker was an avid knitter, often photographed carrying her knitting bag. Actresses who knit included Ginger Rogers and

Angela Lansbury. Elizabeth Bentley, dubbed the "red spy queen," considered her knitting bag the ideal stealth vessel to smuggle clandestine material between U.S. government offices and Russian intelligence agents. Portraying herself as a sort of "Communist June Cleaver" during her spy stage, Bentley stuffed reels of microfilm, government memos, and other critical documents into her knitting bag.[270]

Although 34 percent of women were in the labor force in 1950, yarn companies and the media largely ignored such working knitters in favor of the postwar female icon: the woman turned homeward, the woman who would make a desirable wife for a man and mother for his children, the woman willing to warm home and family with hand knits. "Woo her and she's yours for life," read a typical Ulmann yarn advertisement: "She's a woman worth having. She's a great enthusiast and a firm friend. She's the lady who knits, crochets or embroiders. Show her a new style sweater or a new design in bedspreads and her needles begin to click. . . . There are more of her type today than ever before."[271]

Yarn makers based these expectations on sound demographics. More postwar and 1950s women did in fact marry, and they married younger and had more children. By the end of the 1950s, 70 percent of women twenty to twenty-four years old were married, higher than any other time during the twentieth century. The average woman married at age 21.5 years in 1940 and at age 20 years in 1957. The number of children an American woman would bear averaged 3.6 in 1957, compared with about 2 children in 1936. Women were

Yarn companies developed new yarns and patterns to attract knitters. In Spinnerin Yarn Company's Fifth Avenue showroom, designers collaborated with "yarn experts" to create new yarns like Marvel Twist for afghans and Pilgrim for "masculine" gloves and stockings. *Spinnerin Men's Hand Knits*, 1946.

Patterns for socks, mittens, scarves, and gloves were especially plentiful after the war. Two-needle mittens were knit flat, then sewn up the sides.

Knitters could tuck this handy book into their knitting bags. Learning to knit was not enough. Knitting instructor Barbara Abbey showed knitters ways to avoid the "numerous little traps" that knitting presented, courtesy of a leading manufacturer of knitting needles.

Many teenagers and "almost teens" were enthusiastic knitters. *Bernat Fashions and Fun for the "Almost Teens,"* 1957.

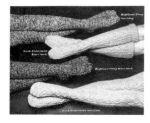

Irish Fisherman and Highland Fling stockings and knee socks appealed to high school and college girls. *Bear Brand hand-knit Socks for Men, Women, Children*, 1950.

expected to show loyalty to their men, too. When Milo Radulovich was wrongly accused as a Communist sympathizer and fought for his career during the "red scare" hysteria, press photographs showed his wife Nancy knitting while she waited to be called as a witness at his hearing.[272]

Welcome Back, Knitters

Department store needlework studios struggled with yarn shortages but not with a lack of enthusiasm for knitting. When new yarns arrived at Barney's in Schenectady, New York, only a small ad was placed as quantities permitted. "The response to just a small ad is terrific," said needlework buyer Marion Dillard. Buyers and knitting instructors anticipated and welcomed regular customers and newcomers alike. Younkers in Des Moines, Iowa, moved its postwar needlework studio to a more spacious, remodeled, high-traffic location and built a new women's lounge nearby. Younkers' buyer Ann K. Bryan attracted new customers with exhibits of hand knits and positioned skeins of yarn on new-style fixtures that let customers touch and select yarn without the help of a salesperson. At Walker's in San Diego, knitters responded enthusiastically to a well-publicized Art Needlework Fair with special demonstrations and displays of hand knits made by customers. Miss Jeanette Pierson, Walker's art needlework buyer, also organized a contest for knitting argyle socks (first prize $15).[273]

Knitting instructors continued to play a key role in the success of needlework studios, and many stores believed the instructors clinched sales that would oth-

erwise have been lost. The occasional magazine article that offered knitting instruction appeared no substitute for personal attention from a knitting instructor. At the John Bressmer Company in Springfield, Illinois, assistant buyer Miss F. Thoma considered herself not only a "tactful, helpful adviser" but also a "friend and confidant" for knitters.[274] Barney's in Schenectady enticed knitters with a homey, secluded atmosphere and their "instructress in the art of knitting." Buyer Mrs. Dillard observed that women preferred knitting to other types of needlework during the winter months and reported February as her company's "top month." Henshey's in Santa Monica, California, believed "free instruction to all the department's customers" was the key component that had kept its needlework department strong during the wartime years. According to buyer Mrs. E. Donald, any customer who bought yarn was welcome to the friendly needlework department's free knitting instruction from 10:00 A.M. to 12:00 P.M. and 2:00 P.M. to 4:30 P.M. six days a week.[275]

Teen Knitters

Nowhere was the importance of the knitting instructor felt more keenly than in promoting knitting to teenagers, a segment of the population with growing economic clout. At the White House in Santa Rosa, California, buyer Mrs. B. E. Ott targeted "younger needlework enthusiasts" through aggressive advertising and free knitting instruction available 11:00–4:00 daily. The Emporium Department Store in St. Paul, Minnesota, started a knitting fad among teenagers with free instruction for Norwegian-style ski sweaters

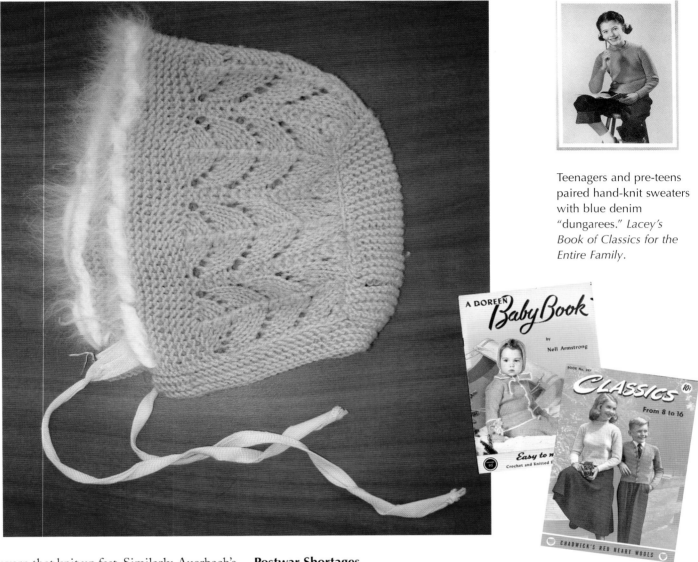

Teenagers and pre-teens paired hand-knit sweaters with blue denim "dungarees." *Lacey's Book of Classics for the Entire Family*.

Postwar knitters found knitting instructions for babies and children in pattern books designed and published by yarn companies. *A Doreen Baby Book*, 1947; *Classics from 8 to 16*, 1948.

Left: A delicate baby bonnet trimmed with angora, circa 1949. One of many postwar baby hand knits lovingly preserved and donated to textile collections. (Washington State Historical Society)

in chunky yarn that knit up fast. Similarly, Auerbach's in Salt Lake City, Utah, advertised directly to teenage girls and emphasized free instruction. A "crowd of teenagers" always gathered at the Henshey's in Santa Monica, thanks to a friendly instructor and spurred by a fad for couples wearing identical sweaters. Girls brought their boyfriends to help choose knitting yarn. Miss Mary Rankin of Lichtenstein's Inc. in Corpus Christi, Texas, filled summer knitting classes with twelve- to sixteen-year-olds, soon joined by eager eight- to ten-year-olds. Knitting class graduates surprised Rankin by telling friends they learned to knit their new sweaters and mittens at Lichtenstein's — bringing the store their next batch of knitting students. The youngsters liked to tackle the more difficult sweater patterns. Another department store in St. Louis not only organized free summer knitting classes, but also awarded prizes that enticed groups of nine- to sixteen-year-olds to finish nearly all their hand-knit sweaters.[276]

Postwar Shortages

When yarn was available, knitters helped combat post-war clothing shortages. At the Ben F. Smith Dry Goods Company in Texarkana, Texas, "homemaker industrialists" from Texas, Kansas, and Louisiana profited by knitting and selling infant clothing that manufacturers still could not supply as late as July 1946. Smith's sold yarn to the knitters at retail price and paid cash based on the estimated time required to knit each piece. Knitters produced shawls and wraps for the women's departments, but the best sellers were bibs, booties, sacques, mittens, blankets, and caps for infants. According to Smith's manager Paul D. Morris, the $1,500 worth of hand-knit merchandise sold during 1945 "saved the day for the infants' department."[277] Knitters could also cope with postwar clothing shortages by knitting their own sweaters, socks, mittens, gloves, scarves, and baby clothes. Mittens and sock patterns were especially easy to find among the many knitting books, including those from Jack Frost Yarn,

Government regulation of civilian clothing had "frozen" women's fashions during World War II, and women continued to wear wartime styles with broad, padded shoulders until spring 1947, when Christian Dior introduced the "New Look" for women's fashions. *Jack Frost Speed-Knit Sweaters*, 1946.

Right: A finely knit (7 stitches to 1 inch) skirt, jacket, and cape ensemble named Empire Silhouette was photographed in the Metropolitan Museum of Art's Louis XVI collection. The skirt was assembled with 4 gores, each beginning with 124 cast-on stitches (size 14). The upscale New Look included a small waist, flared hips, and long skirt. *Minerva Fashions in Hand Knits*, 1948.

Women's magazines sold mail-order instructions for classic hand knits. Close-fit sweaters with round shoulders and nipped-in waists show the "New Look" silhouette. *Woman's Home Companion*, May 1949.

Lacey's, Doreen, Beehive, Chadwick's, Spinnerin, and Hilde's Fashions in Wool.[278]

Knitters who lived far from department stores and instructors could buy learn-to-knit books. In 1946, the aspiring knitter learned the basics from Spool Cotton's *Learn to Knit Book* (No. 234) for 10¢. Aimed at teen knitters, the instructions moved quickly from the basics of casting on, knitting, and purling to a cabled vest, Fair Isle sweater, pattern-stitch gloves, and Argyle socks. Knitters who needed instructions beyond the basics could turn to Barbara Abbey's *101 Ways to Improve Your Knitting*, from needle manufacturer C. J. Bates & Son, Inc. Abbey, who had studied for a career as a concert musician, turned to needlework and established a knitting studio in Pell Lake, Wisconsin.[279]

Any postwar knitter who did not live near a needlework shop and needed to order yarn from the 1946 Sears, Roebuck & Company Catalog found a limited selection: only three kinds of knitting wool, one nylon knitting yarn, and one cotton knitting yarn. Sears' Golden Crown four-ply Germantown Zephyr (29¢ for a one-ounce ball) was popular for baby things and fine gauge sweaters, gloves, and bed jackets. Sears' Golden Crown four-ply worsted (96¢ per four-ounce skein) — the "aristocrat of knitting worsteds" — was recommended for afghans, shawls, winter caps, sweaters, and mittens. Golden Crown two-ply floss twist yarn (27¢ for a one-ounce ball) resembled fine Shetland wool, soft enough not to irritate baby skin and fine enough for adult sweaters and scarves. These knitting wools were available in white, black, brown, yellow, and a limited range of reds, blues, and greens. Enterprise Cotton Knitting Yarn was sold to make

practical items like rugs and baby soakers, and Sears' 94 percent nylon/6 percent rayon yarn was recommended for socks and hats for those allergic to wool. The catalog carried accessories: a wool winder, plastic and wooden knitting bag handles, and aluminum, plastic, and wood needles in pairs, sets of fours, and circular styles (prices ranged from 14¢ to 23¢). For those with money to burn, Sears sold a Deluxe Knitters' Kit with six pairs of plastic single-point needles size 1 to 6, six pairs of plastic double-point sock needles size 1 to 6, stitch holder, crochet hook, and knit counter all in a rayon moiré case for $4.39.[280] Supply had begun to catch up with demand.

Baby Boom Knitting

Even before the yarn shortage eased, postwar knitting patterns for the entire family were widely available. Yarn companies commissioned designs to sell their yarn, and knitters ordered patterns or pattern books from their ads, including Bear Brand and Fleisher's Yarn, Spinnerin Yarn, Frederick Herrschner, James Lees & Sons, Emile Bernat & Sons, Spool Cotton, John Dritz & Sons, and American Thread Company. Knitters also ordered instruction sheets for patterns from women's magazines like *Good Housekeeping*, *Ladies' Home Journal*, and *Woman's Home Companion*. Knitting for baby-boom offspring was especially popular. In the *Ladies' Home Journal*, a Mrs. Olsen recommended sweaters to knit for children. Olsen and her youngsters wore cotton sweaters, including hooded sacques that tied at the neckline for her baby, pullovers and cardigans for her children older than six months, mother-and-daughter styles for her young girls, and a doll sweater to match her little girl's sweater.[281] The Bear Brand pattern book *Hand Knits for Children* and Star's *Kid's Sweater 4 to 14* featured everyday sweaters for boys and girls. There were also pattern books for babies, among them *Lacey's Baby Book*, the *Doreen Baby Book* by Nell Armstrong, and the *Jack Frost Baby Book*. Layette sets knit in lace were favorites.[282] Some of these baby hand knits were lovingly preserved and donated to textile collections, in particular a delicate, treasured piece like the lacy bonnet with angora trim in the Wisconsin State Historical Society. Collections also have an occasional baby soaker that mothers continued to knit.

Fashion Knitting

Knitting patterns in magazines and yarn companies also targeted the flourishing teen knitting market. Minerva Yarn published *Teen Age Togs* with patterns for sweaters, socks, and a ribbed top with matching shorts. *Good Housekeeping* offered new patterns to knit and crochet. In the *Ladies' Home Journal*, teenagers found sweaters in "gay colors, new designs" to make themselves: cardigan with dolman sleeves, pullover with drawstring waist and cap sleeves, off-the-shoulder evening sweater, pullover with bare midriff, and loose-stitch shawl trimmed with multicolored seashells. Fashion-conscious young women found an abundance of new patterns. The knitting woman found that "your new collection is ready" in the *Ladies' Home Journal*. Among the up-to-date styles were weskits worn under jackets, cardigans designed to fit like tweed jackets, a close-fitting ribbon-knit skirt and jacket, and a winter-white knit jacket with jet buttons and crocheted black chenille collar with coordinated crocheted muff (5¢ a pattern). Similar styles appeared in *Good Housekeeping*, though designs tended toward more casual twin sets, ski sweaters, cardigans, and snug-fitting pullovers with cap sleeves.[283]

Knitters chose among many knit postwar fashion styles. In 1949, *Woman's Home Companion* advised readers, "You'll hear the click of busy knitting needles everywhere — for knitted fashions are the big news of the year — they are as practical as they are good-looking and they are inexpensive if you make them yourself." Patterns at 10¢ each included a ribbon-knit halter top and scoop-neck blouse, a triangular wool stole, and a finely knit wool three-quarter-sleeve sweater with ribbed yoke. In its "Lots for Little" feature, *Woman's Home Companion* showed fashion-appropriate, hand-knit separates: "Sweaters this year are smart for all occasions, all ages, and are worn as jackets or as blouses with your skirts and suits. This fall's lines have a soft fitted look, best achieved with the care that only your own hands can give." Short fitted cardigans (one knit in cashmere) were worn as blouses, a cable-stitched cardigan served as a suit jacket, and separate blouses

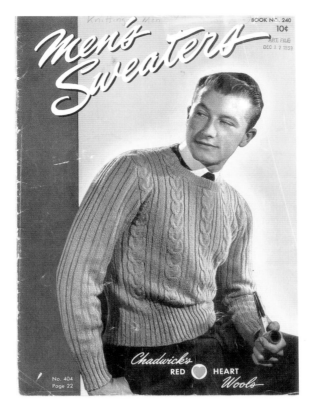

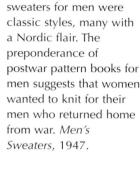

Postwar hand-knit sweaters for men were classic styles, many with a Nordic flair. The preponderance of postwar pattern books for men suggests that women wanted to knit for their men who returned home from war. *Men's Sweaters*, 1947.

(camisole and sweater-blouse) and single rib-knit skirts from boucle yarn created two outfits. An upscale pattern book from James Lees & Sons, *Minerva Fashions in Hand Knits*, featured twelve elegant suits and dresses hand-knit in Minerva Yarns and photographed against a background of masterpieces at New York City's Metropolitan Museum of Art. Knitters pressed for time, on the other hand, could follow Jack Frost instructions for "Speed-Knit Sweaters" on size 8 needles, quickly knitting vests and short-sleeved sweaters.[284]

Knit for Your Man

Men who liked the hand-knit sweaters and socks they received during the war often wanted their wives to keep knitting for them. Pattern books obliged those who knit for men, among them Lacey's, Fashions in Wool, Doreen, Spool Cotton, Minerva, Spinnerin, Jack Frost, and Ayr Scotch Wools. Besides the ever-popular socks, knitters favored a variety of classic cardigan and pullover sweaters for men. Ayr presented "unusual and practical designs which are adapted to the fine quality of Ayr yarns." Using imported cashmere and Shetland wools, knitters indulged the men in their lives with classic sweater vests, cardigans, and pullovers knit in a variety of textures. In Spool Cotton's *Men's Sweaters*, Chadwick's Red Heart wool was used to knit gentlemanly pullovers like the "Rugged Individualist" (a patterned vest in two colors), the "Stag at Ease" (*lice*-pattern ski sweater), and the "Good Mixer" (tattersall pullover worn with bowtie). Minerva

Red Heart yarn, 1950s.

Nearly every postwar knitting book included an argyle pattern, especially for socks. Argyle designs became national favorites "for young men and women who are always young."

Below: Appreciation in postwar America for intricate, distinctive Scandinavian sweaters and mittens rode the wave of popularity for skiing. Traditional designs were derived from stars, snowflakes, trees, or animals in the winter landscape but also included flowers, hearts, and abstract geometric shapes.

Knitting Nancy child's kit, 1950s.

Yarns provided similar patterns for classic, practical men's sweater vests, cardigans, and pullovers. A teenage girl could also order patterns for a matching sweater-and-socks set from *Good Housekeeping* or from Spinnerin Yarn to knit for the man in her life: "Want to impress the man in your life? Here's a sweater-and-socks set that really will take his eye. He'll be contender for the best-dressed man on campus, and you'll be the smartest gal he knows. You may start a fad, and you'll be ahead of the game. Knit this set for him, and he'll call it a labor of love, but you'll know it was fun."[285]

Argyle Socks and Scandinavian Sweaters

During the late 1940s, knitters were enamored with Scandinavian sweaters, often interpreted as ski sweaters. In *Scandinavian Sweaters* (1946), Kajsa Lindqvist and Natalie Hebert explained that knitters in the old days kept their entire family in hand-knit sweaters, and the patterns must have enlivened their otherwise tedious work. The designers offered ten Scandinavian variations with pattern-knit stars, squirrels, hearts, bears, diamonds, flowers, reindeer, pine trees, and dancing boys and girls. Lindqvist followed with *Scandinavian Snow Sets* in 1947 and *Scandinavian Mittens* in 1948. Mittens bore Swedish snowflake, star, rococo, modern, tulip, rose trellis, brownie, and lamb designs sized from infant through adult.[286]

The popularity of Scandinavian styles paled in comparison with the craze for knitting argyle patterns, however. Nearly every knitting pattern book included the mandatory argyle or a variation of argyle for men, women, babies, children, and teenagers. Socks were the favorite argyle project, worked with a daunting maze of bobbins that held colored yarns. Two-needle sock patterns offered some relief from the tangled yarn and bobbin dilemma. The Frederick Herrschner Company of Chicago sold an argyle sock knitting kit advertised for one-fifth the cost of comparable socks: "Just imagine . . . you can Knit a pair of the colorful and popular argyle Socks for just $1.00! The Fun . . . the colorful interest involved you can't afford to miss! This complete Kit of materials includes sufficient Beige or Maroon background yarn with argyle colors to knit a pair of socks up to size 12, also 4 Sock Needles, 10 Yarn Bobbins and complete easy to follow instructions. 100% satisfaction or your money back."[287] The even more ambitious knitter could tackle argyle sweaters, perhaps resorting to duplicate stitch for fine lines that crisscrossed argyle diamonds.

NORWEGIAN SWEATERS
The Easy Way

Almost no purling of alternate pattern rows—no twisting together of yarns—pattern rhythms that can be memorized—and a simplified way to hold the yarns

Design 1

By ELIZABETH ZIMMERMANN
A WOMAN'S DAY NEEDLEWORK FEATURE

I HAD, all my life, determinedly set my face against making any form of Norwegian Ski Sweater for what I consider four excellent reasons: *One*—I hate purling back; *two*—I hate twisting yarns at each color change; *three*—I hate complicated graphs and translating dots, asterisks, and funny squiggles into colors; *four*—and much the worst, I hate the interminable putting down of one color and picking up the other whenever the pattern demands it—sometimes every second stitch.

But my children were equally determined to have ski sweaters! So I beat my brains out and licked all four difficulties, evolving a Norwegian garment which was the envy of the sixth grade; and now I make such sweaters in all sizes for my growing-up family.

Before going into the four points, I must advance the theory that patterned sweaters are never meant to be s-t-r-e-t-c-h-e-d, for fear of distorting the pattern. They must be roomy enough to fit without binding anywhere and should cling only at the ribbed lower edge, cuffs, and neckline—turtle or semi-turtle, according to taste. By the same token, they should be designed on the simplest lines possible: The armhole should have no shaping; and the sleeves should be straight across the top, with a knitted-in gusset, to give a dropped shoulder line that is classic, effective, and comfortable. Now for the solving of my four problems.

One: I found I could avoid purling pattern rows except on the first rows at neck. I do all the rest of the job, round and round, on circular needles, using shorter ones for sleeves. A pattern is much simpler to follow if you are always looking at it from the right side, without the constant necessity of

Design 2

PHOTOGRAPHS BY HOWELL
AND WOMAN'S DAY STUDIO

Design 1: Light gray with white and charcoal-

Knitwits?

Postwar American knitters offset early clothing shortages, welcomed the baby boom generation with warm hand knits, kept up with fashionable sweater trends, and satisfied teenage knitting fads. Yarn companies and department stores alike indulged the growing number of knitters with plenty of new patterns. But all this knitting got on some people's nerves, as Janet Graham wrote in *Good Housekeeping* in January 1948:

Don't Be a Knitwit
Walking, riding, standing, sitting —
Where she goes, there goes her knitting.
When the bus is bursting full,
Down the aisle rolls her wool.
Anxious passenger soon wheedles,
"Lady, will you watch those needles?"
But the knitwit keeps on going
Though her absent mind is showing.
Socially, she's just a bore,
Turning sock heels by the score,
Grabbing friend's unfinished sweater,
Claiming *she* can do it better.
At the parties she attends
All the conversation ends:
How can you chatter with a girl who
Only answers, "Knit two, purl two?"
Hardly any girl bewitches
When she's always counting stitches.[288]

In one of her early articles, Elizabeth Zimmermann tackled the pattern for a man's Scandinavian sweater with a personable verve that would lead so many knitters to feel she was their knitting grandmother — or godmother perhaps. This dog-eared copy of her article, torn from a magazine, was well used and eventually donated to the art file at the Seattle Public Library. *Woman's Day*, January 1955.

Knitters often incorporated colorful characters, like these elves, into children's mittens, perhaps another Scandinavian influence. (Private collection)

Knitting for Korea

During the 1950s, Americans sought stability at home and abroad, and the genial Eisenhower years brought reassurance to the nation. Inflation and unemployment fell, and American's suburban population increased 47 percent. Unprecedented prosperity and phenomenal growth in media and science counterbalanced a burgeoning, hysterical fear of communist subversion. Soviet and American world views quickly

Historical Pattern
1950s Men's Argyle Socks and Anklets

No longer dull and drab, stockings knit in argyle patterns grew even more popular with knitters during the 1950s. The pattern is for the gray argyle socks shown here.

This pattern comes from the Bear Brand hand-knit Socks *book, Vol. 340, 1950.*

Instructions are for Socks; changes for Anklets are in parentheses.

Materials: Bear Brand Win-Spint (1 oz. skeins); or Bear Brand Ever-Match Sock and Fingering Yarn, (1 oz. skeins), Main Color A, 2 skeins; Colors B and C, 1 skein each; Colors 0 and E, about 20 yds. each.

Bucilla Nylon "Heel 'n Toe" yarn, 1 card.

1 set Yarn Bobbins.

Knitting Needles: "Boye" Sock Needles, 1 set Size 1.

Gauge: 9 sts = 1 inch

13 rows or rounds = 1 inch

Note: Chart and instructions call for cross lines to be knitted in. Cross lines may be embroidered in duplicate st after sock is completed, in which case diamonds are worked in solid color and cross lines are embroidered after sock is completed.

Cuff — With color A, cast on 68 sts loosely. Using 2 needles only, work back and forth in k 2, p 2 ribbing for 3 Ins.

Inc. row — Work ribbing, increasing 7 sts evenly spaced across row; 75 sts. Wind 2 bobbins of each color, or use color A from skeins.

Use separate strand for each color. Do not carry colors across on wrong side of work, except for single st of cross lines. To prevent a hole when changing colors, always bring color to be used under last color used. Begin pat.

Sock — Leg — Row 1 — Join C, k 1; with A, k 17; join D, k 1; join E, k 1; with A, k 17; join B, k 1; join 2nd strand of A, k 17; join D, k 1; join B, k 1; with A, k 17; join C, k 1.

Row 2 — P 2 C, 15 A, 1 E, 2 A, 1 D, 15 A, 3 B, 15 A, 1 E, 2 A, 1 D, 15 A, 2 C.

Anklet — Leg — Row 1 — Join B, p 1; with A, p 17; join E, p 1; join D, p 1; with A, p 17; join C, p 1; join 2nd strand of A, p 17; join E, p 1; join D, p 1; with A, p 17; join B, p 1.

Row 2 — K 2 B, 15 A, 1 D, 2 A, 1 E, 15 A, 3 C, 15 A, 1 D, 2 A, 1 E, 15 A, 2 B.

Continue pat. in stockinette st — k 1 row, p 1 row — until 74 (37) pat. rows.

Next row — With A, k 19 sts, slip on holder for heel; work next 37 sts in pat.; slip remaining 19 sts on holder for other half of heel. Continue pat. on 37 sts to end of chart, working 1 complete B diamond (Anklet — work 1 B and 1 C diamond). Break off.

Take up 38 sts from holders to 1 needle with side edges at center of needle. Join yarn and Nylon "Heel 'n Toe" Yarn on wrong side.

Heel — Row 1 — Slip 1 st as to p, p to end.

Row 2 — * Holding both strands at back of work, slip 1 st as to p, k 1; repeat from * to end. Repeat last 2 rows until there are 36 rows on heel, end with row 2.

Turn heel as follows: Wrong side — Slip 1, p 20, p 2 tog., p 1, turn. Slip 1, k 5, slip, k and pass, k 1, turn. Slip 1, p 6, p 2 tog., p 1, turn. Slip 1, k 7, slip, k and pass, k 1, turn. Slip 1, p 8, p 2 tog., p 1, turn.

Continue to work toward sides of heel, having 1 st more before dec. on each row until 22 sts remain. Break off "Heel 'n Toe" Yarn.

Gussets and Foot — With free needle and A, from right side, pick up and k 18 sts on side of heel, k 11 sts of heel to same needle; with another needle, k remaining 11 heel sts, pick up and k 18 sts on other side of heel to same needle; 58 sts.

Turn, p back across sts on 2 needles. Turn, k 1, slip, k and pass, k to end of first needle; k to within 3 sts of end of 2nd needle, k 2 tog., k 1. Repeat last 2 rows 10 times; 36 sts.

Place all sts on 1 needle for sole. P 1 row, k 1 row until 37 (74) rows from where sts were picked up on sides of heel.

Place 18 sole sts on each of 2 needles and 37 instep sts on 1 needle. Join, k 1 round, decreasing 1 st at center of instep. K around on these 72 sts until foot measures 2 ins. less than desired finished length from tip of heel, allowing these 2 ins. for toe. Join "Heel 'n Toe" Yarn.

Toe — Begin at center of sole. Round 1 — K to within 3 sts of end of first needle, k 2 tog., k 1; on 2nd needle, k 1, slip, k and pass, k to within 3 sts of end, k 2 tog., k 1; on 3rd needle, k 1, slip, k and pass, k to end. K 1 round even.

Repeat last 2 rounds until 20 sts remain. K 5 sts of first needle and slip to 3rd needle. Break off, leaving end for weaving. Weave sole and instep sts tog.

Sew back seam, matching pats. Sew seams at each side of foot. Steam.

At times, women who spent their days in far-flung suburbs turned to knitting to meet their needs for creativity and social connection. *Sweaters of Nylon or Wool,* 1952.

Nylon knits were ideal for the postwar lifestyle. *Minerva Hand-Knits in Nylon for the Family,* 1948.

Knitting Spool Outfit, 1950s.

surfaced and faced off with irreconcilable hostilities. In 1949, the United States joined with Western Europe for military defense through the North Atlantic Treaty Organization (NATO), and the Soviet Union exploded its first test atomic bomb and was entrenched in Eastern Europe. By 1950, America dedicated its resources, four times more for military defense alone than previously planned, toward resisting communism worldwide. Bolstered by decades of mutual distrust and suspicion, the United States and Soviet Union locked into a postwar ideological struggle for world domination — the Cold War.

Americans who craved postwar peace and prosperity saw the 1950s begin with the North Korean invasion of pro-Western South Korea. President Truman sent support forces for a "police action" that led to prolonged but limited military commitment. Predictably, knitters responded sympathetically to the call for warm knit clothing for Korean children, refugees, and the elderly. Knitters from World War II simply picked up their needles once again to make socks and mittens sent across the Pacific. The U.S. Army purchased 100 million pounds of raw wool for the reserve needs of the armed services, some designated for knitting wool. In 1951, the American Council of Voluntary Agencies for Foreign Service established American Relief for Korea, which sponsored the "Knit for Korea" campaign. The Women's Society of the First Baptist Church of Mount Vernon, New York, founded the first knitting circle in the relief organization's campaign to recruit one hundred thousand women to knit for the Korean people. In New York City, more than three thousand women volunteered to knit wool garments for war-devastated Koreans after American Relief for Korea provided the yarn. In 1953, the Americans Knit for a Korean Child project distributed mittens through its Seoul Presbyterian Mission.[289] Knitters once again donated their time generously, though never on a scale approaching that of World War II.

Knitting into 1950s Prosperity

The Korean War helped ignite the American economy of the 1950s, and the American Gross National Product jumped 250 percent between 1945 and 1960. In addition, the baby boom that peaked in 1957 fed economic growth and consumer demand. Although postwar immigration slowed to a trickle, the introduction of vaccinations and the first antibiotics meant Americans lived longer. The American population increased from 150 to 170 million during the decade, and Americans were more mobile than ever before. City dwellers fled to suburbs. The suburban population grew 47 percent during the decade, their exodus sparked by easier credit and sprawling housing developments. African-Americans moved by the thousands from the rural South to north-

ern cities, often sequestered into decaying neighborhoods. In 1956, the first enclosed shopping mall was built in a Minnesota suburb. The number of people who owned cars doubled, and the nation built more highways, including interstate highways. Suburban sprawl had arrived, trailing a culture of restless, monotonous alienation for many Americans. Middle-class suburban women who felt the social pressure to forego career for family were perhaps most likely to confront isolation and aimlessness in the suburbs — the "problem that has no name" Betty Friedan would label it in her landmark book *The Feminine Mystique.*[290]

Reading between the lines, the brisk trade in knitting suggests that department stores and yarn shops met some of the middle class, suburban woman's need to feel connected and productive. Bernhard Ulmann yarn ads showed women knitting together in social groups. Although knitters could order patterns and even yarn, at times, directly from yarn companies, needlework departments and yarn shops remained profitable businesses. In fact, the growing demand for yarn and instruction was behind the new "Knitting Shop" set up at Stampfer's department store in Dubuque, Iowa. In 1950, Knollenberg's department store in Richmond, Indiana, expanded its needlework department with knitting yarns in particular to meet the rising demand for yarn. Many stores shifted toward self-service and let knitters touch yarn and select their own supplies, including the Joseph Spiess Company in Elgin, Illinois. At Parker's in Davenport, Iowa, buyer Minnette Padden pronounced large, colorful self-service yarn racks very successful.[291]

During the 1950s, America fell in love with the beautiful and feminine perfection of actress Grace Kelly — knitting in *The Country Girl*, 1954. (Photofest)

A sampler afghan assembled from 50 different knitting patterns was a true "Adventure in Knitting."

"Father, mother, sister, brother — every single member of your family — can always use another sweater . . . in fact, the more the merrier!" One or more knitters made good use of a dog-eared pattern book, 1952.

Hand knits kept all the new babies looking especially adorable during the 1950s.

Knitting patterns reinforced gender roles of the 1950s. *Bear Brand Baby Book Infants to 4 Years,* 1950.

Knitting instructors were friends and confidantes for knitters. The full-time knitting instructor at the Popular Dry Goods store in El Paso, Texas, advised some thirty to fifty customers every day. Needlework buyer W. R. Dorris said he would never think of eliminating knitting instruction. Although the Trask, Prescott & Richardson department store in Erie, Pennsylvania, hired a part-time instructor to buffer the slower summer months, most stores had provided classes for so long that their customers expected to find instructors on hand. The Petersen-Harned-Von Maur department store in Davenport, Iowa, not only advertised free instruction but considered full-time instructors indispensable. Ada Clark, knitting instructor for a Washington department store, was proud of her devotion to each customer's success. Clark considered instruction "the biggest drawing card the department ever had."[292] At the Hager & Brother department store in Lancaster, Pennsylvania, "instructress" Alice McQueney loved to knit and had taught knitting since 1935. McQueney was so dedicated to her students that, for any knitter who became so "hopelessly confused in her work that she can't see her way out," she would tote the project home and straighten it out herself. "You've got to really like your job," said McQueney.[293]

High school and college girls were especially enthusiastic knitting students and were armed with cash from part-time jobs like babysitting. The argyle sock craze was still in full swing, especially among college girls. Miss Vivian Vinall at Petersen-Harned-Von Maur noticed her argyle sock knitters would "make them for their favorite fellow, and some of them [would] make them to sell. I've known girls to sell them for $10 a pair. They get to be experts and can turn out a pair in a short time."[294]

At Purcell's department store in Lexington, Kentucky, buyer Vernon Trammell convinced the university football team to pay for yarn that university girls knit into wool socks for the complete team roster. In preparation, Trammell staged sock-knitting contests among the women, with complimentary lessons in knitting argyle and plain socks. In all, 184 women entered the contests and some knit as many as five pairs of socks.[295] Yarn companies provided plenty of sock patterns. The Nomis Yarn Company published *The All-American Sock Book* with twenty-one original designs for men, women, and children — argyles, Fair Isle, lace-rib, and striped, among others. Similarly, Bernhard Ulmann encouraged knitters to "Step right out in FASHION" with argyles, argyle variations, and cable design patterns in *Bear Brand hand-knit Socks for Men, Women, Children*: "Gone are the days when socks were just things to wear under one's shoes. No longer are they drab, everyday necessities. Socks today are lovely to look at, delightful to own — and, with Bear

Brand, heaven to knit. For the men in your life — for children — and for yourself, too, hand-knit socks are high fashion . . . colorful . . . and an essential accessory for every wardrobe."[296]

Another yarn-marketing strategy recruited youngsters in schools across America. The Institute for Hand-Knitting, a conglomerate of yarn manufacturers, jumpstarted knitting interest with a nationwide knitting contest, for which an estimated 1 million teenagers learned to knit. The contest included a category for girls, who said they liked to knit for creativity, and boys, who said they liked to knit while listening to the radio. Knitting and women's magazine editors selected the winning dress (girls' category) and ski sweater (boys' category) from among 5,476 entries preselected by knitting shops around the country. Winners received a week's stay in New York City. According to winner David McGee, many young men in his high school liked to knit. An Institute representative explained that many European men knit, and "only in this country is hand-knitting considered purely a woman's occupation."[297]

Knitters who ordered from the Sears, Roebuck & Company Catalog during the mid-1950s found a far better selection of knitting yarns than in 1946. Sears encouraged knitters to "Knit for the whole family with Sears quality knitting yarns for sweaters, socks, afghans, hats, booties, scarves, mittens and stoles." Hearthside 100 percent virgin wool knitting worsted was available in a wider range of colors. Although Sears offered several knitting yarns in wool, it also sold the new synthetic "miracle yarns" of acrylic and nylon. Presumably, knitters had split into two factions: traditional wool knitters and knitters who liked the new acrylic and crimp-set nylon yarns. As a compromise, Sears offered blends like 50 percent crimp-set nylon and 50 percent wool. Nylon stretch yarn meant "miracle fit," and nylon-wool blends had greater strength for sock knitting. A knitting kit for youngsters taught them to knit a quick and easy tied collar with plastic charm decoration. Afghan kits came in several colors of virgin wool, and a bolero sweater kit offered quick and easy-to-knit fashion with a "glamorous" metallic ribbon trim that Sears assured its customers only looked expensive. Knitting bags and fabric coordinated with yarn were also available.[298] Clearly, yarn companies had geared up for the knitting demands of the 1950s.

The popularity of knitting spurred several postwar inventions for knitters. In 1950, Bett Morrison patented the Morrison knitting needle, equipped with a removable end cap and designed to slip a row of stitches from the needle onto a length of yarn in one swift movement. In 1955, Rollin W. Woodruff and Irene V. Swadberg patented a knitting needle with a working tip fitted with ridges and grooves that prevented dropped stitches, even while the knitter was not

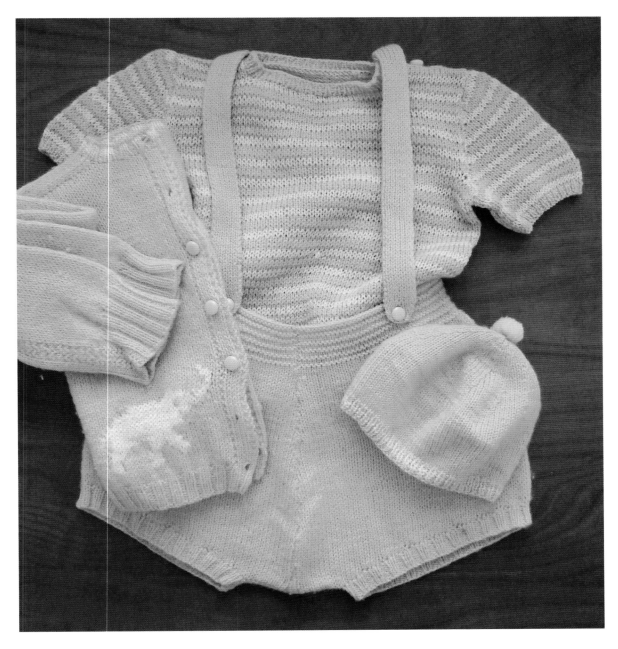

COAST-TO-COAST KNITTER MAKES
SWEATER ON 10¼-HOUR FLIGHT

The bulky look was sweeping the country. *Woman's Day*, November 1953.

looking at her work. Several other inventors patented improvements in circular needle production and design during the early 1950s.

Patterns for the 1950s

Yarn companies stimulated the knitting market with an array of patterns for home and family — most subtitled "for the entire family." Knitting patterns during the 1950s had a practical nature but also a lively flair that entertained and challenged hand, mind, and eye. The adventurous knitter with plenty of leisure time could whip up the sampler afghan (patented, number 121954) as "a lasting record of your Knitting Skill" with the fifty stitch patterns shown in the *Bear Brand — Fleisher Knitting Primer*.

Patterns for classic mittens and gloves for everyone in the family could be knit in plaid or figurative color variations, knit-lace, fancy cables, or duplicate stitch in everything from snowmen and reindeer to hearts and flowers. Knitters had discovered angora as a favorite for gloves, mittens, and caps or a bit of fanciful edging on a bonnet. Among many others, knitters could choose the Bucilla *Gloves and Mittens to Knit and Crochet for the Entire Family*, J. & P. Coats and Clark's *Accessories in Wool . . . for Men, Women, Children*, Bernat *Handicrafter Gloves and Mittens for the Family*, and J.& P. Coats and Clark's *Sweaters for the Family*. Even pattern books that targeted women's classic sweater styles on covers claimed "Hand Knits for the Family" inside.[299]

The newness of knitting with ribbon attracted knitters during the mid-1950s. Ribbon was knit using large needles (size 10) with a loose gauge (4 stitches to 1 inch), taking care to hold the ribbon stitches flat. A two-piece ribbon suit used 22 100-yard spools of "silky" Ruban d'Art. The fluid texture of ribbon knits complimented the curvaceous 1950s silhouette. *Nomotta Ruban d'Art*, 1953.

Right: When she was nine years old in 1947, Merle Terry of Chicago wore this sweater vest, knit by her mother, over a yellow dress. (Chicago History Museum)

Knitting for favorite small fry in the family was as popular as ever. More married women were having more children, after all, during the 1950s. And more babies and small children were working their way through the major part of the fifteen-year baby boom, while more grandparents lived longer and healthier lives than ever before. Women's magazines like *Woman's Day* and *Good Housekeeping* obliged doting parents and grandparents with patterns at 15¢ each for a toddler-size Eisenhower jacket, baby creepers, and tiny sweaters. More and more yarn companies (Bear Brand, Fleisher, Spinnerin, Bernat, and Jack Frost among many) hired knitting designers — typically anonymous — to supply adorable patterns for youngsters: snow suits, sun suits, jodhpurs, stocking caps, bonnets, buntings, argyle sweaters, tennis sweaters, cabled cardigans, carriage covers, baby sacques, bootees, and mittens. Tiny patterns traced duplicate-stitch squirrels, kitties, elves, and such. There were, of course, the ever-popular soakers — some baby girl versions with lace-knit edgings and ruffles. Knitters could have them all in an astonishing range of designs.[300] Bear Brand promoted its instruction book for baby hand knits as "so easy to understand, even your baby could almost knit them!"[301] Prices for pattern books ranged from 25¢ to $1, with the cost tending to edge up a bit during the decade. Some books provided gauge and interchangeable yarn charts.

Classic knits were popular for school-age boys and girls. *Good Housekeeping* offered patterns for an "authentic ski sweater" for a young man and striped skirt, hat, and sweater outfits for a little girl's favorite doll. Jack Frost Yarn published pattern books with simple stockinette cardigans, pullovers, vests, and mittens. Patterns from Fleisher Yarns elaborated on basic styles for school and play. Little girls could have knits "just like Mother's" flower-embroidered cardigan, ruffled blouse, sweater suit, or jumper dress; young boys could have their own knits "just like Dad's" argyle sweater vest, turtleneck Viking theme sweater, or shawl collar raglan cardigan. According to Fleisher, the knitter could "Make the children in your life pretty as pictures" and have fun knitting these unique patterns: "There's nothing like a handknit from Mom, Auntie, Grandma, to make a boy or girl feel delighted . . . look delightful! And you'll have the time of your life knitting any or all of these practical, wearable fashions of famous Fleisher's yarns."[302]

Keeping up with the emerging mohair look and quick-to-knit bulky trends in sweaters, Bernat designed fashion knits for youngsters using two new mohair-wool blend yarns, Cuddlespun and Cuddleshire. Worked on size 9 needles at four stitches to the inch, a little girl could have a cabled coat or pullover, angora-trimmed cardigan, or sailor-collar jacket. A little boy could have a tennis sweater, classic cardigan with pockets, or Fair Isle turtleneck. Bernat yarns expected that "almost teen girls" from eight to fourteen years would be eager to knit their own sweaters, mittens, caps, and socks.

Fifties Fashions

Knitting for fashion and style fit the image of the 1950s knitter as a woman at home with plenty of leisure time. Yarn companies kept publishing new designs, many with clever hooks for the knitter. For $1, Bernat gave knitters sixty new sweaters and jackets — in cable or intarsia — to wear skating, hunting, sailing, bird watching, skiing, golfing, cycling, gardening, and anything else a person could think of doing outdoors. Fleisher and Minerva focused on the curvaceous Dior "New Look" silhouette with a full-skirted sweater dress, close-fitting cardigans and jackets, and dresses with pleated skirts and dolman sleeves. Predictably, men's patterns were still classic rib-knit or stockinette sweaters, sweater vests, and cardigans, although pattern books still included interesting variations for socks, gloves, scarves, and neckties. Botany kept up with the bulky knit style for men's sport cardigans.[303]

Woman's Day magazine in particular was a faithful friend to the knitter throughout the decade, keeping knitters up to date with everything from aristocratic knit-lace to the popular bulky sweater look. Perhaps a bit retro even for 1953, patterns featured a lace-knit sunburst doily, chair set, tea cloth, and early American–style bedspread. Later the same year, *Woman's Day* stepped up to the fashion plate with eight pages of bulky sweaters knit with cotton rug yarn for less than $3 each. *Women's Wear Daily* claimed the bulky sweater was sweeping the nation. To drive this point home, photographs showed women across the Country knitting and wearing the new sweaters. One knitter completed a *Woman's Day* bulky sweater during an almost eleven hour flight from New York to Los Angeles. Even the magazine's stylist, Jack Bodi, gave in and knit one of the bulky rug yarn sweaters.[304]

During the mid-1950s, *Woman's Day* needlework editor Roxa Wright featured patterns for sporty knit fashions for women. Highlights included a crosswise knit pullover, giant popcorn-stitch "polka-dot" cardigan, ski sweater with drawstring neckline, and Scandinavian sweaters that still intrigued knitters and fashion divas alike. Wright was especially proud of her grand prize–winning sweaters — elegant designs from a Paris knitting competition juried by French fashion editors. Knitters also followed directions for Aran Island knee socks and two-finger matching mittens patterns, or they ordered the *Woman's Day* leaflet, *Hand Knits from the Aran Islands*, free with purchase of Rygja Homespun yarn imported from Ireland ($1.29 per skein, thirteen skeins for a medium-size hip-length coat).[305]

Knitting Scandinavian sweaters was too tedious for some knitters. Innovative designer Elizabeth Zimmerman — destined to occupy a special place of affection in the hearts of American knitters — licked the "interminable" problems of purling back, twisting yarns for color changes, following complex graphs, and

dropping and picking up yarns required for Scandinavian knitting. First, she knit her Norwegian sweater in the round on circular needles, machine-stitched the sections destined for armholes, and then cut out the armholes with shears before hand sewing in the sleeves. Second, she chose patterns with short color repeats to eliminate twisting yarns when she changed colors. Third, she designed sweaters with wide bands of repeats to simplify charts. Fourth, she learned to knit the German way with one color in her left hand and knit the English way with a second color in her right hand. And with the creative spark that would endear her to knitters everywhere, Elizabeth encouraged knitters to make their own patterns from old cross-stitch books and samplers.[306] Zimmermann also designed a knit pillbox hat for *Woman's Day*. Knit with two skeins in contrasting colors in about four hours, the pillbox was "young and jaunty-looking cocked on the back of the head — not pulled down about the ears."[307]

Other magazines had knitting patterns, too. Knitters found homey house slippers, two-needle mittens, gloves, sweaters, and baby raglan sweaters and bonnets in *Woman's Home Companion* and *Good Housekeeping*. In 1950, *Good Housekeeping* highlighted Mrs. Richardson and her five children from Connecticut, all wearing sweaters knit from one versatile *Good Housekeeping* pattern (Mr. Richardson also got a sweater but could not make it home in time for the photo).[308] "Patterns of The Times" columns in *The New York Times* promoted fashion hand knits — cardigans with striped trim, sleeveless sweater, ski sweaters, knit blouses with dressmaker details, and an angora shrug "for the busy needles of women who seek the smart handmade look." The needlework editor for the *Times* recommended that women "take along a knitting bag filled with some of the lovely new yarns and a few good patterns" because "hand-knits were never more important in the fashion world."[309]

If women were knitting even a portion of the patterns that appeared in women's magazines, newspapers, and pattern books, they did indeed have leisure time and money for yarn during the 1950s. Mainstream Americans would look back on the Fabulous Fifties as another postwar golden age, a time of unprecedented prosperity and general agreement on appropriate values for family and nation. But social tensions in civil rights, women's rights, and family structure brewed beneath this patina of self-satisfaction. Prosperity, opportunity, and world dominance were not as universal as the mainstream family wanted to believe, and Americans would meet the subsequent cultural and political crises head-on during the 1960s.

Coats & Clark's *Style Parade* offered 1955 knit fashion at its peak.

Chapter Eleven
Worldly Knitting

Americans who expected a prosperous, predictable future faced a rude awakening during the 1960s and 1970s. The 1960s opened brightly enough with the election of John Fitzgerald Kennedy as president. First Lady Jacqueline Bouvier Kennedy brought sophistication and style to the White House. Formerly marginalized voices — women, youth, and minorities in particular — challenged traditional beliefs and authority. In 1962, Rachel Carson launched the environmental movement with her book, *The Silent Spring*, and Ralph Nader exposed corporate indifference to car safety in *Unsafe at Any Speed*. Dr. Martin Luther King Jr. channeled the crusade for civil rights into a massive, peaceful march on Washington, and passage of the Civil Rights Act followed in 1964. Betty Friedan published *The Feminine Mystique*, denouncing the 1950s female stereotype, and in 1966 she became the first president of the National Organization for Women. Americans dressed for the new ideologies. Black pride and Afros. Mini skirts and Nehru jackets. A-line skirts and flip hairdos. Hippies and love beads. The Beatles and bellbottoms. Bouffant hairdos and pillbox hats. Pop art and polyester double-knit. Consciousness raising and pantsuits. Disco and leisure suits.

In 1963, millions watched in horror as President Kennedy was assassinated on live television, an event fixed in collective American memory. By 1968, protestors staged tumultuous demonstrations against an undeclared war in Vietnam. Although the Red Cross worked actively in Vietnam during the war, information about knitting for the soldiers does not leap out of the historical record. Probably there was little call for hand-knit wool stockings for soldiers in steamy Vietnamese jungles. Most likely knitting was not part of this war because America was divided, not united over Vietnam. America continued sending CARE (Cooperative for American Remittances to Europe) packages overseas during the 1960s, first with emergency food rations and later with books, blankets, tools, and knitting supplies.[310]

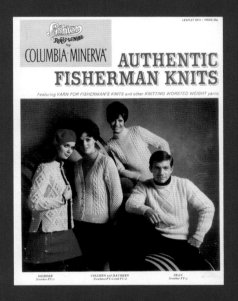

Knitting traditions from nations around the world, especially the intriguing stitches used for Aran Isle ("fisherman") knits, captivated knitters during the 1960s and 1970s. *Authentic Fisherman Knits*, 1968.

The world was going mod. Bulky knit (2 stitches = 1 inch) mini-dresses in harvest gold, avocado green, and orange — knitting patterns kept pace with fashion styles. *The Best of Spinnerin*, 1969.

Knitters chose from new fibers and yarns. Miracle Sayelle Wintuk (acrylic) assured knitters it was the "closest in appearance and texture to fine wool . . . yet it's machine washable and dryable — holds its rich colors forever — and never needs blocking!" *The Workbasket*, March 1972.

Although roles for women were changing during the 1960s, the image of the knitter remained decidedly maternal. The mother in a Hero knitting needle advertisement works up a trendy bulky knit on extra large needles. *Needle and Yarn*, 1964.

Knitters could make their own mohair sweaters in bright, clear colors, just like the expensive Italian imports. *Campus Hand Knits for Men and Women*, 1963.

Women received mixed messages about social and gender roles during the 1960s. The image of the knitter seemed similarly conflicted at the beginning of the 1960s. Maurine Neuberger, the third woman elected to a full term in the U.S. Senate, first served as a representative in the Oregon state legislature along with her husband, state Senator Richard Neuberger. She reasoned, "I might as well be speaking for my sex in the House of Representatives as knitting socks and sweaters while I watched Dick in the Senate gallery." Perhaps she continued to knit while she worked on education, health, and consumer legislation during the 1960s.[311]

Conflicted or not, knitters bought pattern books. Prices ranged from 40¢ to 75¢ during the 1960s and shot up to $3–$4 during the 1970s. Reynolds and Unger focused on upscale designer collections for coats, suits, and dresses. European sophistication found a place in knitting patterns. Fashion-conscious knitters purchased patterns for "hand-knit fashions from PARIS" in books from Laines du Pingouin Yarns (made in France). Emile Bernat & Sons Company emphasized classic sweaters, and knitters found "masterpieces that never go out of fashion" in *Bernat Classics for Women* (1961). Bernat listed thirty-five varieties of yarn, all interchangeable, for delicate cabled or seed-stitch cardigans and feminine twin sets — all worn with ladylike, and mandatory, short white gloves. Spinnerin books targeted both elegant and outdoorsy knitters. Vests and hats were popular knitting projects later in the 1970s, as shown in Leisure Arts' *Vests for Women* (1979) and *Woman's Day*'s quick-knit caps.[312]

Knitters had an ever-widening range of yarns and fibers from which to choose. In 1950, DuPont introduced Orlon acrylic yarn, marketed as a machine washable and dryable substitute for wool.[313] Knitters liked acrylic yarn for soft, easy-care baby layettes and children's sweaters. American Thread sold acrylic yarn as Dawn Sayelle Orlon, and Coats & Clark advertised Red Heart "Wintuk" acrylic yarn as virtually indestructible. Mrs. Fred Bard of Isleton, California, salvaged her hand-knit Red Heart "Wintuk" sweater-coat that had been buried in mud for five months after her home flooded. She hosed it down, tossed it into the washer and dryer, and claimed it looked as good as new.[314]

Inventors also patented new products for knitters. In 1962, N. T. Sanders received a patent for a counting device that the knitter slipped onto a knitting needle and twisted to reveal numbers that kept track of rows. Abby Tracy patented a new style of compact yarn and needle holder in 1962, and in 1969 G. L. Ingersoll patented an adjustable knitting needle designed to accommodate different widths of knitting. Lee D. Gilchrist received a patent in 1973 for a knitting method that created a dense, stable fabric texture.

Knitting fads were there and gone as fast as paper dresses and hot pants. After Virginia Harvey brought back the Victorian craze for macramé in 1967 with her book *Macramé: The Art of Creative Knotting*, crafters tried their hands making macramé jewelry, plant hangers, bags, or wall hangings. Knit wall hangings that mimicked macramé never quite caught on, though.[315] Another short-lived fad surfaced for bulky sweaters knit from Aunt Lydia's Heavy Rug Yarn — a fad no doubt cut short after knitters watched their rug yarn sweaters sag out of shape. The American Thread Company, maker of Aunt Lydia's rug yarn, promoted the idea in its knitting pattern book, *Sweaters*. A whim for dresses, sweaters, and socks knit with broad, bold-colored stripes attracted knitters for a short while during the early 1970s. Knit swimsuits, buttoned capes, and — shades

of the 1940s and 1950s! — argyles surfaced and faded.[316] Other knitting patterns followed the granny look of the early 1970s. *Woman's Day* encouraged knitters to reinterpret crocheted granny squares by knitting little knit squares and borders to make pillows, afghans, and long skirts.[317] Crocheted granny-square vests proved a more popular fashion choice (especially in orange and brown).

Mohair

During the early 1960s, any knitting book worth its salt included something, *anything* in mohair. Long, roomy mohair sweaters looked youthful and trendy, especially when worn with sleek stretchy ski pants and sporty boots. Knitters found co-ed sweaters in fluffy Bear Brand and Fleisher mohair yarns among the cabled slipovers and classic jackets in *Campus Hand Knits for Men and Women* (1963). Spinnerin Yarns sold kits for mohair sweaters knit in large-scale plaids with trendy wide collars in a choice of four popular colorways. Designer Hilde Fuchs' *Mohair Fashions in Wool* (1963) and *The Mohair Look in Orlon Fashions in Wool* (1964) capitalized on the fluffy look with patterns for mohair shells, wide-collared cardigans, cabled and

turtleneck slipovers, Chanel-style jackets, stoles, popcorn-stitch pullovers, and even a sleeveless sheath dress.

Bear Brand and Fleisher Yarns' *Hand Knit Mohair Fashions* (1961) recommended their brand of Supra Mohair for simple stockinette cardigans and slipovers — many with wide collars. Other patterns included mohair pullovers jazzed up with broad stripes and textured ribbing; a fringed mohair skirt coordinated with an overblouse and a long stole; and a cabled mohair slipover designed for men. Long mohair coats required either two strands of mohair or a strand of mohair and wool held together for bulky, quick-knit fashion.

The Mohair Book by Bernat (1964) brought the mohair look into the realm of classic fashions for men and women with interchangeable Bernat Mohairspun and Astrakhan boucle yarn. Even outdoorsy Mary Maxim styles got into the mohair look, offering knitters eighteen shades and kits for mohair headbands (only 98¢), a mohair V-neck sleeveless pullover ($5.95), and mohair pullovers and cardigans knit from the top down ($7.98). In 1975, knitting patterns for mohair sweaters still appeared in *McCall's Sweater Book*.[318]

Bulky Knits

Bulky knitting offered fashion in a fraction of the time. Fashionable bulky giant-rib or cable-knit hat patterns in Ulmann's *The New Hand Knit Hats* (1960) and *Hits in Hats* (1965) were knit to a gauge of two-and-one-half stitches per inch with Fleisher's "Gigantic" or Botany's "Colossal" brand yarn and size 15 needles. *Boys and Girls Bulky Knits* (1960) assured knitters that "in the world of 'children's fashions' . . . the big idea is BULKY KNITS!" Doting knitters could outfit children size 2 to 16 in casual, practical bulky knit cardigans, vests, slipovers, and turtlenecks

The Spinnerin Yarn Company sold kits for mohair sweaters knit in plaid. *Spinnerin American Couturier Look*, 1961.

Left: A mohair coat hand-knit by Irma Hoar of Glen Ellyn, Illinois, during the early 1960s.

Mohair sweaters looked young and trendy worn with stretch ski pants and boots. *Mohair Fashions in Wool*, 1963.

Bulky knits — worked with large knitting needles and yarns with names like Gigantic and Colossal — promised popular styles in half the time. *Boys and Girls Bulky Knits*, 1960.

An Aran sweater and hat hand-knit in natural Irish wool by Mary Snell of Chicago, during the 1960s.

Elegant interpretations of Aran Isle sweaters were popular project for knitters. *Woman's Day*, January 1973.

Icelandic Lopi Wool, yarn that was carded but not spun, knit quickly into warm, cozy sweaters — photographed on the Arctic Circle Island of Grimsey, Iceland. *Reynolds New Icelandic Fashions.*

— even a bulky Aran Isle pullover. Botany's *Hand Knit Bulkies for Children* (1960) had even more patterns for kids.

Knitters made bulky sweaters well into the 1970s. The big bulky look of two stitches to the inch made the covers of *McCall's Sweater Book* (1975) and *Family Circle* (June 1970). Lopi Icelandic wool from Reynolds Yarn suited the bulky style at three to three-and-a-half stitches to the inch. Sheared from Icelandic mountain sheep, Lopi was carded but unspun wool in natural colors. Geometric motifs in bold contrasts either covered the sweater surface or balanced across yoke, lower edge, and cuffs. Reynolds Yarns President Tom Reynolds invested in photo essays for Lopi pattern books: the Arctic Circle island of Grimsey for *New Icelandic Fashions for Men and Women* and a windjammer in *New Icelandic Patterns for the Great Outdoors* (1975).

Knitting for men tended toward classics slipovers, cardigans, and vests made with worsted wool yarn. In *Men's Classics* (all styles — all weights — all sizes to 46), Bernhard Ulmann gave knitters greater variety with its Choose-O-Matic Selector that specified light, medium, and heavy weights in Ulmann's Bear Brand, Fleisher, and Botany yarns. Gauges ranged from lightweight yarn

(7 stitches = 1 inch), to medium and heavyweight (5 stitches = 1 inch), to extra heavyweight (13 stitches = 4 inches), and finally to gigantic weight (5 stitches = 2 inches). There was, of course, a mohair cardigan pattern in the book as well. Occasional articles in *The New York Times* called attention to men who knit. The art needlework department at the Abraham Straus store in Brooklyn reported that women bought knitting needles and yarn for their husbands. Nick Andrews, a Broadway dancer, knit sweaters for fellow cast members, and a group of men learned to knit, confident that, if women could knit, men could learn, too.[319]

Worldly Knits

Knitters took considerable interest in knitting traditions around the world. Aran Isle sweaters in particular challenged knitters with the ingenious stitches — trellis, double-seed, cluster, and cable variations. *Woman's Day* magazine recommended unbleached, moisture-resistant Aran wool for its child's Aran sweater for boy or girl.[320] William Unger imported natural Norwegian yarn for classic Aran sweater patterns in *Rygja, The Natural Homespun Yarn from Norway* (1963). *Sportswool Arans* (1969) was among many instruction books published by Sirdar Wools, a British company that sold Sirdar Sportwool for natural-colored Aran knits and for Greek fishing sweaters named for the Greek islands (Rhodes, Kos, Corfu, and so on).[321] An occasional Tyrolean sweater popped up in pattern books. In *Reynolds Continental Collection*, a cardigan knit with wishbone cable and diamond-pattern Aran stitches was embroidered with colorful French knots and lazy daisy flowers. The knitter who could not get enough Aran Isle patterning in a sweater or two could knit Aran afghans. *Decorator Afghans* (1963) and *Afghans Knit and Crochet* (1967) had afghan patterns knit with Aran stitches using Coats and Clark's Red Heart knitting worsted. Aran patterns appear in knitting books through the 1970s: a natural brown Aran cardigan in *McCall's Sweater Book* and a cardigan coat, child's turtleneck pullover and pants outfit, tunic pullovers, and even Aran bellbottom pants in *Woman's Day*.[322]

Scandinavian and Fair Isle sweaters knit with elaborate color designs were especially popular, though simplified at times for easier knitting. Spinnerin's *World Wide Fashions* promised knitters an "Around-The-World Look Fashions for All." *Woman's Day* proclaimed

Knitters relied on intricate, colorful techniques inspired by knitting traditions around the world to knit distinctive sweaters. *Woman's Day*, February 1966.

Left: The Aran Isle afghan was "not for beginners" but promised a "sense of accomplishment upon completion." *Coats & Clark's Afghans*, 1967.

Colorful sweaters based on vintage Norwegian patterns found their way into the American knitter's repertoire. *Dale Yarn Company Knit Your Own Norwegian Sweaters*. Patterns by Dale of Norway.

Skirt hand-knit by Irma Hoar of Glen Ellyn, Illinois, during the early 1960s.

A Lopi sweater pattern detail.

"Gifts from many lands" in 1962, highlighting Austrian wool gloves, English cable socks and diamond-pattern scarf, man's ski sweater designed by Mirsa of Italy, and, of course, mohair woman's cardigans — one French, one Italian.[323]

Interest in international sweater styles mushroomed, and *Woman's Day* developed round-the-world sweaters: "Today, everyone wears sweaters everywhere. Here, for you to knit, are 20 of the newest, most distinctive designs and textures from almost every country, as varied and exciting as the wide world itself."[324] Readers could order patterns for the sweater collection inspired by styles from Peru, Bavaria, Mexico, Ireland, Canada, Norway, France, Italy, Holland, Switzerland, Portugal, Denmark, Germany, Finland, Greece, England, Austria, Iceland — even a mohair jacket from the United States. More international sweater collections appeared in *Woman's Day* during the 1960s, and the 1966 international collection of twenty-four sweater patterns cost 50¢.[325] In 1970, the editors compiled a book of sweaters from the magazine, reprinted annually for at least the next six years. On a folk art theme, Mrs. Salme Kolk designed eleven pairs of "imaginative and joyous" gloves and mittens inspired by colorful motifs in her native Estonia (mail-order knitting directions, 50¢). *Woman's Day* continued to give knitters Fair Isle cardigan patterns in vibrant 1970s colors.[326]

Why did traditional knitting styles worldwide intrigue knitters during the 1960s and 1970s? Perhaps the popular peasant look — the long skirts and embroidered blouses of European folk costume — influenced

their tastes. More likely, world travel was at the heart of the matter. More Americans were traveling to more far-flung nations more often than ever before.[327] The 1960s marked the beginning of the commercial jet age, the first operational Boeing 707 rolled out in 1957, and one year later passenger jets were flying from New York to London. Within three years, passenger jet

The ethnic look could be as simple as a striped poncho, a popular style during the early 1970s. American Thread Company.

Right The Mary Maxim company marketed knits and yarns for bulky knit sweaters with designs inspired by the great outdoors.

Youngsters also wore the ethnic look, often fringed and embroidered. *Woman's Day 101 Sweaters*, 1971.

Pauline Denham Yarns published many pattern books characterized by classic, elegant design.

routes stretched across the Atlantic and Pacific, to South America, Australia, Asia, even the Arctic. By 1959, flashy Pan American ads enticed travelers to the first round-the-world jet service.

The Peace Corps, established in 1961, also attracted Americans to overseas adventure. In its founding year, the Peace Corps sent thousands of American volunteers, especially young college graduates, to Ghana, Tanzania, and Colombia, and eventually to a total of 134 developing nations. Volunteers dug wells, immunized children, taught English, and immersed themselves in hundreds of other services. Returned Peace Corps Volunteers infused America with a fresh interest in the material culture of other nations. And a number of volunteers learned to knit while in the corps, especially those who served in countries with strong knitting traditions like Peru or Bolivia. Some Peace Corps volunteers helped to develop entrepreneurial hand-knitting businesses in their host nations.[328]

The New York World's Fair in 1964–1965 also stirred interest in international styles. Alongside exhibitions of advanced industrial achievements, pavilions from many nations — Japan, Spain, China, and many others — staged fashion shows. Perhaps the most

exciting was the Crystal Palace of Fashion at the Better Living Center, modeled on London's Crystal Palace of 1851. An American Thread Company representative rhapsodized about hand knits at the Crystal Palace fashion show in the company's book on designs featured at the fair: "The fairytale architecture of the Orient, the charm of Europe, the romance of Africa . . . Best of all at the Crystal Palace of Fashion in the Better Living Center, I saw a fabulous array of hand-knit and crocheted fashions created with DAWN Yarns that I can make myself. Instructions for each and every exciting fashion . . . sports sweaters . . . shells . . . dresses . . . suits . . . evening shift . . . designs for any time of day . . . any way of life . . . are given in this book."[329] The American Thread Company's book featured original designs in 100 percent wool Dawn yarn for stylish women's cardigans, slipovers, shells, jackets, and dresses seen at the World's Fair.

Knitting Designers

With exceptions, the names of hand-knitting designers seldom appeared with their patterns during the 1960s and 1970s. In 1971, *Woman's Day* began giving name credits for knitting designers, including Helen Bullett, Patti Lawrence, and Erika Loeb. Viola Sylbert was credited for Columbia-Minerva's *Folkloric Sweaters and Accessories* (1974). Gabriele Knecht, an American designer born in Germany, wrote and designed knitting booklets from 1973 to 1982, including patterns with a flair for Columbia Minerva's *Learn to Knit* (1973).

Although knitting designers would take charge of their creative work during the 1980s, a number of entrepreneurs promoted their own patterns and founded knitting enterprises during the 1960s and 1970s. Hilde Fuchs published a series of *Fashions in Wool* pattern books, each with "Styled by Hilde" on the cover. Pattern books listed Hilde Fuchs as editor and designer and focused on such themes as hats or socks and mittens, or targeted campus, pre-teen, or men's fashion markets.

American-born Kaffe Fassett was among the most influential designers to gain knitting fame. A painter from a fine arts tradition that frowned on craft, Fassett settled in England in 1964. During a visit to Holm Mills in Inverness, Scotland, he bought knitting needles and twenty colors of yarn. On the train back to London, he pondered what to do with his yarn purchase. Serendipitously, he sat beside a woman who taught him to knit and suggested he knit the colors together. He knit all twenty colors into one sweater and took it straight to *Vogue Knitting Magazine*, which published his design and led to the beginning of his enormously successful career.[330]

Pauline Denham Yarns in Petaluma, California, published pattern books with classic sweaters, jackets, and dresses knit in a fine gauge (six to seven stitches = one inch). Promoted as California originals, Denham sold sweater yarn with matching worsted wool fabric in heather tones. Yarns included Shan Isle and Tulare (100 percent wool), Nubette (wool-rayon blend), Angora Faerie (angora-wool blend), and Ballet (mohair).[331] Designs in Denham pattern manuals were subdued and graceful. *Pauline Denham Yarns* had a double-breasted blazer, striped slipover with duplicate stitch diamonds, and delicately textured cardigans, with a nod to the mohair trend in a feather-and-fan mohair stole, shell, and short-sleeved cardigan. *Designs in Molana* interpreted the mohair look in Molana yarn (no fiber types indicated), a refined softness knit to a somewhat larger gauge (four stitches = one inch).

Although customers believed Mary Maxim was a knit designer — thousands wrote to "Miss" Mary Maxim asking her advice about knitting — she was the invention of an entrepreneurial station master in Manitoba, Canada. During the early 1940s, Willard McPhedrain, a young Canadian National Railway station master, had assisted in setting up cottage fiber industries to employ impoverished immigrants. McPhedrain opened a small woolen mill, began a mail-order business from his home, and opened his first wholesale and retail store in Manitoba to sell their products. Taking a cue from Betty Crocker, McPhedrain named the business after Mary Maximchuck, a woman who helped around his home.[332] In 1956 Larry McPhedrain, Willard's son, started the U. S. Mary Maxim mail-order company with kits for hand-knit designs inspired by North American wildlife and the great outdoors: camping scenes with pine trees, moose, leaping fish, hunters, hunting dogs, and such. Sweaters with baseball players, birds in flight, and construction equipment appealed to children. The signature bulky-knit style and shape of the signature Mary Maxim sweater was an adaptation of the Cowichan sweater. Advertisements assured knitters that Mary Maxim sweater kits worked up quickly: "Just a few rows work into inches of beautiful sweater — actually just like

Trendy tunic top and A-line skirt knit by Martha Hoar of Chicago during the 1960s.

Left: Actress and comedienne Goldie Hawn tackles knitting. (Photofest)

Knitting and the Handspinning Revival

By Deborah Robson

Deborah Robson has written on knitting and spinning for magazines including *Interweave Knits*, *Spin-Off*, *Threads*, and others. She's the co-author with Priscilla A. Gibson-Roberts of the classic *Knitting in the Old Way: Designs and Techniques from Ethnic Sweaters* (Nomad Press, 2004).

In the early 1970s, anyone who entertained the odd idea of making yarn by hand could not easily obtain a good spindle, a spinning wheel, or decent fiber. Yet the people who were growing into adulthood at that time spurred a crafts revival that included handspinning. Over about two decades, they first reclaimed yarn-making skills and then reconnected them with knitting.

Across the country, significant numbers of young people rejected mainstream American society and followed Timothy Leary's mandate to "turn on, tune in, and drop out." Many sought social change in counterculture movements, including major handcraft revivals. In the 1971 *Whole Earth Catalog*, social critic Gary North advised, "Prestige will come once more to the man who can build with his own hands, the creative person, the man who possesses operational knowledge of how simple things work." Young people researched and practiced skills that were about to be lost. The would-be spinners among them picked up spindles — heavy and unbalanced. They acquired wool, matted, seed- and burr-specked fiber of unremarkable quality. They spun lumpy yarn, frequently working "in the grease" (not a bad thing for those skilled enough to know how to do this right, which they did not). They wove with their handspun, using it as weft in funky so-called wall-hangings, or they knitted crude and irregular, but still warm, hats and mittens and sweaters. Their yarn was "natural" and "individual" and "real."

A few remarkable resources helped these new spinners expand their vision and refine their skill. Elsie Davenport's *Your Handspinning* (1953) held the essential details — from fleece selection to making yarn — that were needed to revive the craft.

Paula Simmons raised sheep with natural color wool that she spun into consistent weights of yarn. Always ahead of her time, Simmons wrote several books that helped new spinners rediscover the sheep-to-fabric continuum.

In 1970, Allen Fannin published *Handspinning — Art and Technique*. Fannin's comprehensive text and photos captured the techniques of precision spinning and efficient production.

Spin-Off, an annual and later quarterly magazine, first appeared in 1977. It put spinners in touch with each other and created a central marketplace that nurtured fledgling businesses that began to provide better and more varied spinning tools and materials.

Davenport, Simmons, and Fannin were all weavers (although Simmons also marketed her yarn to knitters) and *Spin-Off* came from Interweave Press, which began as a service for weavers. To connect knitting with spinning, knitters had to discover the pleasure of working with high-quality handspun yarn and to design their own knitting patterns.

In books and workshops, Elizabeth Zimmermann gave countless numbers of knitters the confidence to design their own patterns or modify published patterns for their own needs. Zimmermann promoted a knitting intelligence that had nearly been forgotten in the United States. She and her daughter Meg Swansen also ran a small business that supplied knitters with high-quality, natural-fiber, imported yarns: they trained knitters' fingers to appreciate the good stuff. Only in the early 1980s were spinning and knitting firmly re-linked, in part with the publication of books by Jacqueline Fee and Priscilla Gibson-Roberts, both of whom were spinners and knitters.

"The ultimate knitting thrill is to work with your own handspun yarn," wrote Fee in *The Sweater Workshop* (1983). Several projects were knit from handspun yarn and quickly upped knitters' skills. The first edition of Priscilla Gibson-Roberts' *Knitting in the Old Way*, 1985, promoted the timeless relationship between the best traditional knitting and superb, handspun yarns made of appropriate fibers. Gibson-Roberts saw no reason why contemporary spinners and knitters could not be as skilled as their predecessors and provided examples, information, and encouragement, along with a world tour of techniques, construction, and patterning.

The reconnection of knitting with handspinning also depended on consistent and appealing handspun yarns. Spinners needed better tools and higher quality fibers, more readily available as the spinning revival continued. In the early 1970s, spinners ordered Ashford wheels from New Zealand, tracked down bulky spinners from the Pacific Northwest and from Canada, and carved too-heavy spindles from backyard wood. As the decade progressed, an array of domestic manufactured and handcrafted spinning wheels were available, along with lighter and more carefully balanced hand-spindles. The American Livestock Breeds Conservancy (then American Minor Breeds Conservancy) began to save the genetics of sheep breeds that produce wool suited for hand, rather than mechanical, spinning. Small businesses processed and sold fibers for handspinners.

Wool festivals gave new spinners access to excellent quality fiber. In 1974, the Maryland Sheep and Wool Festival and the Black Sheep Gathering (Oregon) were the first major national events that supported shepherds who wanted to grow more than generic, mid-grade fiber destined for the low-paying wool market. Through the 1970s and 1980s, more festivals were established: the Massachusetts Sheep and Woolcraft Fair (1975), the New Hampshire Sheep and Wool Festival (1977), the World Sheep and Fiber Arts Festival in Missouri (1980), and the Taos Wool Festival in New Mexico (1984). Beginning in 1983, Interweave Press has sponsored the Spin-Off Autumn Retreat (SOAR) specifically for handspinners. More wool festivals and gatherings of spinners and knitters have been established, often as annual events.

The handspinning revival gave knitters the delight of working with finely crafted handspun yarns. There's nothing like it.

Resources

Fee, Jacqueline. *The Sweater Workshop*. Loveland, CO: Interweave Press, 1983. Second edition, Camden, M.E.: Down East, 2002.

Gibson-Roberts, Priscilla, and Deborah Robson. *Knitting in the Old Way*. Loveland, CO: Interweave Press, 1985. Revised edition, Fort Collins, CO: Nomad Press, 2004.

Last Whole Earth Catalog: Access to Tools. Menlo Park, CA: Portola Institute, 1971.

North, Gary. "Inflation and the Return of the Craftsman." *Whole Earth Catalog*, January 1971, 8.

Zimmermann, Elizabeth. *Knitter's Almanac*. New York: Charles Scribner's Sons, 1974. Reissued by Dover, 1981.

Zimmermann, Elizabeth. *Knitting without Tears: Basic Techniques and Easy-to-Follow Directions for Garments to Fit All Sizes*. New York: Charles Scribner's Sons, 1971. Continuously in print.

magic. You will find it possible to knit a *whole back* in a single evening! You'll see then why Mary Maxim bulky sweaters have become the most popular outdoor hand-knit garment in America today."[333] Working Mary Maxim Northland and Cloudspun bulky wool to a large gauge (often seven stitches and ten rows to two inches) on size 9 needles, knitters turned out warm, wooly sweaters for the whole family. The company also sold kits for lighter-weight bulkies and worsted-weight knitting, and for a "Modernistic Afghan" with knit geometric and a "Sportsman Afghan" with charted hunting and fishing designs.[334]

Fashion Dolls

The Barbie doll made her debut at the 1959 American International Toy Fair in New York. Barbie's voluptuous figure — 39 by 21 by 33 inches in human measurements — shocked parents, but children adored her. Mattel's in-house designers outfitted Barbie with glamorous wardrobes. Could yarn companies and knitting designers be far behind? Hilde Fuchs published *Garments for Fashion Model Dolls* (1964) with fashions for the entire family — the family that was 9 1/2 to 13 inches tall. Knitters ordered "glamorous summer knits for a glamorous model doll" from *Needle and Yarn* magazine, and only 35¢ brought patterns for a knit coat, hat, suit, skirt and blouse, ski pants, and hooded pullover. Knitters also ordered a pattern manual with Barbie's sweater wardrobe from *Woman's Day*.[335] Coats & Clark's *Doll Wardrobe* (1964) had knitting patterns for Barbie: a wide-collar-seed-stitch pullover and slacks set, knit car coat and skirt, and party dress with shrug for the girl doll, and a boat neck shirt and trousers for the boy doll. All of these knitting patterns called for Coats & Clark's 100 percent wool Red Heart Super Fingering yarn. Virginia Lakin of Loveland, Colorado, published *Doll Knitting and Crocheting Magazine* and a series of knit and crochet pattern books for dolls, including fashion dolls. *Virginia Lakin's Doll Knitting and Crocheting* (1966) also had knitting patterns for the popular — but not as popular as Barbie — troll dolls.

Who could have predicted that Barbie (named for Mattel founders Elliot and Ruth Handler's daughter) and her sidekick dolls like Ken and Skipper would become objects of fame, fashion, and knitting?

Practical Knitting

Knitters with a practical side favored simple, useful hand knits. *The Workbasket*, a humble home arts magazine from Kansas City, Missouri, faithfully included knitting patterns in each monthly issue (25¢ in 1966; 50¢ by 1976). In December 1966, *The Workbasket* had simple stretch slippers, a child's cardigan and hooded pullover, and a "Glamor [*sic*] in Glade Green" woman's cardigan in Supra Mohair embellished with crocheted flowers. By the 1970s, conservative but pretty knit sweaters, vests, and coats appeared regularly on *The Workbasket* cover. Another homespun source of practical knitting and crocheting tips was Pat Trexler's newspaper column, "Pat's Pointers." Handy hints ranged from favorite cast-on methods to buttonhole styles. Readers responded *en masse* when Pat admitted she had lost instructions for a favorite corn cob pot holder, and Pat published the pattern sent by Freda Blackburn. Pat sold mail-order patterns (35¢–50¢ when customers provided a stamped, self-addressed envelope) that would "put some real punch" into a wardrobe: a vivid burnt orange and forest green knit suit with Jacquard borders and fringe; tunic-length window-pane check cardigan; and slipover vest with an elephant or donkey for election year.[336]

Knitting for Barbie and other fashion dolls used up small bits of leftover yarn and kept young *fashionistas* happy with their wardrobes.

A subscription to *The Workbasket* delivered practical, simple knitting patterns at low cost. The cape with openings for hands was a popular style.

at age ninety-eight, Minta knit circular rugs from fabric scraps, which became so popular she had a waiting list of people willing to buy the rugs for $7 each.[338] More than one knitter advertised products of home-based businesses in *Women's Circle*. Knitters sold hand-knit slippers and hats or Barbie doll wardrobes; others sold knitting patterns or instruction books:

IMPROVE YOUR KNITTING! Order "Professional Knitting Secrets". Experts' tips on techniques, fitting, finishing, etc. Over 50 pattern stitches. $2. Dept. WC-2, Sis and Jan, 225 Linden, Winnetka, Illinois 600093. Free gift.

An occasional knitter assembled kits to sell:

LADIES Knit this lovely cardigan with 8 oz. yarn, sizes 30-46! My original ideas included which made this worth $50.00. 25¢ & stamped envelope. Box 218. E. Pepperell, Mass. 01437.[339]

At that upscale price, how many knitters would have bought the cardigan kit?

Knitting comfortable, practical little things for babies and small children was a knitting mainstay. Charming patterns for young folks enticed relatives and friends to knit gifts made with love. Yarn companies hired knitting designers (typically unidentified) to create new designs, some with a nod to such fashion trends as the poor boy sweater. Adorable babies and toddlers modeled knit sweaters, coats, caps, leggings, pants, and dresses in Bucilla's *Lovable Hand Knits* (1968) and Columbia-Minerva's *Beautiful Baby Book* (1967). Knitters could choose among patterns with cables, lace, intarsia, smocking, and embroidery, and there were even patterns for an argyle stockings, jumper, and sweater outfit. For older kids, there were mohair and bulky cardigan patterns in books like the *Bernat Classics for Girls and Boys* (1962). Jack Frost's *Gypsy Kids: Unisex Patterns for Boys and Girls* (1977) had plenty of popular vest patterns.

Revival of Handcrafts

During the 1960s and 1970s, youth in particular rediscovered macramé, weaving, crochet, and knitting — some as part of counterculture. Artists also began to explore fiber as a medium for fine art. Mary Walker Phillips' *Creative Knitting: A New Art Form* (1971) treated knitting as an art form. Dover Publications reprinted *Mary Thomas's Book of Knitting Patterns* in 1972 (originally published in London, 1943), and Barbara G. Walker published a series of invaluable books, including *A Treasury of Knitting Patterns*, *Charted Knitting Designs*, and *Sampler Knitting*. Interest in hand-weaving soared, and Linda Ligon

Knitters sought out imported yarn and patterns during the 1960s and 1970s. The Antartex kit, a Scottish import used to knit this rugged sweater, was purchased from a yarn shop in Geneva, Illinois, during the 1960s. The fiber is seventy percent mohair, thirty percent wool. Knit by Martha Hoar of Chicago.

Knitters with plenty of yarn, time, and energy could indulge in warm blankets or afghans. Coats & Clark and American Thread published pattern booklets with afghan designs from plaid to pineapples. *Knit and Crocheted Afghans* had panel-embroidered afghans with patriotic eagle emblems and flower motifs, and *Decorator Afghans* (1963) featured cable panel, butterfly stitch, color block, and Aran Isle afghans using Coats & Clark Red Heart knitting worsted (twelve skeins of four-ply, four-ounce "Tangle-Proof" pull-out). Bernhard Ulmann's *Knitting Primer: 100 Easy-to-Knit Stitches* (1968) shepherded the more ambitious knitter through a series of textured sampler blocks that, sewn together, created an afghan. *Women's Circle* magazine sold inexpensive patterns for such everyday comforts as caps, bed socks, slipper socks (with bunny ears for toddler version), and even a smart cable-knit bathroom mat and toilet lid cover.[337] In 1974 *Women's Circle* profiled 105-year-old knitter Minta Schoonover of Farmington, Illinois. After she retired as town librarian

Knit
Snowsuit
with Hood

LITTLE RED
RIDING HOOD
Number 766-36
(instructions
opposite)

JACK FROST
Number 766-37
(instructions
opposite)

More upscale publications invested in well-designed clothing for youngsters — and took the first steps toward a more inclusive mainstream society. *Beautiful Baby Book*, 1967.

Left: Making practical, pretty clothing for babies and children was a mainstay of knitting, even as changes in society raged during the 1960s and 1970s. *The Workbasket*, December 1974.

started *Handwoven* magazine as part of Interweave Press, a publishing company that grew to include books and magazines about knitting.

Stewart Brand launched the first *Whole Earth Catalog* in 1968 as a tool for the 1960s counterculture. Catalog readers submitted an eclectic assortment of low-cost, mostly mail-order resources that people could use to educate themselves about independent living. Sources for wood stoves and basket-making supplies appeared side by side with books about organic gardening and Eastern religions. The 1971 catalog directed aspiring knitters to *Knitting Dictionary*, Ida Riley Duncan's *Complete Book of Progressive Knitting* (1949), and Gertrude Taylor's *America's Knitting Book* (1968). Illustrations and text sampled from these resources were patchy at best: how

to make a knit stitch, shape armholes, and construct buttonholes. Knitting suited the independent lifestyle that appealed to *Whole Earth Catalog* readers.[340]

By the end of the 1970s, the environmental, civil rights, and women's movements had changed American laws, institutions, and aspirations. American society struggled to become more inclusive. Only in the early 1970s were racial minority populations represented in mainstream knitting books or advertisements for yarn. By 1980, more than half of all college students were women, and the salaried labor force was sixty percent female. Many women knit to relax after long days working in stressful occupations. As the twentieth century wound to a close, Americans continued to knit, although they no longer *needed* the product, they did need the process of knitting.

Chapter Twelve

Knitting Redefined

The tumultuous social changes of the 1960s and 1970s led to a more inclusive society — for women and minorities in particular. For many Americans, a booming stock market and low unemployment during the Reagan years fueled more affluent lives, despite mushrooming national debt and disturbing conflicts in the Middle East. The fabric of American life was changing. For one thing, the United States was an immigration magnet: an estimated 17 million legal immigrants — plus an unknown number of undocumented ones — arrived in America between 1980 and 2000. The American family also changed. Both men and women married later, nearly five years later than in 1950, if they chose to marry at all. By 2000, only one in five married couples had a single male breadwinner working outside the home. Educated women entered professional positions, and households relied on their income.

Women wearing power suits and working outside their homes, it was predicted, would not have time for knitting. Instead they would prefer inexpensive ready-made knits from stores and catalogs, and knitting would become a pastime whose time really had passed. But knitting continued. Rather than spelling the demise of knitting, the increasingly pricy array of new yarns and designer patterns redefined knitting from utilitarian craft to designer fashion statement. Knitting was also redefined as a compassionate gesture that could make the world a better place. Knitting became a serious medium for fine artists and, increasingly, knitting became a source of solace and a way to connect with a world growing smaller each day.

Fashion Sweaters

Fashion designer Perry Ellis had introduced hand-knit sweaters as a sportswear fashion statement during the late 1970s. Marc Jacobs, design director at Perry Ellis, carried on the legacy of distinctive hand knits, and Calvin Klein's collections featured hand-knit classics. Perhaps the oversize sweaters of the

Goddess Throne was crafted by artist Karen Searle blending knitting, crocheting, and weaving with materials from a bent aluminum frame to knit copper wire. (Photograph by Karen Searle)

Opposite page: Katharine Cobey of Cushing, Maine, was one of the pioneers of art knitting. She honored her mother, Clare Raymond Durant, with her hand-knit visual metaphor, *Portrait of Alzheimer's*. (Photograph by David Boyce Cobey)

Classic sweaters of the early 1980s boasted broad shoulders — upper sleeves often gathered and padded — that seemed to reflect the growing opportunity and responsibility that women were "shouldering."

During the 1980s, more children dressed in smaller versions of adult styles. *Good Housekeeping Needlecraft*. Fall-Winter 1980-81.

1980s and early 1990s encouraged more knitters to try their hand at making sweaters. *Vogue Knitting* editor Margery Winter attributed the upsurge in home knitting to young knitters who wanted to duplicate popular designer sweaters.[341] Oversize sweaters that had a boxy silhouette, straight without much concern for shaping, were easy and fast to knit. Sweaters grew larger, longer, and roomier during the 1980s, and broad shoulders bolstered with shoulder pads were in style until the mid-1990s. Shoulder pads could even be knit and stuffed with scraps of mohair.[342] Another popular 1980s sweater style had gathered and puffed sleeve caps that resembled the turn-of-the-century Gibson girl look.[343]

Knitters chose from an ever-widening array of luxurious yarns in natural fibers, including mohair, cashmere, angora, exotic wools, silk, and combed cotton. Mohair was still so popular in 1986 that *Knitting and Design for Mohair* listed seventy-six brands and forty suppliers of yarn containing mohair.[344] An oversize, heavily cabled mohair sweater appeared on the cover of *McCall's Needlework and Crafts* magazine for August 1986, with more jewel-toned, fluffy mohair sweaters inside. Blending natural and manmade fibers gave knitters new yarns that had the best qualities of each. Bernat, for example, marketed Monaco yarn, a blend of 70 percent wool, 15 percent rayon, and 15 percent nylon. Caron International made a cotton terry yarn appropriate for the nautical look comfortable tops. Reynolds sold Sorrento, a blend of linen for crispness, cotton for comfort, and acrylic for easy care. Other specialty yarns included hand-dyed, painted, metallic, and ribbon.

Sweaters were the stars of most pattern books and a growing number of pattern flyers. The familiar Aran, Nordic, and Tyrolean styles carried over from the 1970s. A flyer from William Unger and Co. (1980) had sweater designs for men and women knit using Unger's Skol, a soft and fluffy brushed wool. Knit with size 10 needles, Skol worked up quickly into long (over-the-hip) cardigans and coats in textured and color patterns, many with Aran and Fair Isle details. Designers reinterpreted Nordic patterns with bands of soft floral or vibrant geometric motifs. Favorite colors were jewel tones, rusts, and browns, some with embroidery or duplicate stitch added to the knit surface.

Knitting and needlework magazines sported sweaters on their covers, even the downscale *Workbasket*. Knitters could count on finding patterns for afghans and children's knits inside. More children wore diminutive versions of adult styles during the 1980s. The "little miss is more fashion conscious than

ever," claimed *Good Housekeeping Needlecraft* when cardigan and sweater set patterns echoed grownup styles (1980–1981). Similarly, *McCall's Needlework and Crafts* had lace-knit sweaters for little girls (June 1985). *McCall's Design Ideas for Christmas Knit and Crochet* (1983) provided patterns for children's sweaters and berets in miniature versions of adult Fair Isle designs, with a nod to childhood in such details as a row of little red ducks.

Sweater vests were also popular knitting projects. More than one knitter was happy to dispense with the tedious duplication of sleeves. The classic 1980s sweater vest reached just below the waist or covered the hips, and cardigans and pullovers alike had round or deep V-necks. Typically, the sweater vest had wide shoulders or cap sleeves, perhaps further exaggerated with shoulder pads, and many vest patterns had low patch pockets decorated with cable or color variations.

Knitting as Legend

Pattern books began to extol the heritage and romance of knitting. Knitters who tackled the twists and turns of Aran patterns "continue[d] the lovely allegory that is so much a part of Irish heritage," according to *Irish Knits* (*Bernat Handicrafter No. 516*, 1983). Picturesque thatched cottages, colorful doorways, and ancient stone ruins beside Galway Bay, Ireland, were the background for creamy white Aran sweaters. Knitters savored, or perhaps created, new legends: "Here on these islands of the North Atlantic, at Europe's westernmost point, legend lives. . . . It lives, above all, in authentic Aran knitwear. The hand-knitted garments of these rustic people have developed a significance beyond their primary function of protecting the wearer against biting ocean winds and salt spray. Their elaborate stitch patterns speak eloquently of love, home, faith, and work — the simple threads which form the fabric of Aran life." *Aran Knits* provided a handy key to symbolic Aran patterns: Irish Moss (gift from the sea), Diamond (symbol of success), Basket (fisherman's creel), and so on.

Knitting was part of life on the Aran Isles, although the history and symbolism of Aran knitting were not as deep as suggested in popular movies (*Man of Aran*, 1934) or publications (*Vogue Knitting*, 1956; *The Harmony Guide to Aran and Fair Isle Knitting* by Debra Mountford). The earliest and best documented Aran knitting was a pair of indigo-dyed stockings knit with white cuffs and toes. Gansey sweaters that Aran women knit for husbands and sons were the hardy prototypes of the white Aran sweater, a twentieth century tourist and export item. Aran knitting infiltrated the fashion world when Jean Paul Gaultier included tight-knit Aran trousers, sweater, and cap in his 1985 menswear collection.[345]

Knitting History and Ethnicity

Knitters seemed increasingly curious about the ethnic and historical roots of hand knitting. Interest followed on the heels of the craze for international knitting traditions during the 1970s, though perhaps also spurred by the phenomenal impact of the 1977 television mini-series *Roots*. Based on Alex Haley's best-selling novel about his African ancestry, *Roots* traced seven generations of a slave family and attracted an average 80 million viewers to each episode, culminating in an audience of 100 million people (nearly half the nation) who watched the final episode. *Roots* was an extraordinary American cultural phenomenon that inspired a collective desire to understand family origin and ethnic heritage.

Knitting had received little attention in textile history or knitting books in the past. Kax Wilson, for example, dedicated one page to knitting in *A History of Textiles*.[346] London fashion journalist Mary Thomas had compiled remarkable technical knowledge of knitting patterns but less certain information about knitting history in the two books she published in 1938 and 1943. During the 1980s, this began to change when books about textiles and knitting tackled the ellusive and often misunderstood history of knitting. In *The Illustrated History of Textiles*, a chapter was devoted to knitting and acknowledged the inherent challenge of tracking the history of utilitarian products intended to be worn out. Erica Wilson introduced *Erica Wilson's Knitting Book* with a brief, though somewhat dubious, history of knitting ("one of the most ancient of crafts") and included no references.[347] *Vogue Knitting, The Ultimate Knitting Book* introduced an extensive

compendium of techniques with a brief history of knitting, again without references.[348] In 1987 Richard Rutt, Bishop of Leicester, took readers on a vicarious world tour of knitting in *A History of Hand Knitting*, devoting just five pages to knitting in the Americas (nearly half to Cowichan knitting). Rutt concluded, "Information about the history of hand knitting in the United States is hard to find." In 1988, Anne L. Macdonald took a phenomenal step forward in the history of American knitting in *No Idle Hands: The Social History of American Knitting*.[349] Rutt and Macdonald were the first to treat knitting as a proper topic for comprehensive scholarship.

Beginning in the 1980s, knitters had a growing wealth of knowledge at their fingertips about ethnic knitting traditions. Interest peaked first in Europe and a number of books about traditional knitting were published in Europe and later in the American market. Betsy Harrell researched stocking knitting in Turkey and published *Anatolian Knitting Designs* in Istanbul. The first edition of Sheila McGregor's *The Complete Book of Traditional Fair Isle Knitting* was published in London in 1981 and detailed the history, techniques, and patterns for Fair Isle knitting. *Twined Knitting* first appeared in Sweden and described the historical search for the authentic Swedish folk technique that

By the late 1980s, roomy sweater vests with drop shoulders had replaced the long slim sweaters popular earlier in the decade. *Vests*, Brunswick, 1982.

Left: Yarns and knitting patterns took on an increasingly international flavor, such as the stylish "Bolero" design by Helene Rush. *Knitter's Magazine*, Fall 1990.

Knitters indulged in long, oversized sweaters through the mid-1990s. *Vogue Knitting International*, Fall 1994.

More and more knitters savored knitting as story and tradition, whether legend or reality. *Irish Knits*, 1983.

Year after year, knitters learned more about ethnic knitting traditions.

More business opportunities opened for knitting entrepreneurs like Chellie Pingree and Debby Anderson of North Island Designs. *Maine Island Classics*, 1988.

produced a dense fabric of intense patterning (first introduced to America in 1983 in Rae Compton's *The Complete Book of Traditional Knitting*). Britt-Marie Christoffersson showed historical Swedish knitting patterns as inspiration for early 1990s oversized sweater styles in *Swedish Sweaters*, first published in Sweden. *Knitting in the Nordic Tradition* by Vibeke Lind originally appeared in Norway.[350]

American knitters also explored ethnic knitting traditions, often those outside their own ethnic heritage. Articles from *Threads* magazine were compiled into *Knitting Around the World*, including Aran and Fair Isle knitting, Shetland and Faeroe Islands lace knitting, Bohus Strickning, and argyle knitting.[351] *Knitter's* magazine focused its fall 1990 issue on South American knitting, in particular Peruvian knitting with alpaca. In 1976 Karen Searle and Suzanne Baizerman had founded Dos Tejedoras, a press that by 1984 was publishing books about textile traditions, including *Latvian Mittens* and *Salish Indian Sweaters*. Lizbeth Upitis, inspired by her mother-in-law's hand-knit mittens, documented not only the techniques and patterns, but also the role of Latvian mittens in regional identity and marriage ritual. Priscilla A. Gibson-Roberts captured the story of Cowichan knitters of Vancouver Island in *Salish Indian Sweaters*. Gibson-Roberts also wrote *Ethnic Socks and Stockings* and *Knitting in the Old Way*, guides to working in traditional techniques. Charlene Schurch, of Czech heritage, described a story of assimilation through the history of knitting among Russia's Komi people in *Knitting Marvelous Mittens: Ethnic Designs from Russia*. Wendy Keele documented the techniques of Bohus knitting and the stories of founder Emma Jacobsson and other Swedish women who knit for the Bohus cottage industry. In *Knitting Ganseys*, Beth Brown-Reinsel described the intricate pattern knitting, dropped shoulders, and easy fit of traditional British fishermen's sweaters.[352] Kristin Nicholas, creative director for Classic Elite Yarns, developed a series of ethnic-inspired kits called the World Knits Collection. American authors often relied on previous work by European or Scandinavia knitters;

Brown-Reinsel referred to Gladys Thompson's *Patterns for Guernseys, Jerseys, and Arans* (1971) and Mary Wright's *Cornish Guernseys and Knitfrocks* (1979). In *Simply Socks: 45 Traditional Turkish Patterns to Knit*, Anna Zilboorg acknowledged the work of Betsy Harrell.[353] Additional books highlighted Victorian lace knitting, Orenburg lace shawls, folk shawls, and Estonian folk knitting.

The Business of Knitting

The yarn industry kept the knitting market well supplied with yarns in new fiber combinations, colors, and textures. David Blumenthal, a fourth-generation chief executive officer for Lion Brand yarns (established in 1878), became a marketing cheerleader for knitting yarn. "Hippie" crochet had kept Lion Brand in business through the late 1970s, and the company responded to a subsequent dip in sales by selling at the growing numbers of big-box discount stores. Knitters could also buy inexpensive yarns like Red Heart at the dwindling numbers of five-and-dime stores, or they could purchase upscale yarns from yarn shops in larger cities. In more remote regions, knitters could order specialty yarns and kits from yarn shops or suppliers. Underhill Yarns in Bay Head, New Jersey, sold imported Shetland yarns and sweater kits, for example, and Lambspun of Colorado began a mail-order line of yarns in sweater and accessory kits. Magazines and pattern books encouraged knitters to write or call yarn companies to find the nearest suppliers.

The yarn industry's trade association, the Craft Yarn Council of America (CYCA), formed in 1981 to raise awareness of yarns. CYCA initiated a certification program for knit and crochet instructors and supported Warm Up America! and Caps for Kids, both community-based compassionate knitting projects. The Knit-Out, playing off the "sit-ins" of the 1960s, was originated in 1998 by CYCA as a way to take knitting and crochet into the public arena. People who never set foot in a yarn shop stopped for a quick knitting or crochet lesson when they saw the beautiful yarns and patterns. The first Knit-Out in New York City attracted 1,000 people; by fall 2006, more than 35,000 people visited the New York Knit-Out. Knitting guilds nationwide adapted the idea and took their knitting out to regional parks and malls.

Growing interest in knitting generated business opportunities. In New York City, knitter and designer Suzanne Russell opened Rococo, a retail shop that sold her hand-knit designs to such stores as Bloomingdale's and Saks Fifth Avenue. She began by knitting pictures into sweaters — cats, cancan dancers, Indian designs — and during the 1980s she and her partners employed one thousand knitters in England to meet the demand for their sweaters.[354] In 1985, Chellie Pingree founded North Island Designs, a business that sold sweater kits

and pattern books. North Light was the offspring of a retail store that sold yarn spun from local sheep, plus sweaters, socks, and mittens knit by the islanders who knit during the winter while other work was scarce. Pingree teamed with knitter Debby Anderson, who designed the sweater kits, and they promoted their new business at the National Needlework Show in New York. Within three years, North Island Designs sold sweater kits to more than one thousand stores nationwide and produced a series of pattern books, including *Maine Island Classics: Living and Knitting on a Maine Island*. North Island Designs sent its sheep fleece for spinning to another business, Bartlettyarns. In 1981 Russ Pierce purchased the Bartlett Mill, in Harmony, Maine, a mill established in 1821 to spin yarn for weavers. Bartlettyarns spun fleece into yarn on a spinning mule, a two-hundred-year-old machine that spins yarn with the heather, homespun look popular with knitters.[355]

Individuals also found ways to market new yarns, at times with personal and political messages. The idea for Peace Fleece knitting yarn originated in 1985 when Peter Hagerty and Marty Tracy traveled to the Soviet Union seeking ways to diffuse the threat of nuclear war. Peace Fleece blended American wool with wool from such troubled world regions as Russia, Kyrgyzia, Israel, and the West Bank. Peace Fleece aimed to find common ground for understanding among farmers and craftspeople worldwide. In 1996, Anni Kristensen founded Himalaya Yarn working with Tibetan families in Nepal who sorted and hand spun sari scraps into unique silk yarn for knitters.[356] Although Biddy and Annie Hurlbut had started Peruvian Connection in 1976, the company grew to an international business during the 1980s. Peruvian Connection hired designers to create Andean-inspired patterns for sweaters hand-knit by Andean artisans in luxury fibers, alpaca in particular.

New magazines devoted in part or completely to knitting appeared, among them *Knit 'n Style* (1981), *Spin-Off* (1977), *Knitter's Magazine* (1984), *Vogue Knitting* (1982), *Knitter's* (1984), *Simplicity Knitting* (1985), *Threads* (1985), *Piecework* (1993), *Interweave Knits* (1996), and *INKnitters* (2001). The Knitting Guild Association (TKGA), a non-profit organization dedicated to knitters and knitting, was founded in 1984 as The Knitting Guild of America. Membership in TKGA brought knitters together through their magazine *Cast On, the Educational Journal for Knitters*, first released in summer 1984. Members could enroll in master classes for hand or machine knitting, donate to charitable knitting endeavors, and connect with one another at national

Mary Walker Phillips, Elizabeth Zimmermann, and Barbara G. Walker (left to right) — were knitters, authors, philosophers, and friends. (Photograph by T. S. Zimmermann, 1980; Courtesy of Meg Swansen)

For subscribers to *Wool Gathering*, each issue was like a friend who dropped in for a visit, bringing clever new patterns and the latest on knitting.

knit and crochet conferences. Eventually, they could connect with other knitters day by day through TKGA's website. Over time, knitters could learn about ever larger numbers of yarns and notions, patterns and kits, books and contests, tours and cruises, camps and workshops, shows and conferences that were promoted in all the knitting and needlework magazines.

Around the nation, knitters began to find exhibit venues, sometimes in unexpected places. In 1987, the University of Minnesota's Goldstein Gallery recognized

the creative knitting work of Mary Walker Phillips in the exhibit *The Magic Knitting Needles of Mary Walker Phillips*, curated by Catherine Daly. In the small town of Monticello in southern Wisconsin, a restaurant named the Dining Room turned its walls into exhibit space for textiles, often knitting. Ruth Knight Sybers, a knitter and textile graduate of the University of Wisconsin, Madison, began the exhibits with her own knitting in 1996. Katherine Pence, a graphic designer and author of *. . . And a Time to Knit Stockings* (1997), exhibited sweaters, vests, hats, and socks inspired by Nordic, Bavarian, and Russian designs, including a dramatic double-knit, reversible sweater coat. Joyce Williams of rural Sparta, Wisconsin, exhibited a knit coat that mimicked the Star Tumbling Block quilt pattern and a Bohus-inspired sweater with the soft colors of the Wisconsin countryside. Williams had learned to knit for Britain during World War II and followed patterns until she learned to design her own knits from Elizabeth Zimmermann and Meg Swansen. With editor Lizbeth Upitis, Williams wrote *Latvian Dreams*, a book of knitting inspired by Latvian weaving designs. The Dining Room also brought together the work of ten men who knit: Kevin Ames, Gene Beugler, Greg Cotton, Nino Esposito, Dale Long, Rick Mondragon, Ted Myatt, Robert Powell, Horst Schulz, and Leigh Witchel.[357]

Inventors also found fertile ground for creating new knitting products. The Brittany Company began making knitting needles in 1980. Its first effort was a hand-turned, walnut Victorian needle eagerly purchased

Handspun, hand-dyed skirt and sweater knit by Kathryn Alexander, who loves to use lots of color and small geometric shapes. Hand spinning and dyeing hundreds of colors adds to the whimsy of her work, and knitting releases the energy created when she twists fibers into yarn. The small geometric shapes twist, tilt, curve, and pucker—a never-ending source of entertainment and anticipation.

by knitters. The romantic tale that Brittany Company founders first peddled their knitting needles on a beach in Santa Cruz, California, is a bit of knitting folklore. Another Brittany design, the Art Deco birch knitting needle, has replaced the walnut needle.[358] The Boye Needle Company sold NeedleMaster, a set of circular knitting needles in graduated sizes with four different cable lengths all tucked away in a zipper case. In 1980, Christine M. Vasquez and Linda L. Rawlins patented an adjustable-length circular knitting needle, and in 1984, Anne L. Macdonald patented a device to prevent tangles when knitting patterned fabric using multiple balls of yarn. In 1987, Cornelius Phipps Sr. and Jr. devised an interchangeable knitting needle system. In 1989, Helen M. Slevin patented a knitting needle support apparatus. The knitter sat on a strap with two mounted holders on either side; each holder had sockets into which round-ended knitting needles would fit, supporting the needles in correct knitting position. Also in 1989, Loretta L. Gardiner patented a knitting and crochet needle kit with interchangeable knitting points and crochet hooks on shafts of different lengths. In 1992, Norma Kroh patented a type of ring with an elevated loop designed to carry knitting yarn over the finger. In 2002, Deborah Lynn Poole patented a one-handed knitting aid for knitters who only had use of one hand, and in 2006, Katherine Marie Eley-Holden-Sotnik received a patent for a circular knitting needle with an elastic cord.

Knit Designers

More knit designers began to receive name credit for their patterns during the 1980s. Knitting patterns in Simplicity's *Knit and Crochet* (1980) credited designers, many of whom worked for specific yarn companies. *McCall's Needlework and Crafts*, however, did not list designers until later in the decade. *Vogue Knitting* focused on hand knits created by designers like Missoni, Perry Ellis, and Calvin Klein, who were otherwise well known in the fashion world. In 1979, Saks Fifth Avenue opened a shop that treated sweaters like art to be collected like jewelry.[359] Some designers published their own work. Penny and Janice Straker, for example, created a series of patterns, each with salient pointers for classic, refined Straker hand knits. Other knitting designers published books with extensive instructions that encouraged knitters to seek creative expression in their knitting. In *Erica Wilson's Knitting Book*, the author included more than thirty patterns designed by the author or others given name credit. Wilson encouraged knitting as self-expression. She divided knitting techniques into four categories: texture, texture and color, changing colors, and creative embellishments. Knitters who followed her step-by-step instructions for knitting techniques would emerge armed with skills required to design original sweaters. Although best known for embroidery, Erica Wilson contributed a compact and lively repertoire of techniques for the adventurous knitter.[360]

Similarly, Angela ffrench in *Knitting and Design for Mohair* treated sweaters as "compositions" for knitters to create from her directory of templates, stitch patterns, and neck and cuff variations — something of a mix-and-match approach to knit design. British designer Montse Stanley turned her understanding of architectural structure into a professional knitting career. American publishers distributed her many excellent books about knit design and technology, including *Creating and Knitting Your Own Designs for a Perfect Fit* (1982), *The Handknitter's Handbook* (1986), and *Knitting Plus* (embroidered knitting, 1990). In *Knitting Plus*, Stanley treated knitting as a soft, blank canvas to cover with colorful yarns and threads.[361]

In 1986, knitting instructor Maggie Righetti published *Knitting in Plain English*, a compendium of lessons advertised as the "only book any knitter will ever need." Righetti gleaned her knowledge from years of teaching and held firm ideas about instruction methods. Chapter 1 — You Can Always Tell What's Wrong with the Garment by the Way the Model is Posed — taught students to cast a critical eye on photos of models wearing hand knits. She believed that knitting students invariably chose self-defeating first projects, so she forced students to knit garments that she dubbed fondly "the dumb baby sweater" and "the stupid baby bonnet." The sweater was knit in one piece from the

The progression from knitting sweaters to knitting human figures such as her *Woman Within* from 1999 — seemed natural for Karen Searle of St. Paul, Minnesota.

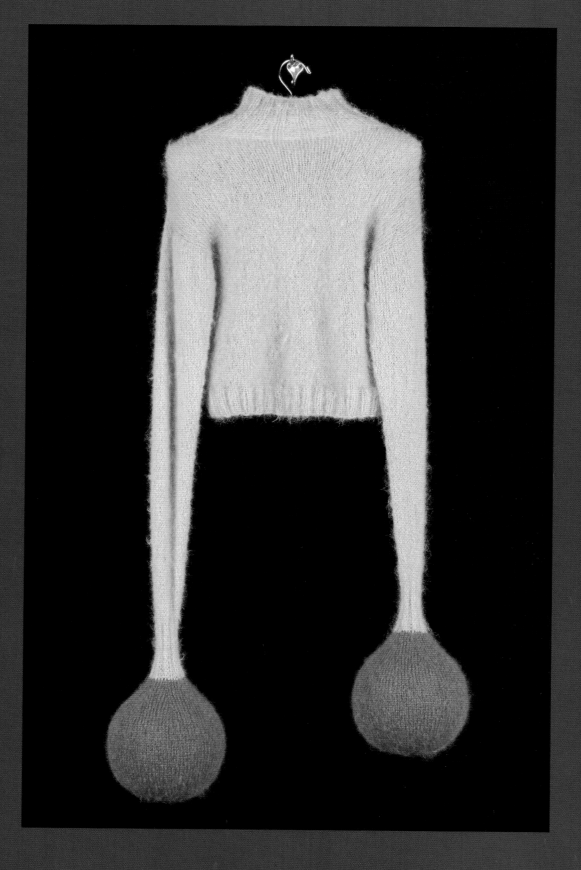

Chicago artist Lindsay Obermeyer hand knit *Weighed Down* in mohair for her "Women's Work" series. (Photograph by Sanders Visual Images)

Elizabeth Zimmermann: The Godmother of Knitting

By Linda Ligon

Linda Ligon is the founder and creative director for Interweave Press in Loveland, Colorado. Her essay on Elizabeth Zimmermann was first published in *Interweave Knits*, Spring 2000.

I'm just not convinced Elizabeth Zimmermann got it right, the title of that first book, *Knitting Without Tears*. It should have been *Knitting Till You Laugh So Hard You Cry*. Or *Knitting with Hilarity and Complete Confidence*. Or more accurately, *The Ya-Ya Sisterhood Takes Up Knitting*.

I first met Elizabeth when she attended our Spin-Off Autumn Retreat (SOAR) in 1985 as a mentor. We'd never invited a mentor who wasn't a serious spinner before, and it felt like a bit of a risk. Our guests were passionately, obsessively involved in making yarn. What they did with it seemed, for many, secondary. Would Elizabeth be able to engage them?

The real question turned out to be how to disengage them and how to get them up out of their worshipful circle to, say, have a meal, or go to bed. We're not talking about Blind Followers here, we're talking about Besotted Ones.

Imagine this: a comfy large room in a rustic mountain lodge. In the center, in the midst of a motley group of jeans-clad, fleece-toting fiber maniacs, is a serene, grandmotherly woman with luminous eyes, a half-made sweater in her lap. She begins to chat — "spin her yarn," as it were. The story is low-key, personal. It's about knitting, but more than that, it's about thinking about knitting. It's about setting aside the rules, challenging the traditional assumptions. The energy builds, and pretty soon it's about

sending those old line-by-line patterns up in flames! It's about being free! This is like nothing so much as an old-fashioned tent revival. Questions, shrieks of laughter, eurekas, for hours on end. And Elizabeth, still serene but with an impish twinkle in her eye, in the middle of the circle.

The whole weekend was like that; it never let up. Knitting versus purling, circular versus flat. Tension and slant, shape and fit, that magic formula. Odd cast-ons, tricky cast-offs, creative mistakes, just pull on this little piece of yarn and see what happens! She taught us to think like artists, like engineers, like sculptors, like plumbers; she taught us to "unvent," she taught us that knitting could be a slapstick adventure.

And her message wasn't just about knitting (depending on how you define it). For Elizabeth, knitting was a family affair. We came to know the children, the grandchildren, the Gaffer, and somehow we felt part of that cozy group, part of that family for which knitting seemed to be a binding metaphor and a source of endless fun.

That was fifteen years ago, and Elizabeth was beginning to wind down her travel commitments. As years went by and memory failed, she wrote less, taught less, knitted less — yet the joy, humor, bravado, and invention with which she buoyed up, going on three generations of us, has somehow prevailed. The legacy is sterling, the memories golden.

---

top down, and the bonnet was worked using short rows. On completion, she assured students they could tackle *any* knitting project.[362]

In 1993, Judith Shangold, working with *Vogue Knitting*, brought the work of prominent knit designers together in *The Designer Collection (for Bears)*, a whimsical book of hand knits for ten-inch teddy bears. There was a Kaffe Fassett cardigan in twenty-three colors, Nancy J. Thomas pink slipover with matching headband, Nicky Epstein pullover with duplicate stitch motifs, Norah Gaughan cabled pullover, and Meg Swansen hooded badger sweater with I-cord border, among other designers whose names and styles had become familiar to American knitters.[363]

The popularity of knitting surged during the 1990s, and knitting designers attracted followers who liked their books, workshops, and personal style. Kaffe

Fassett continued to build his exceptional career as a colorist and textile artist, and American knitters loved the painterly and colorful geometric designs in Fassett's knitting books and kits. In 1996 Melanie Falick captured enlightening portraits of thirty-eight knit designers in *Knitting in America*. Among the American knitters was Kathryn Alexander of New York, who gained recognition for knitting handspun yarn into colorful, whimsical entrelac socks and sweaters. Sarah Swett in Idaho, best known for woven tapestries, designed complex sweaters using her handspun, natural-dyed yarn. In New York, Norah Gaughan combined mathematical precision with creative exploration in her career as a knit designer, and Nicky Epstein parlayed her design work into a series of books on knit embellishments and felting — plus knitting for Barbie!

Sumi Wu of Vancouver, Washington, adapted knitting for her sculpture. For one exhibition, she invented socks intended for space explorers who will need warm socks when they encounter new worlds.

Elizabeth Zimmermann attracted an unprecedented following. She wrote four knitting books in a voice both humorous and intelligent, and readers considered her their friend. Over many years and after knitting scores of sweaters, Elizabeth developed a simple percentage system (dubbed EPS for Elizabeth's percentage system) to make custom-fitted, seamless sweaters. A knitter who followed EPS multiplied individual gauge times the desired body circumference to get a Key Number (K). The number of stitches for other parts of the sweater — sleeve, yoke, neck — were determined with fixed percentages of K. Elizabeth's designs were published in magazines and in a newsletter she began in 1957, a beginning effort that consisted of "two long skinny sheets with various items of woolly interest." The newsletter became *Wool Gathering*, the quarterly publication that Elizabeth, and later she and her daughter Meg Swansen, continued to produce and distribute. Not only was *Wool Gathering* a terrific source of innovative knitting patterns, but Elizabeth, the self-described Opinionated Knitter, considered it her "means of expression, my pulpit, my soapbox."[364] Every issue brought subscribers patterns for such clever knits as the bog shirt, and moebius scarf. She and Meg also collaborated on designs like Box-the-Compass and Meg contributed her own original designs, like Square-Rigged Vest. Knitters pored over issues of *Wool Gathering* to learn about new knitting books and the latest sources for knitting wool, Norwegian pewter or elkhorn buttons, umbrella swifts, ball winders — and even how to knit a section for the ribbon that would be wrapped around the Pentagon on the fortieth anniversary of Hiroshima and Nagasaki (August 1985). She brought together the newsletter, book publishing, instructional videos, and mail-order business for knitting supplies under the name Schoolhouse Press. Elizabeth convened a knitting camp each summer, hosted a knitting program shown on public television stations, and led knitting workshops throughout the U.S. and in New Zealand.

On November 30, 1999, the woman who had set the creativity of so many knitters free in *Knitting Without Tears* died. Stunned by the loss, American knitters felt they had lost a personal friend in Elizabeth Zimmermann, even those who had never met her in person. Knitters poured their grief into letters to her family, and *The New York Times* and National Public Radio honored her memory. Kaffe Fassett acknowledged her extraordinary influence on his life; she had told him to buy a circular knitting needle because it would change his life![365] The millennium was drawing to a close, but for thousands of American knitters Elizabeth Zimmermann's death also marked the end of a knitting era.

Knitting into a New Millennium

During the last two decades of the twentieth century, Americans witnessed the collapse of the Soviet Union,

Yarn and patterns are widely available online, but yarn shops meet needs for instruction and companionship. Knitters gather at Twisted, a yarn shop in Sheridan, Wyoming. In common with knitters nationwide, many women turn to knitting to gain self awareness, connect with the traditional past, and join others to knit for a better world. Shop owner Pam Gable (left) noted that more fathers and daughters knitting together.

the fall of the Berlin Wall, and wars in Yugoslavia and the Middle East. Terrorist attacks stunned the nation, in particular the 1993 attack on the World Trade Towers, but the worst was to come. On September 11, 2001, hijackers flew passenger jets loaded with fuel into the World Trade Center in New York and into the Pentagon in Washington, D. C. Americans watched the assaults in horror. Wars in Afghanistan and Iraq and the devastation of New Orleans by Hurricane Katrina in August 2005 further traumatized the nation.

Once again knitting was a solace that brought grieving Americans together. Knitters poured generosity into

Knitters in Sheridan, Wyoming, made caps to donate for premature babies — one of hundreds of opportunities knitters had to donate their work to those in need.

Knitters by the hundreds continue to enter their work in county and state fairs across the nation, each knitter competing for ribbons awarded to the finest work. Hand knitting entered in the Iowa State Fair in Des Moines in 2006 included a child's cardigan in the shape of an ear of corn and a tubular cover, knit from odds and ends of yarn, that covered the hose of a canister vacuum cleaner.

hand knits that they donated to help alleviate human suffering, spurred by a desire to do something, anything, to make the world a better place. Interweave Press compiled and posted on its website an extensive list of charitable knitting opportunities, from Adopt-A-Native Elder and Afghans 4 Afghans to Newborns in Need and Warm Hearts–Warm Babies. A program called Socks for Soldiers recruited knitters to send military-standard socks in boxes with other comforts to soldiers serving in Iraq. Operation Toasty Toes sent more than forty thousand pairs of slipper socks to military men and women.[366] Other projects that had begun during the 1990s accelerated in number of knitters and products in the new millennium. Evie Rosen of Wausau, Wisconsin, founded Warm Up America! to help the homeless and others in need. She asked knitters to make seven-by-nine-inch pieces that would be sewn together into afghans. When totals donated nationwide overwhelmed Rosen, the CYCA assumed responsibility for the program and added the Caps for the Capital campaign to supply warm hats for newborns around the world.[367] Similarly, Knits for Newborns asked knitters to make baby blankets to send to a health clinic or humanitarian service supported by the United Nations Population Fund. Janet Bristow and Victoria Galo combined spiritual practice with a love of knitting to form the Prayer Shawl Ministry; the knitter prayed and blessed a recipient during a time of special joy or need. Other compassionate knitting campaigns included pink scarves knit for breast cancer awareness, blankets for children in foster care (Project Linus), and comfort blankets for kittens in animal shelters. Whatever and wherever the need, the numbers of donated hand knits have been nothing short of staggering.

Another wave of fine artists began to work with knitting. Although too young for the 1960s hippie crochet or the 1970s women's art movement, this generation of artists knit limited-edition or one-of-a-kind artwear. Jean Williams Cacicedo knit jackets that combined hand- and loom-knitted wool that was dyed, pieced, and appliquéd. Reina Mia Brill hand-knit coated copper wire into jewelry.[368] A gradual number of artists — among them Katharine Cobey, Lindsay Obermeyer, Sumi Wu, and Karen Searle — further redefined knitting as a medium for social expression, a brave statement in the prestigious gallery and museum world. Cat (Catherine) Chow knit one thousand shredded dollar bills (donated one dollar at a time by friends and strangers) into a long gown titled "Not for Sale." At the Massachusetts Museum of Contemporary Art in North Adams, David Cole video-taped *Knitting Machine*, a performance piece with two John Deere excavators hoisting two tapered telephone poles into position to knit an American flag from strips of torn blankets. In January 2007, an exhibition titled

Radical Lace and Subversive Knitting opened at the Museum of Arts and Design. As a reflection of her piece about wartime knitting, artist Sabrina Gschwandtner invited people to knit blankets for Afghan citizens and convalescing soldiers. An occasional graduate student has turned knitting into a topic for an academic thesis. Gail Ann Lambert, for example, wrote *The Taxonomy of Sweater Structures and Their Origins*, a thesis focused on the construction of the hand-knit sweater (North Carolina State University, 2002).

Newspapers and magazines have extolled the many ways that knitting has become hip. Debbie Stoller kickstarted the hip knitting party with her enormously popular book *Stich 'N Bitch* (2003). Students caught up in the knitting craze in schools have rated feature stories in the nation's regional newspapers. Knitters have rushed to knit sweater and scarf patterns like those worn in the *Harry Potter* movies. Members of knitting circles like Seattle's PurlyGirls have began to "kip" (knit in public — knitting has developed its own shorthand slang). Celebrities who have been spotted knitting also have garnered media attention. Prominent knitting designers have been hired as instructors for knitting camps, overseas trips, and cruises. Knitting has been touted as the new yoga, and memoirs and anthologies about knitting stocked bookstore shelves. New yarn stores have sprung up, like the Knit Café in West Hollywood; Chix with Stix in Forest Park, Illinois; and Twisted in Sheridan, Wyoming. The big draws at the winter 2007 Stitching Salon at the Chicago Cultural Center were workshops and movies for knitters ("knitflix"), plus a drop-in collaborative knitting piece. Anyone could pick up yarn and needles and contribute to the hand-knit flourishes on a skirt suspended in the center of the fiber gallery.

It has been online technology, however, that has brought knitting enthusiasts together as never before. Knitting has always been an inherently social activity, and technology has accelerated the ability of knitters to interconnect, exponentially so. For many knitters, the online entry points have been e-mail discussion groups with memberships that have grown into thousands, often splitting into countless spin-off groups to handle the sheer volume of mail. Online knitting magazines have caught on quickly, and virtual yarn stores are selling yarn, books, and every imaginable knitting product. Beginning in the mid-1990s, knitters embraced blogs — personal "web logs" on websites

with chronological online journal entries. Through blogs, knitters share new designers, patterns, yarns, and opportunities to donate their knitting to needful causes. Blogs celebrate in exquisite detail the progress of each new knitting project. Knitters also share photos of pets, children, severe weather, food, books, patterns, and at times their personal lives. Stephanie Pearl-McPhee's "yarn harlot" blog and Mason-Dixon Knitting have had strong followings, as has Men Who Knit (and blog). How else, other than online, could the yarn harlot have invited knitters to her Knitting Olympics, a challenge to cast on a first stitch during the first winter Olympic event and complete an entire hand-knit piece by the last event?

Throughout their history, Americans have kept knitting. In a land of abundance, the business of knitting has generated extraordinary opportunities for designers, manufacturers, writers, instructors, and inventors. Portable and practical, knitting is simple enough to relax the mind, complex enough to challenge the intellect. Knitters have taken pleasure in the fiber that moves through their fingers and in the bit of mystery that unfolds each time a single strand of yarn becomes stitches, then rows, then a sweater or sock. During wartime and natural disasters, American knitters have been moved beyond words to extraordinary levels of productivity and generosity. America is, after all, a knitting nation.

The twenty-first-century knitter can choose from a dazzling variety of yarns and fibers — the yarn stash — and some have become yarn "snobs" who seek exotic fibers from qiviut to microfibers, from hand-painted mohair to elaborate novelty synthetic yarns.

Endnotes

1. Kirstie Buckland, "The Monmouth Cap," *Costume* 13 (1979): 23–37.

2. Cited in Johnson, *A History of the American People*, 68.

3. Elisabeth McClellan, *History of American Costume 1607–1870* (New York: Tudor Publishing Company, 1937).

4. Elizabeth Ewing, *Everyday Dress, 1650–1900* (New York: Chelsea House Publishers, 1984).

5. Mary Merrill, Anne Seamans, Betty Shannon, and Adele Harvey, *17th Century Knitting Patterns as Adapted for Plimoth Plantation*, Monograph One, Second Edition, (Boston: The Weavers' Guild of Boston, 1990).

6. Edward Kimber, *Itinerant Observations in America*, ed. Kevin J. Hayes (Dover: University of Delaware Press, 1998). Reprint, first published mid-1740s in *London Magazine*.

7. Jabez Carpenter ledger, 1750–1754, and journal, 1750–1753; Jabez Carpenter Ledger, 1755–1772, in Ellen Hartigan-O'Connor, "'She Said She did not Know Money': Urban Women and Atlantic Markets," (paper presented at Program in Early American Economy and Society Conference, Philadelphia, PA, October 1, 2004), available from http://www.librarycompany.org/economics/pdf%20files/o'connor.pdf

8. Philbrick, *Mayflower*; Ulrich, *Good Wives*.

9. Mary Rowlandson, "The Soveraignty and Goodness of God, Together, with the Faithfulness of His Promises Displayed," in Richard Van Der Beets, ed., *Held Captive by Indians: Selected Narratives 1642–1836* (Knoxville: University of Tennessee Press, 1973), 54, 58, 74, 80. The first edition of her narrative was published by Samuel Green Jr. in Boston in 1682.

10. Philbrick, *Mayflower*.

11. *Virginia Gazette*, 22 September 1768, in Buckland, "The Monmouth Cap."

12. *Virginia Gazette*, 2 December 1775, in Baumgarten, *What Clothes Reveal*, 132.

13. Plaiding was a type of kersey, an obsolete English term for a diagonal ribbed or twill fabric, which was coarse and heavily fulled and either woven of all wool or with cotton warp and woolen weft. The term is derived from the English town of Kersey, where it was made in the eleventh century. Plaid hose were not necessarily patterned. Isabel B. Wingate, *Fairchild's Dictionary of Textiles*, Sixth Edition (New York: Fairchild Publications, 1979).

14. Edmund S. Morgan, *Virginians at Home: Family Life in the Eighteenth Century* (Williamsburg: Colonial Williamsburg, Inc., 1952), 53–54, in Gloria Seaman Allen, "Slaves as Textile Artisans: Documentary Evidence for the Chesapeake Region," *Uncoverings* 22 (2001): 1–36.

15. Gloria Seaman Allen, "Slaves as Textile Artisans," 1–36.

16. Letter, 23 December 1792, "Black Presence — Textiles," Item 288, *African American Notebooks*, Colonial Williamsburg Foundation; Fritz Hirschfeld, *George Washington and Slavery: A Documentary Portrayal* (Columbia: University of Missouri Press, 1997), 38, in Gloria Seaman Allen, "Slaves as Textile Artisans."

17. Emma L. Powers, "A Biographical Sketch of Mrs. Ann Wager," available from http://research.history.org/historical_research/research_themes/themereligion/wager.cfm.

18. Linsey-woolsey refers to the fabric's combination of linen warp and wool weft (filling), though at times cotton was used in place of linen. Coarse, loosely woven linsey-woolsey originated in England and was popular in the American Colonies. Its name derives from the English village of Linsey, England. Isabel B. Wingate, *Fairchild's Dictionary of Textiles*.

19. Baumgarten, *What Clothes Reveal*.

20. George Mason, April 23, 1769, "Virginia Merchants Association, Plan for Non-Importation of British Goods," in *The George Washington Papers at the Library of Congress, 1741–1799*. Available from http://memory.loc.gov/cgi-bin/query/r?ammem/mgw:@field(docid+@lit(lw030185)).

21. Norton, *Liberty's Daughters*, 169.

22. "George Washington to Clement Biddle, September 26, 1777," in *The George Washington Papers*. Available from http://memory.loc.gov/cgi-bin/query/r?ammem/mgw:@field(docid+@lit(gw090282)).

23. "George Washington to Continental Congress, October 3, 1777," in *The George Washington Papers*. Available from http://memory.loc.gov/cgi-bin/query/r?ammem/mgw:@field(docid+@lit(gw090313)).

24. "George Washington to Patrick Henry, December 27, 1777," in *The George Washington Papers*. Available from http://memory.loc.gov/cgi-bin/query/r?ammem/mgw:@field(docid+@lit(gw100210)).

25. "George Washington to John A. Washington, April 12, 1777," in *The George Washington Papers*. Available from http://memory.loc.gov/cgi-bin/query/r?ammem/mgw:@field(docid+@lit(gw070389)).

26. Rhoda Farrand Chapter, "Daughters of the American Revolution," available from http://www.northshirecomputer.com/VTDAR/RhodaFarrandPoem.html (case-sensitive); Andrew M. Sherman, *Historic Morristown, New Jersey: The Story of Its First Century*, (Morristown, N.J.: Howard Publishing Company, 1905).

27. Carolyn R. Shine, "Scalping Knives and Silk Stockings: Clothing the Frontier, 1780–1795," *Dress* 14 (1988).

28. David Barrows II, "Correspondence 1841–51," The Joseph Downs Collection and the Winterthur Archives, Collection 191 (181), available from http://www.winterthur.org/about/downs_collection_and_winterthur_archives/xhtml/jdcmckinstry.htm#jd.entries.

29. Ellen Hartigan-O'Connor, "Abigail's Accounts," *Journal of Women's History* 17, no. 3 (2005): 35–47.

30. Laurel Thatcher Ulrich, *A Midwife's Tale: The Life of Martha Ballard, Based on Her Diary, 1785–1812* (New York: Alfred A. Knopf, 1990), 287, 237, 312, 168.

31. Pat Gibbs, "Daily Schedule for a Young Gentry Woman," available from http://research.history.org/historical_research/research_themes/themefamily/gentrywoman.cfm.

32. "Knitted Mittens," Object ID: 1979.0980.01, National Museum of American History. Image available from http://americanhistory.si.edu/collections/object.cfm?key=35&objkey=193.

33. "The Treasury," *Godey's Lady's Book*, April 1850, 280.

34. Available from http://www.firstladies.org/biographies/firstladies.aspx?biography=18 and http://www.firstladies.org/biographies/firstladies.aspx?biography=25.

35. "Elizabeth E. Miller," American Life Histories: Manuscripts from the Federal Writers' Project, 1936–1940 (Library of Congress American Memories). Available from http://memory.loc.gov/ammem/wpaintro/wpahome.html.

36. George L. Osgood, *Knitting the Scarf* (Boston: Ditson and Co., 1880). Retrieved from the Library of Congress American Memory website at http://hdl.loc.gov/loc.music/sm1880.19505.

37. Document 219, The Joseph Downs Collection and the Winterthur Archives; Document 8, The Joseph Downs Collection and the Winterthur Archives; Document 300, The Joseph Downs Collection and the Winterthur Archives. All documents available from http://www.winterthur.org/about/downs_collection_and_winterthur_archives/xhtml/jdcmckinstry.htm#jd.entries.

38. Isabella Mary Beeton, *Mrs. Beeton's Book of Household Management* (New York: Oxford University Press, 2000), 28. Reprint of 1861 original.

39. The Library Company of Philadelphia has an extensive collection of crochet and knitting instructional literature published before 1851.

40. "Necktie," *Godey's Lady's Book*, August 1850, 114.

41. "History of Stockings," *Godey's Lady's Book*, June 1853, 503.

42. A sontag is a woman's knit or crochet jacket with long ends that cross over the chest and tie in the back.

43. "Knitted Artificial Flowers," *Godey's Lady's Book*, March 1861, 262; May 1861, 449; June 1861, 550.

44. "Gentleman's Knitted Shirt," *Godey's Lady's Book*, January 1870, 86; "Knee Cap," *Godey's Lady's Book*, January 1870, 83; "Gentleman's Knitted Braces," *Godey's Lady's Book*, February 1870, 180; "Knitted Overshoe," *Godey's Lady's Book*, March 1870, 282; "Bachelik Pelerine (Knitting)," *Godey's Lady's Book*, December 1870, 544.

45. "The Boa," *Godey's Lady's Book*, January 1870, 84; "Rabbit Penwiper (Knitting)," *Godey's Lady's Book*, November 1870, 464–465.

46. "Knitted Workbasket," *Godey's Lady's Book*, September 1870, 270.

47. "Drawers for Child of Four to Six Years Old," *Godey's Lady's Book*, September 1880, 287–288; "Straw Hat, with Knitted Shade for the Neck," *Godey's Lady's Book*, July 1880, 95.

48. Janet Johnson Stephens, "Miss Pruden's Lace Diary," *Piecework*, May/June 1997, 61–62. Miss Pruden's niece, Ruth McGowan, gave the workbook to Edith N. Hippensteel, who donated it to the Smithsonian National Museum of American History in Washington, D.C.

49. Joyce Volk, "The Warner House Bedspread Project," *Piecework,* November/December 1997, 42–47.

50. "Point Lace Pattern," "Palm-Leaf Insertion," "Knitted Socks with Shell Tops," *Ladies' Home Journal,* April 1884, 6; "Coral Tidy," *Ladies' Home Journal,* February 1885, 6; "Leaf Edging," "Deep Shell Lace," "Handsome Fancy Mitt," *Ladies' Home Journal,* November 1886, 6; "Apple Leaf Lace," *Ladies' Home Journal,* February 1887, 6; "Handsome Fancy Mitt," *Ladies' Home Journal,* November 1886, 6.

51. "A Special Offer," *Ladies' Home Journal* advertisement, March 1886, 14.

52. Peter Weis and Ann Feitelson, "The Silk Industry of Florence, Massachusetts," *Piecework,* January 1999, 37–41.

53. *How to Use Florence Knitting Silk,* No. 4 (Florence, MA: Nonotuck Silk Co., 1882), 2.

54. "Nonotuck Silk Company," *Ladies' Home Journal* advertisement, November 1885, 4; December 1885, 4.

55. Jane Weaver, "Knitted Cuff," *Peterson's Magazine,* January 1860, 77; Jane Weaver, "Knitted Scarf," *Peterson's Magazine,* January 1860, 79; Jane Weaver, "Knitted Capuchin," *Peterson's Magazine,* January 1860, 85; Jane Weaver, "Knitted Shells for Counterpane," *Peterson's Magazine,* February 1860, 160; November 1860, 398–399; December 1860, 476–477; Jane Weaver, "Baby's Knitted Shoe and Sock," *Peterson's Magazine,* January 1861, 66; Jane Weaver, "Knitted Leggin," *Peterson's Magazine* April 1861, 348.

56. Warren, "A Norwegian Morning or Bonnet Cap, in Shetland Wool," *Peterson's Magazine,* February 1861, 169; Mademoiselle Roche, "Thibet Knitting," February 1861, 169–170.

57. Jane Weaver, "Knitted Jacket for a Young Girl," *Peterson's Magazine,* May 1869, 395; "Knitted Cravat," *Peterson's Magazine,* August 1869, 150; "Boy's Gaiter," *Peterson's Magazine,* September 1869, 227; "Case for Knitting and Darning-Needles," *Peterson's Magazine,* September 1869, 227; "Knitting-Basket," *Peterson's Magazine,* February 1869, 162.

58. Jane Weaver, "Child's Gaiter, with Knee-Warmer," *Peterson's Magazine,* February 1877, 163; Jane Weaver, "Child's Knitted Shirt," *Peterson's Magazine,* February 1879, 167; Jane Weaver, "Knitted Shawl," *Peterson's Magazine,* May 1879, 400; Jane Weaver, "Nightingale Knitting," *Peterson's Magazine,* March 1879, 244; Jane Weaver, "Knitted Petticoat for a Child," *Peterson's Magazine,* November 1885, 451; Jane Weaver, "Child's Scotch Cap," *Peterson's Magazine,* December 1886, 554.

59. Galer Britton Barnes, "A Matter of Fashion: Beaded Bags of the Civil War Era," *Piecework,* May/June 1994, 48–51; Mary Thomas, *Mary Thomas's Knitting Book* (New York: Dover Publications, 1972), 133–141; "Baby Socks," *Piecework,* January/February 2000, 72.

60. "Children's Dresses," *Godey's Lady's Book,* July 1850, 55.

61. Christina Bates, "How to Dress the Children? A Comparison of Prescription and Practice in Late-Nineteenth-Century North America," *Dress* 24: 1997.

62. Mrs. Child, *The American Frugal Housewife* (Bedford, MA: Applewood Books, 2002). First published by Carter and Hendee, Massachusetts, in 1832.

63. "Child's Stocking in Squares of Three Colors," *Godey's Lady's Book,* August 1880, 190, 191; "Reins for a Child," *Godey's Lady's Book,* August 1880, 191; "Baby's Shoe," *Ladies' Home Journal,* April 1884, 6; "Infant's Jersey," *Ladies' Home Journal,* August 1887, 6.

64. Silber, *Daughters of the Union,* 59.

65. Anne Firor Scott, *Natural Allies: Women's Associations in American History* (Urbana: University of Illinois Press, 1991); Silber, *Daughters of the Union.*

66. Silber, *Daughters of the Union.*

67. Zinn and Arnove, *Voices of a People's History of the United States,* 128–129.

68. Letter of Fanny Pierce, October 13, 1861, in Thayer Family Papers, MHS, cited in Silber, *Daughters of the Union,* 180, 181.

69. William Quentin Maxwell, *Lincoln's Fifth Wheel: The Political History of the United States Sanitary Commission* (New York: Longmans, Green and Co., 1956).

70. "Patriotic Work for Women," *The New York Times,* 12 October 1862, 4.

71. *Greenfield Gazette and Courier,* 14 October 1861, 2; 4 November 1861, 2; 6 October 1862; 30 November 1863, 2.

72. *Hampshire Gazette,* undated clippings in scrapbook in Forbes Library, Northampton, MA and *Northampton Free Press,* December 16, 1864, cited in Beverly Gordon, "Textiles and Clothing in the Civil War: A Portrait for Contemporary Understanding," *Clothing and Textiles Research Journal* 5, no. 3 (1998): 44.

73. T. S. Arthur, "Blue Yarn Stockings," *Harper's New Monthly Magazine* 24, no. 139 (1861): 110; "A Pair of Stockings from the Army," *Continental Monthly* 5, May 1864; Saxe Holm, "Joe Hale's Red Stockings," *Scribner's Monthly* 15, no. 3 (January 1878): 333–352.

74. M. C. Baryton, *Our Acre and Its Harvest: Historical Sketch of the Soldiers' Aid Society of Northern Ohio, Cleveland Branch of the U. S. Sanitary Commission,* Part I

(Cleveland: Fairbanks, Benedict, 1869) 62–63, in Beverly Gordon, "Textiles and Clothing in the Civil War," 45.

75. Silber, *Daughters of the Union.*

76. Silber, *Daughters of the Union.*

77. Gordon, *Bazaars and Fair Ladies.*

78. "Directions for Knitting Soldiers' Mittens," *The New York Times,* 1 December 1861, 6.

79. *Hampshire Gazette,* undated clippings in scrapbook in Forbes Library, Northampton, MA, in Beverly Gordon, "Textiles and Clothing in the Civil War," 43.

80. Karin Timour, "Knitting the 1865 U.S. Sanitary Commission Sock," Atlantic Guard Soldiers' Aid Society. Available from http://agsas.org/howto/patterns/knitting_sock.shtml.

81. "Commend Me to a Knitting Wife" (paper presented at the Ladies and Gentlemen of the 1860s Conference, Harrisburg, PA., March 2006). This paper summarizes Civil War–era knitting needles and gauges information, including contemporary needle and yarn equivalents. See also Formby, Colleen. "Commend Me to a Knitting Wife: A Look at Civil War-Era Knitting," *Civil War Historian,* March/April 2007, 47–51.

82. George W. Briggs to Abraham Lincoln, Tuesday, February 7, 1865 (Send socks; with endorsement), in *The Abraham Lincoln Papers at the Library of Congress,* available from http://memory.loc.gov/cgi-bin/query/r?ammem/mal:@field(DOCID+@lit(d4049000)); Sarah Phelps to Abraham Lincoln, January 1865, in *The Abraham Lincoln Papers,* http://memory.loc.gov/cgi-bin/query/r?ammem/mal:@field(DOCID+@lit(d3987900)); Lucy A. Thomas to Abraham Lincoln, Monday, March 4, 1861, in *The Abraham Lincoln Papers,* http://memory.loc.gov/cgi-bin/query/r?ammem/mal:@field(DOCID+@lit(d0777900)); Mrs. H. S. Crocker to Abraham Lincoln, Monday, January 11, 1864, in *The Abraham Lincoln Papers,* http://memory.loc.gov/cgi-bin/query/r?ammem/mal:@field(DOCID+@lit(d2935600)); Philena M. Upham to Abraham Lincoln, Saturday, November 26, 1864, in *The Abraham Lincoln Papers,* http://memory.loc.gov/cgi-bin/query/r?ammem/mal:@field(DOCID+@lit(d3875700)).

83. Ruth Painter Randall, *Mary Lincoln: Biography of a Marriage* (Boston: Little, Brown and Co., 1953), 23.

84. "Mrs. William Price, Marlin, Texas (White Pioneer)," Federal Writers' Project for the U.S. Works Progress Administration. Available from http://memory.loc.gov/ammem/wpaintro/wpahome.html.

85. Anne Firor Scott, *Natural Allies,* 69–70.

86. Mrs. C. G. Richardson; Mrs. William Craig; Mrs. Josephine Wood; Ella Lassiter, Federal Writers' Project for the U.S. Works Progress Administration. Available from http://memory.loc.gov/ammem/wpaintro/wpahome.html.

87. Shane White and Graham White, "Slave Clothing and African-American Culture," *Past and Present,* no. 146 (February 1995): 171; "Florence Lee, Ex-Slave Narrative," Works Progress Administration (WPA) Ex-Slave Narratives, in *The African-American Experience in Ohio 1850–1920,* the Ohio Historical Society (available from http://dbs.ohiohistory.org/africanam/page.cfm?ID=13923); Ulrich B. Phillips, *American Negro Slavery* (New York: D. Appleton and Company, 1918), 191, in Gloria Seaman Allen, "Slaves as Textile Artisans," 1–36.

88. "Commend Me to a Knitting Wife." This paper summarized references to knitting in diaries and period literature.

89. Mary Boykin Chesnut, *A Diary from Dixie* (Boston: Houghton Mifflin, 1961), 111, 121, 130. Reprint, originally published 1904.

90. Beverly Gordon, "Textiles and Clothing in the Civil War," 41–47.

91. J. L. Underwood, *The Women of the Confederacy* (New York: Neal Publishing Co., 1906), 75.

92. Cornelia Phillips Spencer, *The Last Ninety Days of the War in North Carolina* (New York: Watchman Publishing Company, 1866), 133. Documenting the American South. University Library, The University of North Carolina at Chapel Hill, 2005. http://docsouth.unc.edu/true/spencer/spencer.html.

93. "Carrie Berry Diary, August 1, 1864–January 4, 1865." Available from http://www.americancivilwar.com/women/carrie_berry.html.

94. "Mrs. I. E. Doane," Federal Writers' Project for the U.S. Works Progress Administration. http://memory.loc.gov/ammem/wpaintro/wpahome.html.

95. Upshur, Mary J., 1862, "Knitting for the Soldiers." Documenting the American South. University Library, University of North Carolina at Chapel Hill, 2003. http://docsouth.unc.edu/nc/barn/barn.html.

96. Sarah Phelps to Abraham Lincoln, January 1865, in *The Abraham Lincoln Papers,* available from http://memory.loc.gov/cgi-bin/query/r?ammem/mal:@field(DOCID+@lit(d3987900)).

97. Tony Horwitz, *Confederates in the Attic: Dispatches from the Unfinished Civil War*

(New York: Pantheon Books, 1998), 133, 388.

98. Atlantic Guard Soldiers' Aid Society, available from http://agsas.org.

99. Susan Shelby Magoffin, in Drumm, *Down the Santa Fe Trail and into Mexico*, 22, 31, 168.

100. Mrs. Clifford Merrill Drury, *First White Women Over the Rockies* (Glendale, CA: Arthur H. Clark Co., 1963), 216.

101. Randolph B. Marcy, *The Prairie Traveler* (Old Saybrook, CT: Applewood Books, 1992). Reprint, original published by authority of the War Department, 1859.

102. Stories of women pioneers are collected in such publications as Lillian Schlissel, *Women's Diaries of the Westward Journey* (New York: Schocken Books, 1982) and Riley, *The Female Frontier*.

103. Kate B. Carter, ed., *Our Pioneer Heritage* (Salt Lake City: International Society, Daughters of Utah Pioneers, 1975).

104. Ronald W. Walker, "Rachel R. Grant: The Continuing Legacy of the Feminine Ideal," *Dialogue: A Journal of Mormon Thought* 15, no. 3 (Autumn, 1982): 111; Lenard Arlington, "Blessed Damozels: Women in Mormon History," *Dialogue* 6, no. 2 (Summer 1971): 23; Louise Comish, "Snowflake Girl," *Dialogue* 6, no. 2 (Summer 1971): 102.

105. Jerome E. Petsche, *The Steamboat* Bertrand*: History, Excavation, and Architecture* (Missouri Valley, IA: Midwest Interpretive Association, 1993).

106. Hilda Polacheck, "Pack on my Back," Federal Writers' Project, Works Progress Administration, 1936–1940.

107. "Bucilla's History," retrieved on December 5, 2006 from the Plaid website http://www.plaidonline.com/articleDetail.asp?entry=article&articleID=102.

108. Westward pioneer settlers were interviewed for the Federal Writers' Project, 1936–1940, and their stories can be retrieved from the American Memory website at http://memory.loc.gov/ammem/index.html.

109. Sally Helvenston, "Fashion on the Frontier," *Dress* 17 (1990); Riley, *The Female Frontier*.

110. Sarah Buffington, Curator, Old Economy Village, Economy, PA, personal communication, July 13, 2006.

111. Carolyn Anderson Wilson and J. Hiram Wilson, "Material Culture in the Bishop Hill Colony: Restoration Inventory for Bishop Hill State Historic Site" (Illinois Department of Conservation, 1980, unpublished).

112. Charles Nordhoff, *The Communistic Societies of the United States* (New York: Schocken Books, 1965), 320. Reprint of 1875 original.

113. Kathleen Fernandez, personal communication, June 27, 2006.

114. Gordon, *Shaker Textile Arts*, 22; Sister Elsie McCool, personal conversation, November 1976.

115. *Ibid.*

116. June Sprig, *By Shaker Hands* (New York: E. P. Dutton, 1974), 185.

117. Jennifer Carroll-Plante, Curator of Collections, Canterbury Shaker Village, personal communication, July 3, 2006.

118. Susan Strawn Bailey, "Knitting in the Amanas," *Piecework*, September 1997, 18–21; Renee Driscoll, *Knitting of the Amana Colonies* (Amana, IA: Amana Arts Guild, 1994); Charles Nordhoff, *The Communistic Societies of the United States*.

119. Renee Driscoll, *Knitting of the Amana Colonies*, 2.

120. Barbara Yambura, *A Change and a Parting: My Story of Amana* (Ames, IA: Iowa State University Press, 1960).

121. Driscoll, *Knitting of the Amana Colonies*.

122. Susan Strawn Bailey, "Especially for the Baby: Amana Star-Pattern Knitted Bonnets," *Piecework*, November 2000, 44–48.

123. Illinois Historic Preservation Agency, available from http://www.bishophill.com/history.php; Kathleen M. Fernandez, "Zoar Village State Memorial," *U.S. Department of Interior Cultural Resource Management* 24, no. 9. Available from http://crm.cr.nps.gov/issue.cfm?volume=24&number=09.

124. "Southern Northwest Coast Weavers," Burke Museum, University of Washington. Available from http://www.washington.edu/burkemuseum/baskets/artists/snwc1.html.

125. Priscilla A. Gibson-Roberts, *Salish Indian Sweaters: A Pacific Northwest Tradition* (Saint Paul, MN: Dos Tejedoras Fiber Arts Publications, 1989); Margaret Meikle, "Cowichan Indian Knitting," Museum Note No. 21, *Museum of Anthropology Museum Notes Series* (Vancouver, BC: University of British Columbia Museum of Anthropology, 1987).

126. Charles Francis Saunders, *The Indians of the Terraced Houses* (New York: G. P. Putnam's Sons, 1912).

127. Franciscan Fathers, *An Ethnologic Dictionary of the Navaho Language* (Saint Michaels, AZ: Franciscan Fathers, 1910).

128. Clyde Kluckhohn, W. W. Hill, and Lucy Wales Kluckhohn, *Navaho Material Culture* (Cambridge, MA: Belknap Press of Harvard University Press, 1971). The forced removal of the Navajo people from their homelands began in 1862, and they were interned under tragic conditions at Fort Sumner, New Mexico, until a treaty with the American government returned them to a reservation in 1868. Destruction of the Navajo sheep was part of federal policy to subdue the Navajo tribe before removal.

129. This is a summary of information cited in Clyde Kluckhohn et al., *Navaho Material Culture*.

130. Galer Britton Barnes, "A Glimpse of Color: Amish Wedding Stockings of the Nineteenth Century," *Piecework* 5, no. 2 (March 1997): 25–27; McCauley and McCauley, *Decorative Arts of the Amish of Lancaster County*.

131. Donna Druchunas, "Amish Knitting and Crochet: Preserving Time-Honored Traditions," *Piecework* 13, no. 2 (March 2005), 38–40.

132. Anna Mary Yoder, personal communication, June 26, 2006.

133. "Work for Detained Aliens," *The New York Times*, 7 December 1914, 10; Carol Medlicott, "Constructing Territory, Constructing Citizenship: The Daughters of the American Revolution and 'Americanization' in the 1920s," *Geopolitics* 10 (2005): 99–120; "Sing Sing Convicts Knitting in the Prison Yard While the Prison Mandolin Club Gives A Concert," photo caption, *The New York Times*, 14 March 1915.

134. Jeannette Weir, ed., "The Neat-Handed Girl: Six Pretty Woolen Wraps," *Ladies' Home Journal*, January 1903, 27.; "Mrs. McKinley to Calve: President's Widow Knitted Slippers for Prima Donna," *The New York Times*, 29 November 1905, 1.

135. Lion Brand Yarn advertisement in *Ladies' Home Journal*, January 1903, 27.

136. "Discoveries by Our Observers and Experimenters," *Good Housekeeping*, April 1905, 450; *The Saturday Evening Post*, 20 February 1915, cover.

137. Jeannette Weir, ed., "The Neat-Handed Girl," 27.

138. Helen Marvin, "The Best Designs and Some Brand New Stitches for Knitted Shawls," *Woman's Home Companion*, November 1905, 26.

139. Helen Marvin, "An English Knitted Cape," *Woman's Home Companion*, November 1914, 67; Helen Marvin, "Practical Christmas Gifts," *Woman's Home Companion*, November 1912, 33; Helen Marvin, "Hats and Coats for Little Girls," *Woman's Home Companion*, September 1912, 62.

140. "The New Sweaters You Can Make," *Ladies' Home Journal*, July 1917, 83; *Corticelli Yarn Book, No. 10* (Florence, MA: Nonotuck Silk Co., 1919); "Style Forecast," *Corticelli Yarn Book No. 12* (Florence, MA: Nonotuck Silk Co., 1919).

141. "Some Best Sellers That Cost Little: To Make or to Buy," *Ladies' Home Journal*, August 1917, 77; "The New Sweaters You Can Make," *Ladies' Home Journal*, July 1917, 83; "The New Wool Sweaters and Hats," *Ladies' Home Journal*, September 1917, 86.

142. "The New Things You Can Knit: Novelties to Wear," *Ladies' Home Journal*, October 1917, 149.

143. "Little Folks' Sweaters and Hats that Are New," *Ladies' Home Journal*, October 1917, 138; Bear Brand Yarn Manufacturers, Inc., advertisement in *Ladies' Home Journal*, October 1917, 149.

144. *Corticelli Yarn Book No. 8* (Florence, MA: Nonotuck Silk Co., 1918), 2.

145. "Expense Accounts for Little Boys," *Good Housekeeping*, January 1917, 57.

146. "A Luncheon Set in Knitting," *Needlecraft*, March 1917, 9; Lena Stickney, "The 'Frilly' Slip-On Sweater," *Needlecraft*, August 1919, 14; Fleisher Yarns advertisement in *Needlecraft*, August 1919, 14; Lillius Hilt, "Pretty Laces and Insertions," *Needlecraft*, April 1917, 19; "Knitted Lace and Insertion," *Needlecraft*, August 1919, 23; E. S. Richardson, "Block for Bedspread, Leaf-and-Diamond Pattern," *Needlecraft*, August 1919, 9.

147. W. L. M. Clark advertisement in *Needlecraft*, May 1918, 16.

148. *Woolco Knitting and Crocheting Manual* (Boston: F. W. Woolworth Company, 1916); *Woolco Knitting and Crocheting Manual* (Boston: F. W. Woolworth Company, 1917–1918).

149. *Bear Brand Blue Book of Yarnkraft*, Vol. 20 (New York: Bernhard Ulmann Co., 1919).

150. Fleisher Yarns advertisement in *Needlecraft*, August 1919, 14; Fleisher Yarns advertisement in *Ladies' Home Journal*, December 1917, 59.

151. "Samuel S. Fleisher (1871–1944)," available from http://www.fleisher.org/about/fleisher-bio.php.

152. "Small Gifts that Will Be Welcome for the Great War Christmas," *The Delinator* 93, no. 6 (December 1918): 60.

153. Heather Nicholson, "Warm Socks from Warm Hearts," *Piecework*, July 1999, 34–39.

154. Philadelphia N. Robertson, "A Woman's Prayer," in Nosheen Khan, ed., *Women's Poetry of the First World War* (Lexington, KY: University of Kentucky Press, 1988).

155. Helen Bosanquet, "The Old Woman's War-Work," in Nosheen Khan, ed., *Women's Poetry of the First World War*.

156. "The Latest for Soldiers," *The Woman Citizen*, May 18, 1918; Bear Brand Yarn Manufacturers, Inc., advertisement in *Needlecraft*, May 1918, 14; "Small Gifts That Will Be Welcome for the Great War Christmas," 60.

157. Goodwin, *No Ordinary Time*, 82.

158. Russel Lawrence Barsh, "American Indians in the Great War," *Ethnohistory* 38, no. 3 (Summer 1991).

159. Clarke, *American Women and the World War*.

160. "For Our Boys in France or in Camp," *Ladies' Home Journal*, November 1917, 28.

161. "Knit Only These for the Red Cross," *Ladies' Home Journal*, November 1917, 29, 30; "The Work for the Summer Porch," *Ladies' Home Journal*, July 1917, 85.

162. "Every Cubic Inch to Work for Him," *The Stars and Stripes* (Paris, France) 1, no. 38, October 25, 1918, 9; Gertrude S. Mathews, "Tell *Them* to Knit," *Good Housekeeping*, September 1917, 102.

163. "A Christmas Bazaar for Junior," *Red Cross Magazine*, November 1918, 66.

164. "Knitting," *The Bellman*, September 8, 1917, 261.

165. United States Government Committee on Public Information advertisement in *Needlecraft*, May 1918, 17.

166. Marie Ashley, "Saving Precious Moments," *The Delineator*, November 1918, 92.

167. "Knit Your Bit Don't Quit," *The Woman Citizen*, October 6, 1917, 350, 351; "For Those Who Knit," *The Woman Citizen*, November 17, 1917, 479.

168. "The Knitting Major," *The Woman Citizen*, November 17, 1917, 479.

169. "The Point of View," *Scribner's Magazine*, January 1918, 250; Eleanor Gehan, "When You Come to the End of a Perfect Row," *Catholic World*, July 1918, 529, 530.

170. There are abundant knitting machine inventions patented before 1918. Application for patents related to hand knitting appear to begin during World War I.

171. Henrietta L. Kelsey, Knitting Needle, Patent No. 1,327,918, issued on January 13, 1920, (United States Patent Office).

172. Eleanor Gehan, "When You Come to the End of a Perfect Row," 528.

173. Daniel Low and Co. advertisement, "Jeanne d'Arc — the bag of the hour" in *The New York Times*, 22 September 1918, 7.

174. "What Was in Their Knitting Bags?" *The Woman Citizen*, 13 April 1918, 387.

175. Marie Ashley, "Knit Your Bit for the Navy," *The Delineator*, August 1917, 40, 41.

176. "The Point of View," *Scribner's Magazine*, January 1918, 250.

177. Archibald Craig, "Get This? Socks!" *The Woman Citizen*, March 16, 1918, 314; Archibald Craig, "Men as Knitters," *The Woman Citizen*, May 18, 1918, 497.

178. "The Emancipation of Man," *The Atlantic Monthly*, January 1919, 141, 142.

179. "Why Not to Knit," *Literary Digest*, July 6, 1918, 31.

180. "Every Cubic Inch to Work for Him," 9; "The American Red Cross," *Ladies' Home Journal*, October 1917, 33.

181. "Plenty of Knitting Needles," *Literary Digest*, November 10, 1917.

182. "Reply of the Knitters," *Literary Digest*, August 3, 1918, 31.

183. W. Livingston Larned, "If These Things Came to Pass," *Needlecraft*, February 1920, 3.

184. "Knitting," *Fortune*, July 1935, 14, 18.

185. "Yarns for Knitting," *Literary Digest*," January 24, 1920, 85; "New England Knitters," *The New York Times*, 20 August 1923, 10; Card dated September 7, 1931, Grace Coolidge's son, John, identified a photograph of his mother knitting on the porch, available from http://www.machinecancel.org; Library of Congress photo, LC-US262-112726.

186. Mabel Foster Bainbridge, "Knitted Laces for Household Use," *Ladies' Home Journal*, May 1922, 132; Merle Munn, "Golf Stockings for Father or Son," *Ladies' Home Journal*, October 1926, 221; Merle Munn, "Knitting a Sweater for One to Six Year Olds," *Ladies' Home Journal*, August 1928, 137; Mabel Foster Bainbridge, "Deep-Pile Rugs from Scraps of Yarn," *Ladies' Home Journal*, July 1927, 73; Cornelia Case, "To be Up-to-Date We Knit an Old-Time Afghan," *Ladies' Home Journal*, August 1927, 129.

187. Elsa Krawiec, "New Summer Sweaters for You to Make," *Ladies' Home Journal*, May 1922, 130.

188. Humaira Husain, ed., *Key Moments in Fashion: The Evolution of Style* (New York: Sterling Publishing, 1999); Meg Swansen, "Armenian Knitting," *Vogue Knitting*, Winter 2005–2006, 32, 34; "Seen at the Paris Ritz," *Ladies' Home Journal*, May 1928.

189. "Knitting," 14, 18, 30.

190. Bear Brand Yarns advertisement in *Needlecraft*, November 1921, 6; Texco Yarn advertisement in *Needlecraft*, November 1921, 16; *Virginia Snow's Sweater Book No. 28* (Elgin, IL: Virginia Snow Studios, 1924).

191. Peace Dale Knitting Yarns advertisement in *Needlecraft*, January 1922, 17; Allies Yarn advertisement in *Needlecraft*, November 1921, 18; "Fitting Up the Shop," *Needlecraft*, January 1922, 3.

192. "The Hope-Chest," *Needlecraft*, February 1920, 3; Elba Stratton, "The Song of the Hope-Chest," *Needlecraft*, June 1927, 3; Home Woolen Mills advertisement in *Needlecraft*, January 1922, 14; Concord Worsted Mills advertisement in *The Farmer's Wife*, November 1924, 202.

193. Columbia Yarns advertisement in *Ladies' Home Journal*, 22 May 1922, 133.

194. Virginia Pope, "High-Style Knitting," *The New York Times*, 19 July 1936, p. X8; Ruth Seinfel, "Snarls of Joy," *Collier's*, December 7, 1935, 26, 68; "Once Again the Click of Knitting Needles," *Needlework*, March 1933, 3; Anne Orr, "Knit or Crochet," *Good Housekeeping*, April 1935, 58.

195. "'Back-to-Knitting' Gains," *The New York Times*, 28 April 1935, sec. III, p. 10, col. 1; "Knitting Needles," *Fortune*, July 1935, 18, 30.

196. "They All Knit, One Row Plain, One Purl," *The New York Times*, 6 January 1935, p. 8, col. 1.

197. "Of Woman Knitting," *The Atlantic Monthly*, May 1936, 639–640.

198. "Supreme Court Bars Knitting," *The New York Time*, 2 February 1935, p. 21, col. 6.

199. Catherine Mackenzie, "They All Knit, One Row Plain, One Purl," p. 8, col. 1.

200. Anne Orr, "Something to Crochet for Today's House," *Good Housekeeping*, June 1935, 117; "Knit to Fit," *The Farmer's Wife*, March 1939, 25; Tara Maginnis, "She Saves Who Sews for Victory: Home Sewing on the American Home Front," *Costume* (1992); 64.

201. "Once Again the Click of Knitting Needles," 3; "When a Girl Needs Clothes," *The Parents' Magazine*, September 1933, 56–57; "Man Wins Knitting Prize," *The New York Times*, 15 August 1935, p. 20, col. 5.

202. "New Knit Shop at Racine Store Rapidly Builds Good Following," *Dry Goods Merchants Trade Journal*, November 1934, 80.

203. "They All Knit, One Row Plain, One Purl," p. 8, col. 5.

204. "Knitting," 14, 18. Similarly, manufacturing and marketing undergarments was a Depression-resistant industry, and the bra and girdle "fitter" served a role similar to that of the knitting instructor, as discussed in Jane Farrell-Beck's book, *Uplift: A History of the Bra* (Philadelphia: University of Pennsylvania Press, 2001). Major manufacturers of yarn at this time included the Bernhard Ulmann Co. of New York; James Lees and Sons Co. of Bridgeport, Pennsylvania; William H. Horstmann Co. of Philadelphia; and Emile Bernat and Sons Co. of Jamaica Plain, Massachusetts.

205. "Knitting," 18; "U.S. Knits Again," *Business Week*, 22 February 1941, 50; Ruth Seinfel, "Snarls of Joy," 68.

206. Virginia Pope, "High-Style Knitting," *The New York Times*, 19 July 1936.

207. Kathleen M. LaBarre and Kay D. LaBarre, *Reference Book of Women's Vintage Clothing: 1930–1939* (The Dalles, OR: LaBarre Books, 1999). Two-piece boucle dresses knitted by Kathleen LaBarre in the 1930s are shown on page 444. For one of the dresses, she purchased eleven balls of pink boucle yarn at 35¢ each. She kept the receipt, also shown beside the dress.

208. Sarah Barnes, ed., *Columbia Book of Misses' and Women's Bouclette Suits* (Philadelphia: William H. Horstmann Company, 1932).

209. Julia Coburn, "For You to Knit," *Ladies' Home Journal*, March 1935, 72; Julia Coburn, "Little Knitted Are Perfect Playmates," *Ladies' Home Journal*, May 1935, 17.

210. "An Easy-to-Make Knitted Sweater in the Latest Mode," *Needlework*, July 1933, 17; "Utility Knitteds," *Needlework*, August 1934, 6, 16; Merle Munn, "The Janna — A Modish Knitted Jumper Suit," *Needlework*, March 1935, 5, 11; *Fleisher's Classic Hand Knits for Men and Women*, Vol. 20, (Philadelphia: Fleisher Yarns, Inc., 1936).

211. Anne Orr, "Knitting for the Home," *Good Housekeeping*, September 1936, 101; Available from http://www.historicvermont.org.

212. "The History of Coats and Clark," available from http://www.coatsandclark.com/about+coats/history.

213. Ruth Seinfel, "Snarls of Joy,"68.

214. McCutcheon's advertisement in *The New York Times*, 11 August 1935, 12. Viyella is the trade name for a lightweight British wool/cotton blend (Isabel B. Wingate, *Fairchild's Dictionary of Textiles*).

215. "Knitting," 18.

216. "Knitting Needles," 18, 30.

217. Ruth Seinfel, "Snarls of Joy," 68.

218. "Boy, 16, Wins a Prize in Knitting Contest," *The New York Times*, 12 May 1936, 17; "Man Wins Knitting Prize," *The New York Times*, 15 August 1935, p. 35, col. 2; "Two Men Lead Knitting Class," *The New York Times*, 6 October 1936, p. 26, col. 6; Once Again the Click of Knitting Needles," 3; "Consider the Light Sources in Store Knitting Studios," *Dry Goods Journal*, October 1938, 80–81.

219. "Knitting," 18.

220. "Parade of Customer's Garments Wins Host of New Yarn Patrons," *Dry Goods Merchants Trade Journal*, September 1935, 92.

221. "Continue to Capitalize the Vogue for Knitting," *Dry Goods Merchants Trade Journal*, January 1936, 96.

222. "Why . . . The Emporium's Popular Knitting Studio Secures Constant Profit for This Store," *Dry Goods Merchants Trade Journal*, March 1935, 88; "U.S. Knits Again," 50.

223. "This Mill End Yarn Sale Brought Hundreds Inside," *Dry Goods Merchants Trade Journal*, March 1934, 74; "Yarn Ball and Needles Are Display Novelty," *Dry Goods Journal*, August 1936, 106; "'Stringing' Customers Is Fine This Way," *Dry Goods Merchants Trade Journal*, March 1935, 86.

224. "Knitting Contest Brings 698 Entries," *Dry Goods Journal*, June 1937, 81, 93; "Boy, 16, Wins a Prize in Knitting Contest," *The New York Times*, 12 May 1936, 17; "Knitting Contest Brings 100 Entries," *Dry Goods Merchants Trade Journal*, August 1936, 68, 106.

225. Catherine MacKenzie, "They All Knit, One Row Plain, One Purl," p. 8, col. 4.

226. Ruth Seinfel, "Snarls of Joy," 68.

227. "New Knit Shop at Racine Store Rapidly Builds Good Following," *Dry Goods Merchants Trade Journal*, November 1934, 80; "Why . . . The Emporium's Popular Knitting Studio Secures Constant Profit for This Store," 79; "45% Increase in Yarn Volume Is Store's Record in Four Months," *Dry Goods Merchants Trade Journal*, September 1935, 89.

228. "Consider the Light Sources in Store Knitting Studios," 80; "Knitting," 14, 18.

229. Louise Paine Benjamin, "'You've Got to Keep Fit to Do a Double Job,'" *Ladies' Home Journal*, October 1942, 103.

230. Katharine Fisher, "You're in the Army, too . . . ," *Good Housekeeping*, June 1942, 110, 111.

231. "How to Knit," *Life*, 24 November 1941, 111; "Home Knitting Defended," *The New York Times*, 22 January 1942.

232. "Stitches in Time in These Needy Times," *The American Home*, January 1942, 12–13

233. Cannon Mills, Inc., advertisement in *Dry Goods Journal*, August 1942, 35; General Motors Installment Plan advertisement in *Life*, 24 November 1941, 120; Solo Hair Accessories advertisement in *Dry Goods Journal*, February 1943, 5; Philip Morris cigarettes advertisement in *Good Housekeeping*, June 1942, 98; Cone Export and Commission Co. advertisement in *Dry Goods Journal*, September 1945, 74; Quaker Oats advertisement in *Ladies' Home Journal*, November 1942, 78; *McCall's Magazine* advertisement in *Dry Goods Journal*, November 1945, 104; Gripper Fasteners advertisement in *Good* Housekeeping, June 1942, 164; Listerine Antiseptic, *Good Housekeeping*, October 1945, 3.

234. "Topics of The Times: Etiquette and the War," *The New York Times*, 17 May 1943, p. 14, col. 4.

235. *Ibid.*

236. Goodwin, *No Ordinary Time*.

237. *The Honolulu Advertiser*, 25 May 1940. Available from http://the.honoluluadvertiser.com/article/2006/may/25/ln/150history.html.

238. Available from http://www.redcross.org/museum/exhibits/knits.asp.

239. "U.S. Knits Again," 49; "How to Knit," 111; Robin Hansen, "Husbands Came First . . . and Then We Knitted for the Red Cross," *Piecework* 3, no. 4, 48–49; Sue Lenthe, "Needle In, Wool Round, Needle Out," *Piecework* 3, no. 4, 54.

240. Leslie J. Mangin, "Playgrounds Aid National Defense," *Recreation* 35 (1941), 389, 402; "How to Knit," 111; Paula Becker, "Knitting for Victory — World War II," *HistoryLink.org: The Online Encyclopedia of Washington State History*. August 19, 2004. Available from http://www.historylink.org/this_week/index.cfm.

241. "U.S. Knits Again," 50–51.

242. Bernhard Ulmann Co. Inc. advertisement in *Dry Goods Journal*, September 1944, 179; Lily Mills Co. advertisement in *Dry Goods Journal*, December 1942; American Thread Co. advertisement in *Dry Goods Journal*, August 1942, 75; *Hand Knits for Men in the Service* Vol. 62 (Bridgeport, PA: James Lees and Sons Co., 1941).

243. "Business Books and Dealer Helps," *Dry Goods Journal*, September 1941, 92.

244. *Learn How Book* (New York: The Spool Cotton Co., 1941), 19–34.

245. Notions and Accessories, "Is This What's Wrong with Your Department?" *Dry Goods Journal*, September 1941, 90.

246. Notions and Accessories, "Variety of Appeals Increases Art Needlework Interest," *Dry Goods Journal*, May 1944, 140.

247. *Make Wonderful Things with Bucilla Wonder-knit Vol. 145* (New York: Bernard Ulmann Co., 1943), 9, 11.

248. "Keep Your Art Needlework Section Alive," *Dry Goods Journal*, May 1941, 88, 95; "Help the Needlework Section Speak for Itself via Display," *Dry Goods Journal*, November 1945.

249. Notions and Accessories, "Related Location Benefits Gifts, and Needlework," *Dry Goods Journal*, November 1941, 74.

250. "Segregation Helps Knitting and Closet Shops," *Dry Goods Journal*, February 1942, 82.

251. Spool Cotton Co. advertisement in *Dry Goods Journal*, December 1943, 212.

252. Helene Wright, "Teens of Our Times," *Good Housekeeping*, May 1942, 75; "Look, Mother, I Can Knit!" *Woman's Home Companion*, December 1942, 55; "Store Sponsors Knitting School for Girls," *Dry Goods Journal*, November 1945.

253. "Knit Yourself A Year-Round Suit and Hat," *Good Housekeeping*, February 1942, 173.

254. *Wonoco Journal of Knitting*, Vol. 2 (New York: Wonoco Yarn Co., 1941); "U.S. Knits Again," 50; "How to Knit: European Knitters Now in U.S.," *Life*, 24 November 1941, 114.

255. *Wonoco Journal of Knitting*, Vol. 2; *F and K Style Book* (New York: F and K Yarn Company, no date, but pattern styles date to the early 1940s).

256. Elizabeth Ward, "The Mittens That Multiplied Like Rabbits," *The Atlantic Monthly*, August 1945, 125–126.

257. "Price-Winning Knitting," *Woman's Day*, April 1943, 31–34.

258. *Woolies for Babies* Book No. 197 (New York: Spool Cotton Co., 1943); *Hand Knits by Beehive for Babies* Book No. 129 (Darlington: Patons and Baldwin, 1945); "Cradle Snatchers," *Ladies' Home Journal*, October 1942, 111.

259. Dawn Crowell, "Use Your Wool Power," *Ladies' Home Journal*, September 1942, 80.

260. Knit a Sweater You'll Always Love," *Good Housekeeping*, April 1942, 66; "Knit with Cotton," *Good Housekeeping*, June 1942; American Viscose Corporation advertisement in *Dry Goods Journal*, March 1941, 87; patterns using small amounts of yarn were published in *Good Housekeeping* (May 1942, 112; July 1942, 43–49; November 1942, 78, 89, 116); Tara Maginnis, "She Saves Who Sews for Victory: Home Sewing on the American Home Front," *Costume: Journal of the British Costume Society*, 1992, 66; *Good Housekeeping*, November 1942; Lesley Stanfield and Melody Griffiths, *The Encyclopedia of Knitting* (Philadelphia: Running Press, 2000), 147.

261. The War Relocation Authority photographs of Japanese-American evacuation and resettlement and other records are held at the Bancroft Library, University of California, Berkley.

262. Jeanne Wakatsuki Houston and James D. Houston, *Farewell to Manzanar* (New York: Bantam Books, 1973), 120.

263. Japanese American National Museum, 47.4A and 4B, 2001.

264. Jane Nakasako, research assistant, Hirasaki National Resource Center, Japanese American National Museum, personal communication, July 26, 2006.

265. Jeanne Wakatsuki Houston and James D. Houston, *Farewell to Manzanar*, 85.

266. Bernhard Ulmann Co. Inc. advertisement in *Dry Goods Journal*, November 1944, 173, and January 1945, 193.

267. Art Needlework, "Postponed Personal Projects Keep Needlework Sales on an Upward Curve," *Merchants Trade Journal*, March 1947, 200.

268. Bernhard Ulmann Co. Inc. advertisement in *Dry Goods Journal*, November, 1944, 173; Bernhard Ulmann Co. Inc. advertisement in *Dry Goods Journal*, January 1945, 193; July 1945, 187.

269. Obituary for Mrs. Fred A. Graber, *The New York Times*, 12 January 1950, 27.

270. Kathryn S. Olmsted, *Red Spy Queen: A Biography of Elizabeth Bentley* (Chapel Hill: University of North Carolina Press, 2002), 46, 126, 166.

271. Bernhard Ulmann Co. Inc. advertisement in *Dry Goods Journal*, July 1945, 187 and August, 1946, 195; Cone Export and Commission Co. advertisement in *Dry Goods Journal*, September 1945, 74; Listerine Antiseptic advertisement in *Good Housekeeping*, October 1945, 3; Bernhard Ulmann Co. Inc. advertisement in *Dry Goods Journal*, August, 1946, 195.

272. Julie Morris, "The Man Who Fought McCarthy's Red Smear," *The Detroit News*. Available from http://info.detnews.com/history.

273. Art Needlework, "For Lasting Needlework Interest," *Dry Goods Journal*, March 1946, 194; Art Needlework, "To Keep Needlework Interest Alive, Show shoppers Something Different," *Dry Goods Journal*, February 1946, 215; Art Needlework, "It's Always Been a Busy Department . . . Now It's Busier," *Merchants Trade Journal*, October 1948, 155; Art Needlework, "Exhibits Put Over Needlework Events," *Merchants Trade Journal*, July 1948, 163–164, 173.

274. Art Needlework, "Boosting art Needlework for Tomorrow," *Dry Goods Journal*, December 1946, 158; Dorothy Steen, "How to Make a Sweater Fit," *Good Housekeeping*, June 1945, 61; Art Needlework, "Postponed Personal Projects Keep Needlework Sales on an Upward Curve," 200.

275. Art Needlework, "For Lasting Needlework Interest," 194; Art Needlework, "Young and Old Like the Knitting School Idea," *Dry Goods Journal*, January 1947, 202.

276. Art Needlework, "Boosting Art Needlework for Tomorrow," *Dry Goods Journal*, December 1946, 158; Art Needlework, "Needlework Sections Woo the Teen-Ager," *Dry Goods Journal*, April 1946, 198; Art Needlework, "Young and Old Like the Knitting School Idea," 202; Art Needlework, "In June, July and August . . . Texas Teen-agers Learn to Knit," *Merchants Trade Journal*, May 1947, 198, 208; "Store Sponsors Knitting School for Girls," *Dry Goods Journal*, November 1945, 228.

277. Art Needlework, "Shortages Stimulate Needlework Interest," *Dry Goods Journal*, July 1946, 166.

278. *Jack Frost Two-Needle Mittens* Vol. 56 (New York: Jack Frost Yarn Co., n.d.); *Lacey's Socks, Gloves-Scarfs and Two Needle Mittens* Vol. 22 (Hackensack, NJ: T. M. Lacey, n.d.); Nell Armstrong, *2 Needle Socks* (Lowell, MA: Doreen Knitting Books, 1946); *Hand Knitted Socks by Beehive* (n.d.); Hilde, *New Sock Fashions in Wool* Vol. 69 (Mount Vernon, NY: Fashions in Wool).

279. *Learn to Knit* (New York: Spool Cotton Co., 1948); Barbara Abbey, *Susan Bates Presents 101 Ways to Improve Your Knitting* (New York: Viking Press, 1949).

280. Sears, Roebuck and Co. catalog, fall and winter 1946–1947, 813, 815, 818.

281. "Young Things . . . To Knit," *Ladies' Home Journal*, October 1946, 204.

282. *Lacey's Baby Book* (Little Falls, NJ: T. M. Lacey, n.d.); Nell Armstrong, *A Doreen Baby Book* (Lowell, MA: Doreen Knitting Books, 1945); *Jack Frost Instruction Books* (New York: Jack Frost Yarn Co., n.d.).

283. *Teen Age Togs* Vol. 69 (Bridgeport, PA: James Lees and Sons Co., 1946); Dorothy Wagner, "Campus Knitting," *Good Housekeeping*, August 1945, 105; Good Housekeeping Fashion, "Knit Warmth," *Good Housekeeping*, November 1945, 254; "A Sub-Deb Knits for Spring," *Ladies' Home Journal*, March 1946, 42–43, 193; "Knitting Beauties," *Ladies' Home Journal*, November 1946, 44–45; "Two-Way Sweater," *Good Housekeeping*, January 1948, 178; "Knit Two Pieces," *Good Housekeeping*, April 1948, 227; "30 Things to Make," *Good Housekeeping*, July 1948, 56–57; "Two Ski Sweaters," *Good Housekeeping*, December 1948, 218.

284. "Wool or Ribbon Knit," *Woman's Home Companion*, May 1949, 126–127; Patricia Young, "Separates to Knit," *Woman's Home Companion*, August 1949, 80–81; *Jack Frost Instruction Book* Vol. 50 (New York: Jack Frost Yarn Co., n.d.).

285. Art Needlework, "Postponed Personal Projects Keep Needlework Sales on an Upward Curve," 200; *Men's Hand-Knit Classics* (Green's Farms, CT: Ayr Scotch Wools Inc., 1946); *Men's Sweaters* No. 404 (New York: Spool Cotton Co., 1947); *Minerva Men's Book* Vol. 70 (Bridgeport, PA: James Lees and Sons Co., 1946); "Knit for Him," *Good Housekeeping*, April 1948, 229; Spinnerin Yarn Co. Inc. advertisement in *Good Housekeeping*, December 1948, 237.

286. Kajsa Lindqvist and Natalie Hebert, *Scandinavian Sweaters* (Boston: Plays, Inc., 1946); Kajsa Lindqvist, *Scandinavian Snow Sets* (Boston: Plays, Inc., 1947); Kajsa Lindqvist, *Scandinavian Mittens* (Boston: Plays, Inc., 1948).

287. "Now . . . Knit Argyle Socks," Frederick Herrschner Co. advertisement in *Good Housekeeping*, March 1948, 254.

288. Janet Graham, "Don't Be A Knitwit," *Good Housekeeping*, January 1948, 20.

289. Marie J. Kelleher, "Bits and Pieces — Childhood Memories," *The Melrose Mirror*, available from http://melrosemirror.media.mit.edu; "Bid for 30,000,000 Lbs. Starts Army Wool Buying," *The New York Times*, 21 October 1950, p. 24; "Knitters for Korea Get Scroll," *The New York Times*, 1 September 1953, p. 25, col. 4; "Yarn Sought in Korea Aid," *The New York Times*, 23 February 1943, p. 19, col. 6; "Warmth from America," *The New York Times*, 20 December 1953, p. 4, col. 2.

290. Betty Friedan, The Feminine Mystique (New York: Norton, 1963).

291. "Well-rounded Plan Keeps Needlework Growing," *Merchants Trade Journal*, September 1950, 124; "Small Knitting Shop More Than Pays Its Way," *Merchants Trade Journal*, November 1950, 128, 141; "How Needlework Offset Loss of First Floor Location," *Merchants Trade Journal*, February, 1950, 154; "Wall Bin Display Steps Up Yarn Sales," *Merchants Trade Journal*, October 1950, 118; "V-Bin Units Adapted for Yarns," *Merchants Trade Journal*, October 1950, 118.

292. "New Fixtures Show More . . . Sell More," *Merchants Trade Journal*, July 1950, 124, 140; "Teach 'Em How to Knit!" *Merchants Trade Journal*, August 1955, 116; "Free Instruction Draws Traffic," *Merchants Trade Journal*, May 1955, 104; "Sticks by Customer until Garment Is Done," *Merchants Trade Journal*, August 1955, 114.

293. "You've Got to Really Like Your Job," *Merchants Trade Journal*, August 1955, 114, 116.

294. "Free Instruction Draws Traffic," *Merchants Trade Journal*, May 1955, 104.

295. "Well-Rounded Plan Keeps Needlework Growing," *Merchants Trade Journal*, September 1950, 124.

296. Melitta Guthrie, and Josephine Springer, *The All-American Sock Book* Vol. 8 (Stoughton, MA: Nomis Yarn Co., 1954); *Bear Brand Hand Knit Socks for Men, Women, Children* (Vol. 340) (New York: Bernhard Ulmann Co. Inc., 1950).

297. "California Girl, 16, Wins Knitting Prize," *The New York Times*, 4 October 1950, p. 36, col. 5; "2 Teen-Age Knitters Visit City as Award," *The New York Times*, 6 December 1950, p. 43, col. 1

298. Sears, Roebuck and Co. catalog, 1956–1957, 195, 215, 218–219.

299. *Bear Brand — Fleisher Knitting Primer* (no publisher or date listed); *Gloves and Mittens to Knit and Crochet for the Entire Family* (New York: Bucilla, 1953); *Accessories in Wool . . . for Men, Women, Children* (New York: Spool Cotton Co., 1952); Carleen Goldsmith, ed., *Bernat Gloves and Mittens for the Family* (Jamaica Plain, MA: Emile Bernat and Sons Co., 1959); *Sweaters for the Family* (New York: Coats and Clark, July 1953); *Sweaters Are Fashion News!* (New York: Coats and Clark, 1955).

300. "A Whole Family of Sweaters," *Woman's Day*, September 1953, 66; "Knit for Baby," *Good Housekeeping*, November 1950, 262; "Tiny Knits for Tiny Tots," *Good Housekeeping*, May 1950, 250; *Bear Brand Baby Book Infants to 4 Years* Vol. 353 (New York: Bernhard Ulmann Co., 1956); *Bear Brand Baby Book Infants to 4 Years* Vol. 339 (New York: Bernhard Ulmann Co., 1950); *Bernat Handicrafter Book No. 57: The Big Book of Hand Knit Fashions for Small Fry, Infants and Toddlers* (Uxbridge, MA: Emile Bernat and Sons Co., 1957); *Fleisher's Baby Book Infants to 4 Years* Vol. 101 (Philadelphia: Fleisher Yarns, Inc., 1957); *Fleisher's Baby Book Hand Knits for Infants to 4 Years* Vol. 87 (Philadelphia: Fleisher Yarns, 1950); *Jack Frost Baby Book* Vol. 60 (New York: Jack Frost Yarn Co., n.d.); *Spinnerin Baby and Toddler Hand Knits* Vol. 137 (South Hackensack, NJ: Spinnerin Yarn Co., 1957).

301. *Bear Brand Knitting Book* (New York: Bernhard Ulmann Co., 1950).

302. "Knit for Pond or Ski Slope," *Good Housekeeping*, September 1950, 210; "Knit Clothes for Dolly," *Good Housekeeping*, March 1950, 244; *Jack Frost Sweaters for Boys and Girls* Vol. 58 (New York: Gottlieb Bros., 1952); *Fleisher's Hand Knits for Boys and Girls Sizes 6 to 14* (Philadelphia: Fleisher Yarns, Inc., 1956).

303. "Fashions: Yarn and a Touch of Venus," *Good Housekeeping*, July 1950, 64–73; "Glamorize Your Wardrobe," *Good Housekeeping*, October 1950, 280; *The Bernat Book for All Sports* Vol. 71, (Jamaica Plain, MA: Emile Bernat and Sons Co., 1958); *Fleisher's Hand Knit Fashions* (Philadelphia: Fleisher Yarns, Inc., 1953); *Minerva Fashions in Hand Knits* (Bridgeport, PA: James Lee and Sons Co., 1952); *Jack Frost Sweaters* (New York: Gottlieb Bros., 1954); *Botany Hand Knits for Men* (Botany Yarns, Inc., 1958).

304. Roxa Wright, "An-Knit Lace Has an Air of Its Own," *Woman's Day*, June 1953, 40; "The Bulky Look Is Sweeping the Country!" *Woman's Day*, November 1953, 37–43.

305. Roxa Wright, "From the Tyrol," *Woman's Day*, December 1954, 109, "Scandinavian Sweaters," January 1957, 72; "Prize-Winning Sweaters from France," *Woman's Day*. April 1955, 57; Roxa Wright, "Hand Knits from the Aran Islands," *Woman's Day*, November 14, 1956, 46, 64, 80.

306. "Norwegian Sweaters the Easy Way," *Woman's Day*, January 1955, 42–43, 119–120.

307. Elizabeth Zimmermann, "Knitted Pillbox," *Woman's Day*, 14 December 1955, 76, 78.

308. *A Woman's Home Companion Leaflet* (n.d.); "One Plan: Seven Sweaters," *Good Housekeeping*, July 1950, 68–73.

309. Patterns of the Times, "Simple Hand-Knit Sweaters," *The New York Times*, 30 June 1952, p. 16, col. 1; "Back-to-School Hand Knits," *The New York Times*, 18 August 1952, p. 14, col. 1; "Back-to-School Hand Knits," *The New York Times*, 15 November 1954, p. 20, col. 2.

310. "CARE Package," Available from http://americanhistory.si.edu/collections/object.cfm?key=35&objkey=245.

311. Senator Maurine B. Neuberger (Democrat-Oregon). Available from http://memory.loc.gov.

312. "The Quick-Knit Cap: One Theme, Thirty Variations," *Woman's Day*, October 1971, 70–71.

313. Available from http://www.heritage.dupont.com.

314. Red Heart "Wintuk" advertisement in *Good Housekeeping Needlecraft*, fall-winter, 1974–1975, back cover.

315. "Playing with Knitting Patterns," *Woman's Day*, June 1972, 34, 154, 156, 159; "Knit Wall Hangings in a Palette of Colors," *Woman's Day*, April, 1971, 30. Mail-order pattern.

316. "Stripe Up the Bands," *Seventeen*, fall-winter 1971; *Woman's Day*, January 1971, cover; "Electric Stripes to Knit," *Woman's Day*, February 1971, 24; "Knit the Perfect Swimsuit," *Family Circle*, April 1972, 38; "Knitting," *Family Circle*, May 1972, 115; *Spinnerin Cape Caper Minibook 344* (Hackensack, NJ: Spinner Yarn Co. Inc., n.d.).

317. "Great Things to Knit and Crochet from Clever Little Squares and Borders," *Woman's Day*, February 1975, 45–47.

318. Mary Maxim advertisement in *Needle and Yarn* 1, no. 3 (1964): 10; *McCall's Sweater Book* (New York: McCall's Pattern Co., 1975).

319. "Men Turning to Knitting And Therein Lies a Yarn," *New York Times*, 20 august 1959, 28; "Male Dancer Turns Knitting to Profit; Nick Andrews Sells to Cast Members of Show He Is In Completed Two Sweater," *New York Times*, 1 February 1962, 46; "Out With the Boys? Yes, but for a Knitting Lesson," *New York Times*, 16 February 1971, 38.

320. "A Sweater Worth Making," *Woman's Day*, April 1960, 70, 93.

321. "Greek Fishing Sweaters to Knit," *Woman's Day*, February 1969, 59.

322. *McCall's Sweater Book*, 27; *Woman's Day*, January 1972, 37; *Woman's Day*, January 1973, 26, 28. *Woman's Day* patterns are mail-order.

323. "Gifts from Many Lands," *Woman's Day*, November 1962, 34–35.

324. "Round-the-World Sweaters," *Woman's Day*, February 1963, 58–61.

325. "Our Brilliant, International Sweater Collection 1964," *Woman's Day*, February 1964, 39–42; "A Superb International Collection of High Fashion Sweaters," *Woman's Day*, February 1965, 78–81; "An International Collection of New Knitted Sweaters Classic Sweaters Pour Le Sport," *Woman's Day*, February 1966, 28–31.

326. *The Woman's Day Book of Knitted Sweaters* (New York: Simon and Schuster, 1976); "Folk Art Designs," *Woman's Day*, October 1964, 24; "Knitter's Boutique," *Woman's Day*, January 1972, 29–30; September 1974, 68–69.

327. Roger Bilstein, *Flight in America: From the Wrights to the Astronauts*, Revised Editon (Baltimore: Johns Hopkins University Press, 1994).

328. "About the Peace Corps," available from http://www.peacecorps.gov.

329. *Knitted and Crocheted Designs as Featured at the Better Living Center at the New York World's Fair* (The American Thread Co., 1965).

330. Available from http://www.kaffefassett.com/biography.htm.

331. *Pauline Denham Yarns* Book 7 (Petaluma, CA: Pauline Denham Yarns, n.d.).

332. Brian Harris, Vice President of Mary Maxim, Inc., personal communication.

333. Mary Maxim advertising letter (n.d.), Port Huron, MI: Mary Maxim.

334. *Mary Maxim Double Knitting Picture-Graph Pattern* (Paris, Ontario: Miss Mary Maxim Ltd., 1960).

335. *Knit a Wardrobe of Sweaters for Your Favorite Doll* (New York: Fawcett Publications, Inc., 1966).

336. Pat Trexler, "Make a 'Corn Cob' Potholder." *Seattle Times*, 13 June 1972; Pat Trexler, "Pat's Pointers," *Seattle Times*, 4 January 1972; 13 June 1972; 31 December 1974; 26 August 1975.

337. "For the Gift-Makers," *Women's Circle*, October 1967, 52–53.

338. "Minta's Mats," *Women's Circle*, July 1974, 12–13.

339. "Handicrafts for Sale or Exchange," *Women's Circle*, October 1967, 55–61.

340. "Knitting Craft," *Whole Earth Catalog*, (Menlo Park, CA: Portola Institute, Inc. June 1971), 171; Lee Worden, "The Rise and Fall of the Whole Earth Catalog," (paper presented to the West of Eden: Communes and Utopia in Northern California Conference, Berkley, CA, March 25, 2006).

341. Deborah Hofmann, "Inspiring: Designer Collections Spur Increase in Home Knitting," *St. Louis Post-Dispatch*, 23 November 1989, 3S, 7.

342. Angela ffrench, *Knitting and Design for Mohair* (New York: St. Martin's Press, 1987).

343. *Finn Time*, Eila, Vol. 6; *Bernat Handicrafter* No. 509, 1983; *McCall's Needlework and Crafts*, May/June 1981.

344. Angela ffrench, *Knitting and Design for Mohair*.

345. Deirdre McQuillan, *The Aran Sweater* (Belfast: Appletree Press, 1993); Rutt, *A History of Hand Knitting*. McQuillan and Rutt describe the complex and fascinating history of making and marketing Aran knits.

346. Kax Wilson, *A History of Textiles* (Boulder, CO: Westview Press, 1979).

347. Irena Turnau, "Knitting" in Madeline Ginsburg, ed., *The Illustrated History of Textiles* (London: Studio Editions, 1991); Erica Wilson, *Erica Wilson's Knitting Book* (New York: Charles Scribner's Sons, 1988).

348. *Vogue Knitting* (New York: Pantheon Books, 1989).

349. Macdonald, *No Idle Hands*.

350. Betsy Harrell, *Anatolian Knitting Designs: Sivas Stocking Patterns Collected in an Istanbul Shantytown* (Istanbul: Redhouse Press, 1981); Sheila McGregor, *The Complete Book of Traditional Fair Isle Knitting* (London: B. T. Batsford Ltd, 1981); Birgitta Dandanell and Ulla Danielsson, *Twined Knitting* (Loveland, CO: Interweave Press, 1984); Britt-Marie Christoffersson, *Swedish Sweaters: New Designs from Historical Examples* (Newtown, CT: Taunton Press, 1990); Vibeke Lind, *Knitting in the Nordic Tradition* (New York: Lark Books, 1984).

351. *Knitting Around the World* (Newtown, CT: Taunton, 1993).

352. Lizbeth Upitis, *Latvian Mittens* (Pittsville, WI: Schoolhouse Press, 1997); Priscilla A. Gibson-Roberts, *Salish Indian Sweaters*; Charlene Schurch, *Knitting Marvelous Mittens: Ethnic Designs from Russia* (New York: Lark Books, 1998); Wendy Keele, *Poems of Color: Knitting in the Bohus Tradition* (Loveland CO: Interweave Press, 1995); Beth Brown-Reinsel, *Knitting Ganseys* (Loveland, CO: Interweave Press, 1993).

353. Anna Zilboorg, *Simply Socks: 45 Traditional Turkish Patterns to Knit* (New York: Lark Books, 1994).

354. Anne-Marie Schiro, "A Thousand Knitters Flourish," *The New York Times*, 23 December 1980, B8.

355. Chellie Pingree and Debby Anderson, *Maine Island Classics: Living and Knitting on a Maine Island* (North Haven, M.E.: North Island Designs, 1988); available from http://www.bartlettyarns.com.

356. "What is Peace Fleece?" available from http://www.peacefleece.com/thestory.htm; available from http://www.himalayayarn.com/

357. Joyce Williams and Lizbeth Uptitis, Latvian Dreams (Pittsville, W.I.: Schoolhouse Press, 2000); available from http://www.monticellowi.com/textilesSep01a.htm.

358. Galer Barnes, personal communication, January 29, 2007.

359. Bernadine Morris, "Sweater Designers Create a Warm and Wearable Art Form," *The New York Times*, 31.

360. Erica Wilson, *Erica Wilson's Knitting Book* (New York: Charles Scribner's Sons, 1988).

361. Angela ffrench, *Knitting and Design for Mohair*; Montse Stanley, *Knitting Plus* (New York: Henry Holt and Company, 1990).

362. Maggie Righetti, *Knitting in Plain English* (New York: St. Martin's Press, 1986).

363. Judith Shangold, *The Designer Collection (for Bears).* (Medford MA: A Bear in Sheep's Clothing, 1993).

364. *The Opinionated Knitter Elizabeth Zimmerman Newsletters 1958-1968* (Pittsville, WI: Schoolhouse Press, 2005), 8.

365. Ibid.

366. Available from http://www.interweave.com/knit/charities.asp; available from http://groups.yahoo.com/group/SOCKFORSOLDIERS/; available from http://www.house.gov/latourette/issues_toasty_toes.htm.

367. Available from http://warmupamerica.org/home.html.

368. Melissa Leventon, *Artwear: Fashion and Anti-Fashion* (New York: Thames and Hudson, 2005).

References

Barney, William L. *The Passage of the Republic: An Interdisciplinary History of Nineteenth-Century America.* Lexington, MA: D. C. Heath and Company, 1987.

Baumgarten, Linda. *What Clothes Reveal: The Language of Clothing in Colonial and Federal America.* New Haven, CT: Yale University Press, 2002.

Clarke, Ida Clyde. *American Women and the World War.* New York: D. Appleton and Company, 1918.

Countryman, Edward. *The American Revolution.* New York: Hill and Wang, 1985.

Dick, Everett. *The Sod-House Frontier 1854-1890.* New York: D. Appleton-Century Company, 1937.

Drumm, Stella M., ed. *Down the Santa Fe Trail and into Mexico: The Diary of Susan Shelby Magoffin, 1846-1847.* Lincoln: University of Nebraska Press, 1982.

Earle, Alice Morse. *Costume of Colonial Times.* New York: Empire State Book Co., 1924.

Freidel, Frank, & Brinkley, Alan. *America in the Twentieth Century*, 5th ed. New York: McGraw-Hill, Inc., 1982.

Goodwin, Doris Kearns. *No Ordinary Time.* New York: Simon & Schuster, 1994.

Gordon, Beverly. *Bazaars and Fair Ladies: The History of the American Fundraising Fair.* Knoxville: The University of Tennessee Press, 1980.

Gordon, Beverly. (1980). *Shaker Textile Arts.* Hanover: The University Press of New England, 1983.

Gutek, Gerald, and Patricia Gutek. *Visiting Utopian Communities: A Guide to the Shakers, Moravians, and Others.* Columbia SC: University of South Carolina Press, 1998.

Hartmann, Susan M., *The Home Front and Beyond: American Women in the 1940s.* Boston: Twayne Publishers, 1982.

Hayden, Dolores. *Seven American Utopias: The Architecture of Communitarian Socialism, 1790-1975.* Cambridge, MA: The MIT Press, 1976.

Johnson, Paul, *A History of the American People.* New York: Harper Perennial, 1999.

Klamkin, Marian. (1972). *Hands to Work: Shaker Folk Art and Industries.* New York: Dodd, Mead and Company.

Klein, Herbert S. (2004). *A Population History of the United States.* Cambridge, UK: Cambridge University Press, 2004.

Macdonald, Anne L. *No Idle Hands: The Social History of American Knitting.* New York: Ballantine Books, 1988.

McCauley, Daniel, and Kathryn McCauley. *Decorative Arts of the Amish of Lancaster County.* Intercourse, PA: Good Books, 1988.

McCullough, David. *1776.* New York: Simon and Schuster, 2005.

Norton, Mary Beth. *Liberty's Daughters: The Revolutionary Experience of American Women, 1750-1800.* Cornell, NY: Cornell University Press, 1996.

Opdyke, Sandra. *The Routledge Historical Atlas of Women in America.* New York: Routledge, 2000.

Philbrick, Nathaniel. *Mayflower: A History of Courage, Community, and War.* New York: Viking, 2006.

Riley, Glenda. *The Female Frontier: A Comparative View of Women on the Prairie and the Plains.* Lawrence, KS: University Press of Kansas, 1988.

Rutt, Richard. *A History of Hand Knitting.* London: B. T. Batsford Ltd., 1989.

Schlissel, Lillian. *Women's Dairies of the Westward Journey.* New York: Schocken Books, 1992.

Scott, Anne Firor. *Natural Allies: Women's Associations in American History.* Urbana: University of Illinois Press, 1991.

Silber, Nina. *Daughters of the Union: Northern Women Fight the Civil War.* Cambridge, MA: Harvard University Press, 2005.

Steinberg, Ted. *Down to Earth: Nature's Role in American History.* New York: Oxford University Press, 2002.

Tortora, Phyllis G., and Eubank, Keith. *Survey of Historic Costume* (4th ed). New York: Fairchild Publications, 2005.

Ulrich, Laurel Thatcher. *The Age of Homespun: Objects and Stories in the Creation of an American Myth.* New York: Alfred A. Knopf, 2001.

Ulrich, Laurel Thatcher. *Good Wives: Image and Reality in the Lives of Women in Northern New England, 1650-1750.* New York: Oxford University Press, 1982.

Ulrich, Laurel Thatcher. *A Mid-wife's Tale: The Life of Martha Ballard, Based on Her Diary, 1785-1812.* New York: Alfred A. Knopf, 1990.

Varney, William L. *The Passage of the Republic: An Interdisciplinary History of Nineteenth- Century America.* Lexington, MA: D. C. Heath and Company, 1987.

Weissman, Judith Reiter, and Wendy Lavitt. *Labors of Love: America's Textiles and Needlework, 1650-1930.* New York: Alfred A. Knopf, 1987.

Woloch, Nancy. *Women and the American Experience: A Concise History*, 2nd ed. Boston: McGraw Hill, 2002.

Yellin, Emily, *Our Mothers' War: American Women at Home and at the Front during World War II.* New York: Free Press, 2004.

Zinn, Howard. *A People's History of the United States: 1492 –Present.* New York: Harper Perennial, 2005.

Zinn, Howard, and Anthony Arnove. *Voices of a People's History of the United States.* New York: Seven Stories Press, 2004.

Periodicals reviewed include *The American Home, The Atlantic Monthly, The Bellman, Catholic World, Collier's, The Delineator, Dry Goods Merchants Trade Journal, Family Circle, The Farmer's Wife, Fortune, Godey's Lady's Book, Good Housekeeping, The Ladies Home Journal, Life, The Literary Digest, Needlecraft, The New York Times, Montgomery Ward Catalog, Peterson's Magazine, The Red Cross Magazine, Scribner's Magazine, Sears Roebuck and Company Catalogs, The Woman Citizen, Woman's Day, Woman's Home Companion,* and *Women's Circle.*

Index

Abbey, Barbara, 158, 160
Abdominal Band, 84
Afghans, 165
African slaves, 15
Alaskan Native knitting, 71
Albino, C. G., 128
Alexander, Kathryn, 190, 193
Allies Yarn, 114
Amana colonies, 58, 60, 62, 64, 66
American Thread Co., 144, 160, 172, 176, 180
Amish knitters, 65
Anderson, Debby, 186, 187
Antartex kit, 180
Aran Island sweaters, 169, 171, 174, 175, 180, 184
Argyle Socks and Anklets, 162, 164
Automobile Helmet, 83
Babbette Jacket, 116
Babies' Knitted Sack, 37
Baby bonnet, 29, 62, 159
Baby bootees, 63, 84
Baby Bunting Set, 116
Baby Soaker, 127
Baby stockings, 63
Baby's Hood, 52
Baby's Sock/Slipper, 37, 52
Bachelik Pelerine, 28
Bags, 112
Baizerman, Suzanne, 186
Balaclava, 143
Bartlettyarns, 187
Barton, Clara, 92
Bead-knit purses, 34, 35
Bear Brand Yarn, 77, 82, 87, 113, 119, 144, 157, 160, 161, 166–168, 173
Bedspreads, 131
Bellman, The, 97
Bernhard Ulmann Co., 87, 124, 128, 144, 148, 157, 165, 173, 174, 180
Blackwell, Elizabeth, 41
Bolero design, 185
Botany Woolen Mills, 148, 174
Boy's knee breeches, 14
Boye Needle Co., 123, 128, 190
Brill, Reina Mia, 196

Bristow, Janet, 196
Brittany Co., 189, 190
Brown-Reinsel, Beth, 186
Bucilla Co., 57, 80, 129, 130, 144, 157, 167, 180
Bulky knits, 173, 174
Butterick, 32, 33
C. J. Bates & Son, Inc., 160
Cacicedo, Jean Williams, 196
Cape, 36
Cappers Act of 1571, 13
Caron International, 184
Cast On, 187
Chanel, Gabriel "Coco," 110
Child's Cardigan Sweater, 84
Chow, Cat, 196
Christoffersson, Britt-Marie, 186
Civil War, 36, 39–49, 45
    Reenactment knitters, 49
Classic Elite Yarns, 186
Close-fit sweaters, 160
Coats & Clark, 128, 167, 172, 174, 179, 180
Cobey, Katharine, 183, 196
Cole, David, 196
Collingbourne Mills, 113
Colonial Revival style, 131
Columbia Bouclette Suit, 126, 130
Columbia Minerva, 176, 180
Columbia Yarns, 117
Compton, Rae, 186
Concord Worsted Mills, 117
Convent Tuxedo Sweater, 118
Coolidge bedspread, 128, 131
Coolidge, Grace, 110, 111, 128, 131
Corticelli Silk Co., 32, 80, 82, 87
Counterpane pattern, 128
Cowichan sweater, 66, 67
Craft Yarn Council of America, 186, 196
Craig, Archibald, 103, 105

Cravat sweater, 113
Crawford, Joan, 123
Cycle or Golf Stocking, 79
Daisy Sweater, 116
Dale, Samuel S., 105, 106
Daphne Scarf, 131
Delineator, The, 87, 103
Designers, 176, 190
Devos scarf sweater, 114
Dior, Christian, 160, 169
Dos Tejedoras, 186
Dresses, 150, 151
Eaton Rapids Woolen Mills, 114
Egg holder, 29
Ellis, Perry, 183, 190
Emile Bernat & Sons Co., 128, 160, 168, 169, 172, 184
Empire Silhouette, 160
Enterprise Cotton Knitting Yarn, 160
Epstein, Nicky, 193
Evening bags, 85
Eye bandage, 103
F. W. Woolworth Co., 78, 80, 87
Fair Isle sweaters, 174, 184
Falick, Melanie, 193
Fassett, Kaffe, 177, 193, 195
ffrench, Angela, 190
Filieres, 30, 119
Finger Bowl Doilies, 131
Flat cap, 13
Fleisher Yarns, 85–88, 113, 119, 128, 128, 144, 148, 157, 160, 167–169, 173
Fleisher, Simon and Moyer, 87
Florence Knitting Silk, 32, 33
Foot-Ball Sweater, 33, 78
Frederick Herrschner Co., 160, 162
Friedan, Betty, 165, 171
Fuchs, Hilde, 173, 176, 179
Gable, Pam, 195
Galo, Victoria, 196
Gauges, 30, 119
Gaughan, Norah, 193
Gaultier, Jean Paul, 184
Gentleman's Neck-Tie, 44

Gibson-Roberts, Priscilla A., 186
Godey's Lady's Book and Magazine, 23–25, 27–29, 31, 36, 41, 57
Good Housekeeping Needlecraft, 184
Good Housekeeping, 121, 128, 131, 146, 160–163, 168
Great Depression, 123, 124
Gschwandtner, Sabrina, 197
H. K. H. Silk Co., 113
Handwoven, 181
Harpoon scarf, 71
Harrell, Betsy, 185, 186
Harrow Sweater, 116
Hats, 80
Highland Fling stockings, 158
Hill, Helen, 97, 99, 100
Himalaya Yarn, 187
Hoar, Irma, 173, 175
Home Arts, 62
Home Woolen Mills, 117
Houston, Jeanne Wakatsuki, 152, 153
Immigrant knitters, 53–57
Imogene Scarf, 115
Infant's Jersey, 36
INKnitters, 187
Institute for Hand-Knitting, The, 166
Instructors, 133, 135
Interweave Knits, 187
Irish Fisherman stockings, 158
J. A. Kirven Co., 145
Jack Frost Yarn Co., 148, 168, 180
Jacobs, Marc, 183
Jacobsson, Emma, 186
James Lees & Sons, 128, 145, 160, 161
Japanese-American knitters, 152–153
Jeanne d'Arc Knitting Bag, 100, 102
Jefferson, Thomas, 15–17
Jiffy-knit sweater kits, 129
Jiffy-made suit, 134
John Dritz & Sons, 160

Johnson, Eastman, 23, 26, 39
Johnson, Eliza McCardle, 25
Joseph Spiess Co., 165
Kelly, Grace, 165
Kimono sweater, 85
Klein, Calvin, 183, 190
Knee cap, 30
Knit 'n Style, 187
Knit Motor Coat, 83
"Knit One Purl Two," 145
Knit Picot Stitch Shawl, 78
Knit Thread Lace, 113
Knit Tie, 119
Knit-Pick, 135
Knitted Winter Spenser, 41
Knitter's Magazine, 187
Knitter's, 187
Knitting as Art, 183, 189, 191, 192, 194, 196, 197
Knitting bag, 100, 102
Knitting Guild Association, 187
Knitting machine, 12, 18, 41, 114
Korea, 163, 165
Kristensen, Anni, 187
Lace knitting, 31, 85
Ladies' Athletic Sweater, 81
Ladies' Bicycle Mitten, 79
Ladies' Cozy Jacket, 77
Ladies' Fancy Silk Mittens, 30
Ladies' Home Journal, The, 23, 31, 32, 34, 36, 75, 78, 80, 82, 96, 110, 126, 148, 160, 161
Ladies' Motor Cap and Scarf, 82
Lady's Travelling Cap, 51
Laines du Pingouin Yarns, 172
Lambert, Frances S., 28, 30, 51
Lambert, Gail Ann, 197
Lansbury, Angela, 157
Laydown Sweater, 79
Learning to knit, 102, 103
Legends, 184
Life, 137, 138, 146
Ligon, Linda, 180, 193

Lily Mills Co., 144
Lincoln, Abraham, 45, 46
Lincoln, Mary Todd, 46
Lion Brand yarn, 186
"Listen to the Knocking at the Knitting Club," 74
Lopi sweater, 175
Macdonald, Anne L., 185, 190
Magoffin, Susan Shelby, 51, 52
Male knitters, 103, 105, 128, 130
Mary Maxim, 176, 177, 179
Mason-Dixon Knitting, 197
McCall's Needlework and Crafts, 184, 190
McGregor, Sheila, 185
McKinley, Ida Saxton, 25, 75
Men Who Knit, 197
Men's golf stockings, 110
Mennonite knitters, 65
Mid-Riff Sweater, 146
Minerva Yarn, 161, 169
Miser's Purse, Victorian, 35
Mittens, 13, 33, 55, 59, 163
Mittens, baby's, 33
Mittens, poetry, 20, 21
Monmouth cap, 12, 14
Moore, Amy Clarke, 188—189
Movies, 123, 125, 126, 138, 147, 157, 165, 185
Music, 74, 95, 97, 143, 145
Native American knitters, 50–51, 66–71, 105
Navajo knit leggings, 67, 70
Navajo sweater, 119
Navy Boy vest, 82
Necktie Scarf, 32
Needlecraft, 62, 85, 87, 110, 114
Needles, 67, 87, 92, 100, 102, 114, 128, 130, 140, 166, 167, 172, 190
Needlework, 121, 124, 126
Nelson Island Diamond pattern, 71
Nicholas, Kristin, 186
Nightcap, 18, 19
Nightingale Cape, 36
Nomis Yarn Co., 166
Nonotuck Silk Co., 31–33, 87

Nordhoff, Charles, 58, 62
North Island Designs, 186–187
Nylon knits, 164
Obermeyer, Lindsay, 192, 196
Orr, Anne, 121, 124
Over the Top Scotch Cap, 82, 83
Parent's Magazine, The, 124
Pauline Denham Yarns, 176, 177
Peace Dale Mills, 114
Peace Fleece yarn, 187
Pearl-McPhee, Stephanie, 197
Pence Jug, 34
Penwiper, rabbit, 29
Pershing Coat, 82, 83
Peterson's Magazine, 33, 34, 57
Phelps, Sarah, 45, 46
Phillips, Mary Walker, 180, 187, 189
Pickford, Mary, 110
Piecework, 187
Pingree, Chellie, 186–187
Pinwheel pattern counterpane, 55
Plimpton, Amos, 18, 19
Poetry mittens, 20, 21
Poetry, 16, 17, 25–27, 44, 66, 91, 92, 110, 117, 163
Poncho, 176
Post, Emily, 140
Prayer Shawl Ministry, 196
Prison knitters, 75
Public aid programs, 195, 196
Qiviut lace knitting, 71
Queen Victoria, 20, 23
Radulovich, Milo and Nancy, 158
Red Cross Soldiers' Socks, 107
Red Cross Soldiers' Wristlets, 95
Red Cross, 92, 96–99, 103–106, 137, 138, 140–142, 171
Reticules, 34, 35
Revolutionary War, 15–17
Reynolds Yarn, 174, 184
Reynolds, Debbie, 157
Ribbed bonnet, 124
Ribbed slip-on sweater, 148

Righetti, Maggie, 190
Robson, Deborah, 178, 179
Rococo, 186
Rogers, Ginger, 138, 157
Roosevelt, Eleanor, 123, 140, 142, 95
Rosen, Evie, 196
Rosenthal, Polly, 146, 148
Royal Society, Inc., 145
Rush, Helene, 185
Russell, Suzanne, 186
Rutt, Richard, 185
Rygjia Homespun Yarn, 169
Saturday Evening Post, 73, 77
Scandinavian sweater, 162, 163, 174, 175, 184
Schiaparelli, Elsa, 113, 124, 126
Schurch, Charlene, 186
Searle, Karen, 186, 191, 196
Sears, Roebuck & Co., 89, 128, 160, 166
Separatists of Zoar, 59, 64
Sessions, Frank L., 87, 100
Sewing case, 20
Shakers, 59, 60
Simplicity Knitting, 187
Simultaneous Socks, 103
Sirdar Wools, 174
Skirts, 129, 177
Slippers, 16, 36
Snow, Virginia, 113, 118
Soldier's hood, 47
Spalding, Eliza, 52, 53
Spinnerin Yarn Co., 158, 160, 162, 168, 173
Spin-Off, 187
Spool Cotton Co., 128, 145, 146, 160, 161
Spool-knitting kits, 118, 162, 164
Star pattern counterpane with border, 48
Star patterns, 86
Stitch 'N Bitch, 197
Stockings, 55, 63, 64, 126
Stoller, Debbie, 197
Suffrage, 82, 83
Suits, 150, 151
Swagger Frocks, 135
Swansen, Meg, 189, 193, 195
Women's Wear Daily, 133, 169
Sweater vests, 97, 168, 184, 185

Sweaters, 77, 106, 112, 113, 126, 128, 132, 159, 161, 174, 183, 184
Swett, Sarah, 193
Taft, William Howard, 106
Tam-O'Shanters, 114
Teen knitters, 158, 159
Threads, 186, 187
Thrum cap, 13
Trevor, Claire, 138, 142
Trianon Bedjacket, 113
Trompe l'oeil, 113, 130
Truth, Sojourner, 40, 41
Tunic top, 177
Turner, Lana, 126
Twin sets, 129
Tyrolean, 126, 184
U.S. Navy Iceland Sweater, 149
Ulmann, Bernhard, 57
Underhill yarn, 186
Union Army Socks, 42, 43
Upitis, Lizbeth, 186, 189
Utopian knitters, 57–66
Vietnam, 171
Vogue Knitting Magazine, 177, 184, 187, 190, 193
W. L. M. Clark Co., 87
Waistcoat, 15
Walker & Co., 45
Walker, Barbara G., 180, 187
Warm Up America!, 196
Washington, Martha, 15–17
Watson, William, 20, 21
"We'll Do Our Share (While You're Over There)," 95
Weaver, Jane, 33, 34, 36
Whisk-broom cover, 86
William Unger and Co., 184
Wilson, Erica, 185
Winter, Margery, 184
Woman Citizen, The, 102, 103
Woman's Home Companion, 78, 160, 161
Women's bedroom slippers, 110
Women's Circle, 180
Women's Day, 148, 168, 169, 173–176

Wonoco Yarn Co., 144, 148
Wool Baby's Mittens, 117
Wool Gathering, 187, 195
Wool helmet, 97
Workbasket, The, 179, 184
World War I, 91–107
World War II, 137–153, 155
Wu, Sumi, 194, 196
Yarn, 87–89, 113, 114, 117, 128, 144–146, 197
  Acrylic, 172
  Mohair, 173, 184
York sweater, 114
Yurka, Blanche, 123, 125
Zimmermann, Elizabeth, 163, 187, 189, 193, 195
Zoar Mittens, 61

Historical Pattern Index
Baby Bunting Set (1920s), 116
Baby Soaker (1930s), 127
Daphne Scarf (1930s), 131
Imogene Scarf (1920s), 115
Knit Tie (1920s), 119
Ladies Fancy Silk Mittens (1880s), 30
Ladies' Cozy Jacket (1910s), 77
Men's Argyle Socks and Anklets (1950s), 164
Monmouth Cap (1600s), 12
"Necktie" Scarf (1850s), 32
Picot Stitch Shawl (1910s), 78
Red Cross Soldiers' Socks (World War I), 107
Red Cross Soldiers' Wristlets (World War I), 95
Simultaneous Socks (World War I), 103
Thread Lace (1920s), 113
U.S. Navy Iceland Sweater (World War II), 149
Union Arm Socks (1865), 42–43
Victorian Miser's Purse (1890s), 35
Zoar Mittens (1880s), 61

Acknowledgments

I relied on the knowledge and expertise of so many people along my way to researching and writing this book. At Voyageur Press, I thank Michael Dregni for shepherding the manuscript through the final stages. Actually, he had to tear it from my hands while I wanted more time to add just one more intriguing story or photo. Thanks as well to Acquisitions Editor Kari Cornell and Designer Sara Holle. I will always be grateful to Dr. Jane Farrell-Beck, who is my model for academic integrity and unabashed enthusiasm in historical sleuthing. I also thank Dr. Mary Littrell, Mary Swander, Dr. Sara Kadolph, and Dr. Hsain Ilahiane who guided me through doctoral studies that led to my teaching and writing life — and who in the process became lifelong friends and mentors.

Before I took up the academic life, Linda Ligon hired me as her staff artist at Interweave Press. As an Interweave illustrator and photostylist, it was my enormous privilege to touch and see close up an array of contemporary and historical handmade textiles, including knitting. Many were nothing short of wondrous. I am indebted to Linda for the opportunity that set me on my true career path. I also learned from her that although we no longer need handmade textiles, we do need the process of making them. During my time at Interweave, I was fortunate to meet Deb Robson, who recommended me to Voyageur Press as an author for this book, and Melanie Falick, who has shared words of wisdom at just the right times.

I also thank each of the writers who enriched this book by contributing sidebars on their areas of expertise. Karen Searle directed me to fine artists who work with knitting as a medium. Meg Swansen shared an especially significant photo of the "knitting summit" with Elizabeth Zimmermann, Mary Walker Phillips, and Barbara G. Walker. I thank each person who responded to requests for information (typically of an obscure and unusual nature). Civil War re-enactors Colleen Formby and Karin Timour were notably generous. Business representatives were also helpful and included Sigrun C. Robertson of the Musk Ox Producers' Co-Operative, Mary Colucci of the Craft Yarn Council, Galer Britton Barnes of Brittany, and Mike Mullins of the Hindman Settlement School. Thank you to the yarn makers, in particular Brian Harris at Mary Maxim at www.marymaxim.com, who gave permission to reproduce photos and advertisements.

I am grateful to each museum curator and librarian who sought information for me, especially to those who gave me access to hand knits in their collections. These include Lynette Miller at the Washington State Historical Society; Alden O'Brien at the Daughters of the American Revolution Museum; Doris Bowman at the Smithsonian Museum of American History; and Jennifer Engelkemier at the Museum of Amana History. Jane Nakasako of the Japanese American National Museum searched their collection for relevant hand knits, as did Wendell Zercher at the Heritage Center of Lancaster County; Laurann Gilbertson at the Vesterheim Norwegian-American Museum; Jennifer Kitlos at the Mt. Vernon Ladies' Association; Kathleen Fernandez of the Zoar Village State Memorial; and Kari M. Main of the Daughters of the Utah Pioneers, Pioneer Memorial Museum. In addition, Kitty Rhoades kept me supplied with interlibrary loan books at the Dominican University Library. You are all too numerous to mention, but you librarians and curators are the keepers of civilization and have become my heroes, each and every one of you.

I appreciate all the knitters I have met along the way who cheered the idea of a new book about the history of knitting, and I am especially grateful for the friendly group of creative knitters at Pamela Penney's Textile Arts on Harrison Street in Oak Park, Illinois. Thanks for welcoming me into your circle. I wish to thank in particular my son Christopher Strawn and my friend Dr. Norma Wolff for their kind and encouraging voices, always just a phone call away.

I deeply regret that contributions to this book from knitting scholar Deborah Pulliam were not possible due to her untimely illness.

About the Author

Susan Strawn teaches history of costume and various other textiles courses as an assistant professor in the Apparel Design and Merchandising department at Dominican University in River Forest, Illinois. Before entering academic life, she was an illustrator, photostylist, and sometimes writer at Interweave Press in Loveland, Colorado. When she was eight years old, her grandmother taught her knitting basics, and she has never since been without a knitting project. During the summer, she knits in Seattle.